STRANGE WEATHER LATELY

Written, drawn and painted by Metaphrog

Strange Weather Lately
Published by Metaphrog, 34 Springhill Gardens,
1/R, Shawlands, Glasgow G41 2EY, Scotland.
e-mail: metaphrog@pmail.net
www.geocities.com/SoHo/Square/5993
www.metaphrog.freeserve.co.uk

This volume comprises the last five issues of Strange Weather Lately
originally serialised.

(Paperback) ISBN 0 9534932 3 7
(Hardback) ISBN 0 9534932 2 9

Printed in Scotland by Clydeside Press Ltd.,
37 High Street, Glasgow G1.

In general, nobody gives a shit if you scream.

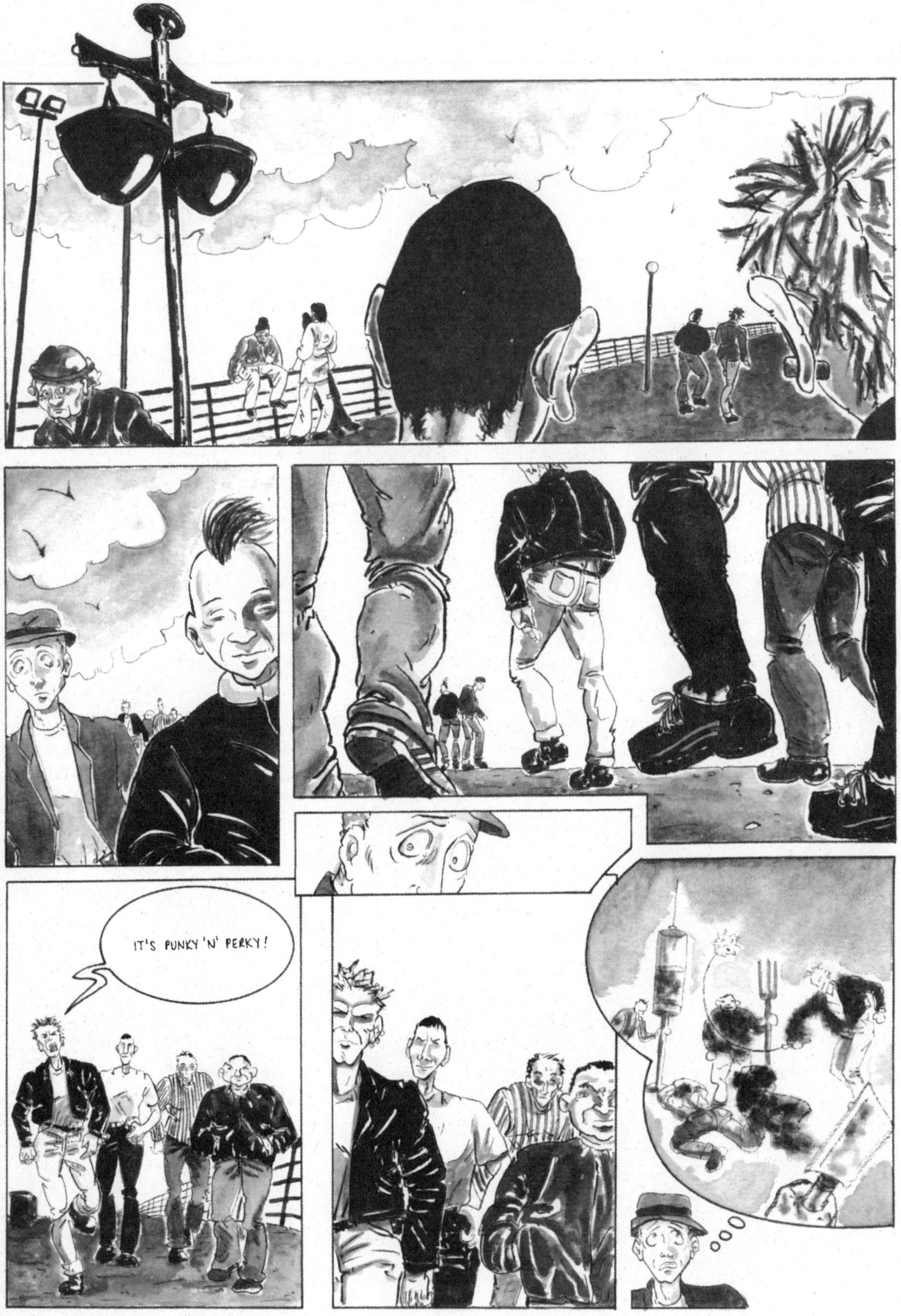
IT'S PUNKY 'N' PERKY!

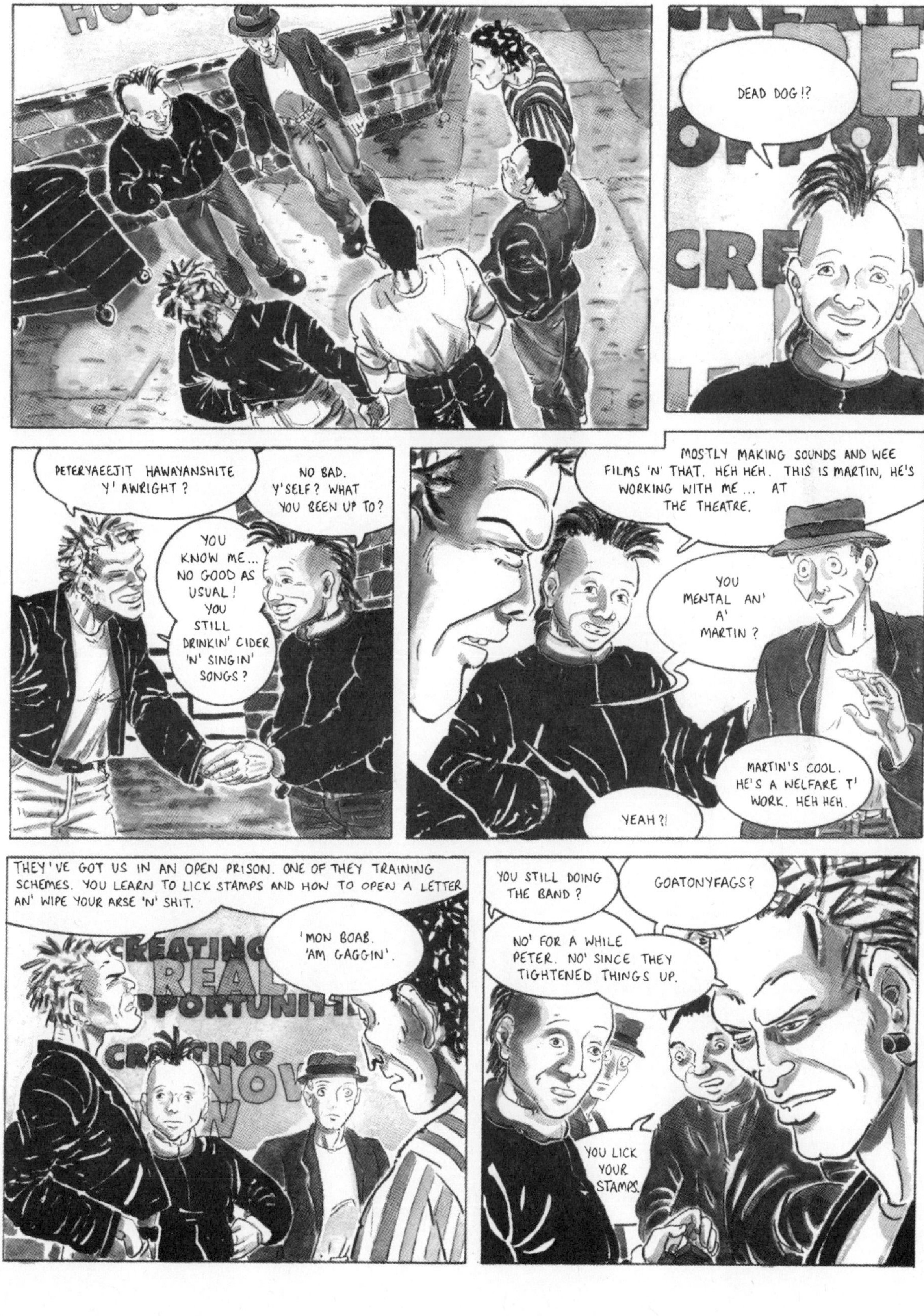
DEAD DOG!?
PETERYAEEJIT HAWAYANSHITE Y' AWRIGHT?
NO BAD. Y'SELF? WHAT YOU BEEN UP TO?
YOU KNOW ME... NO GOOD AS USUAL! YOU STILL DRINKIN' CIDER 'N' SINGIN' SONGS?
MOSTLY MAKING SOUNDS AND WEE FILMS 'N' THAT. HEH HEH. THIS IS MARTIN, HE'S WORKING WITH ME... AT THE THEATRE.
YOU MENTAL AN' A' MARTIN?
MARTIN'S COOL. HE'S A WELFARE T' WORK. HEH HEH.
YEAH?!
THEY'VE GOT US IN AN OPEN PRISON. ONE OF THEY TRAINING SCHEMES. YOU LEARN TO LICK STAMPS AND HOW TO OPEN A LETTER AN' WIPE YOUR ARSE 'N' SHIT.
'MON BOAB. 'AM GAGGIN'.
CREATING REAL OPPORTUNITIES
CREATING NOW
YOU STILL DOING THE BAND?
GOATONYFAGS?
NO' FOR A WHILE PETER. NO' SINCE THEY TIGHTENED THINGS UP.
YOU LICK YOUR STAMPS.

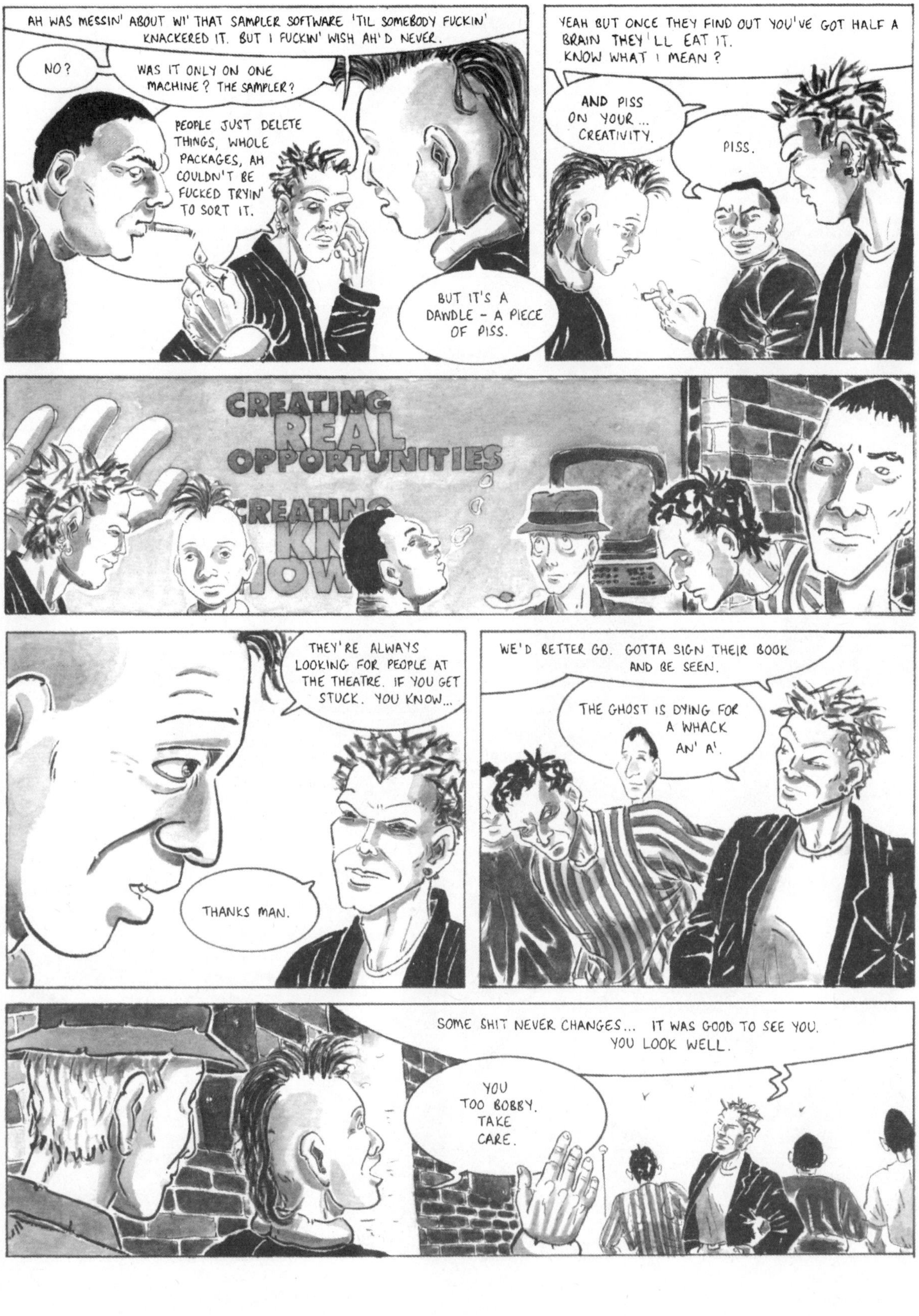
AH WAS MESSIN' ABOUT WI' THAT SAMPLER SOFTWARE 'TIL SOMEBODY FUCKIN' KNACKERED IT. BUT I FUCKIN' WISH AH'D NEVER.
NO?
WAS IT ONLY ON ONE MACHINE? THE SAMPLER?
PEOPLE JUST DELETE THINGS, WHOLE PACKAGES, AH COULDN'T BE FUCKED TRYIN' TO SORT IT.
BUT IT'S A DAWDLE - A PIECE OF PISS.
YEAH BUT ONCE THEY FIND OUT YOU'VE GOT HALF A BRAIN THEY'LL EAT IT. KNOW WHAT I MEAN?
AND PISS ON YOUR... CREATIVITY.
PISS.
CREATING REAL OPPORTUNITIES
THEY'RE ALWAYS LOOKING FOR PEOPLE AT THE THEATRE. IF YOU GET STUCK. YOU KNOW...
THANKS MAN.
WE'D BETTER GO. GOTTA SIGN THEIR BOOK AND BE SEEN.
THE GHOST IS DYING FOR A WHACK AN' A'.
SOME SHIT NEVER CHANGES... IT WAS GOOD TO SEE YOU. YOU LOOK WELL.
YOU TOO BOBBY. TAKE CARE.

COME ON MARTIN MAN. I'LL MAKE YOU A CUPPA.

SORRY PETER. I'M A FUCKIN' NERVOUS WRECK.

I THOUGHT THEY WERE GOING TO JUMP US.

I KINDA WISH THEY HAD.

'UH !!?

YOUR PAST CATCHING UP WITH YOU ?

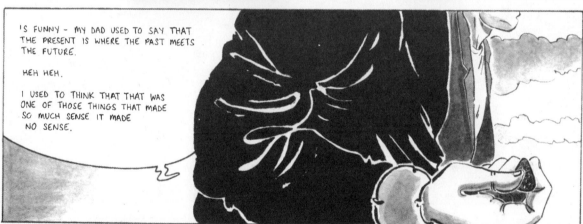

'S FUNNY — MY DAD USED TO SAY THAT THE PRESENT IS WHERE THE PAST MEETS THE FUTURE.

HEH HEH.

I USED TO THINK THAT THAT WAS ONE OF THOSE THINGS THAT MADE SO MUCH SENSE IT MADE NO SENSE.

SUPPOSE SO.

I USED TO BE IN A BAND WITH BOBBY, DEAD DOG. WE WERE SO CLOSE WE BECAME ALMOST THE SAME PERSON. EXCEPT I'M SHORT AND UGLY HEH HEH.

OH, YOU KNOW WHAT I MEAN. WE HAD THE SAME TASTES.

WE DRIFTED APART.

I'M NOT VERY WITH IT TODAY.

YOU'RE DECENT MAN, DEAD OPEN. FEEL LIKE I FUCKED YOU UP. GIBBERING ON LIKE THAT ABOUT HARI:

I FILLED YOU UP WITH BAD THOUGHTS ...

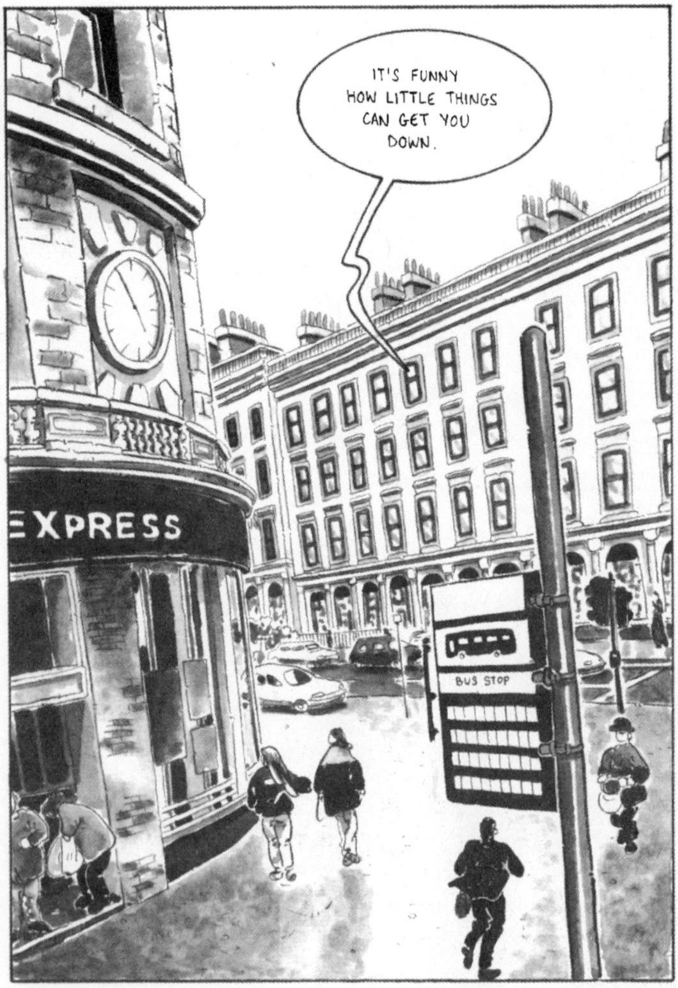
IT'S FUNNY HOW LITTLE THINGS CAN GET YOU DOWN.
EXPRESS
BUS STOP

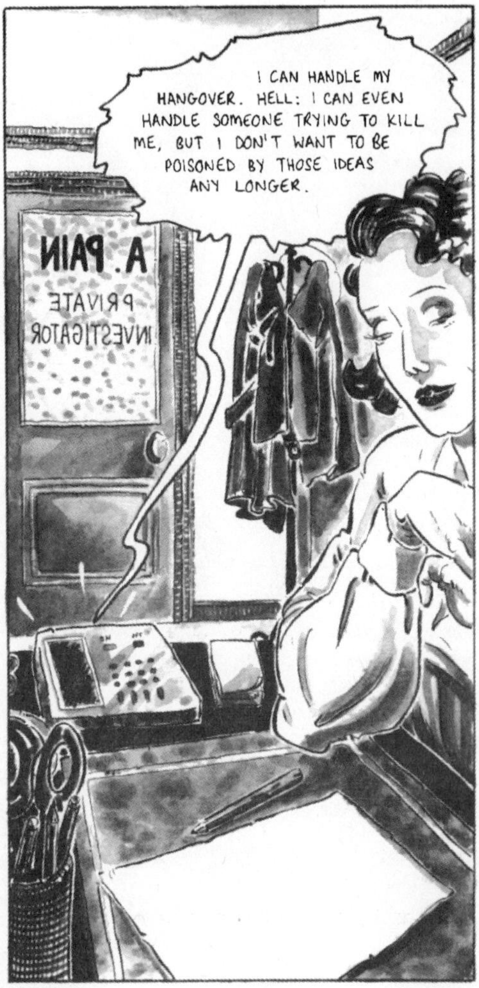
I CAN HANDLE MY HANGOVER. HELL: I CAN EVEN HANDLE SOMEONE TRYING TO KILL ME, BUT I DON'T WANT TO BE POISONED BY THOSE IDEAS ANY LONGER.
A. PAIN
PRIVATE
INVESTIGATOR

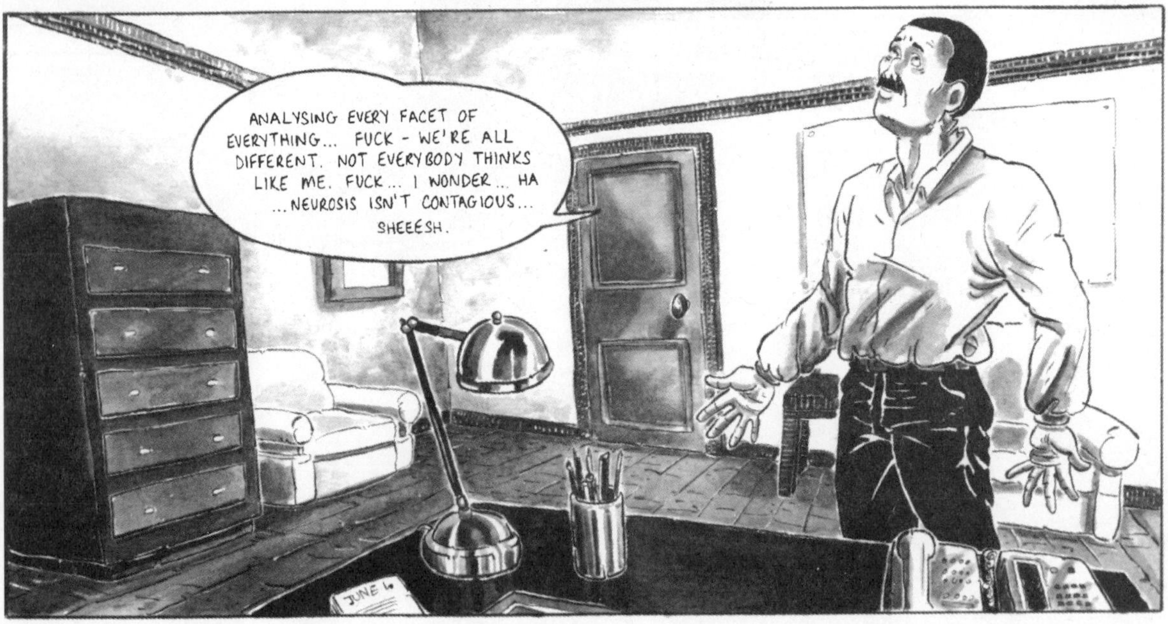
ANALYSING EVERY FACET OF EVERYTHING... FUCK - WE'RE ALL DIFFERENT. NOT EVERYBODY THINKS LIKE ME. FUCK... I WONDER... HA ...NEUROSIS ISN'T CONTAGIOUS... SHEEESH.
JUNE 6

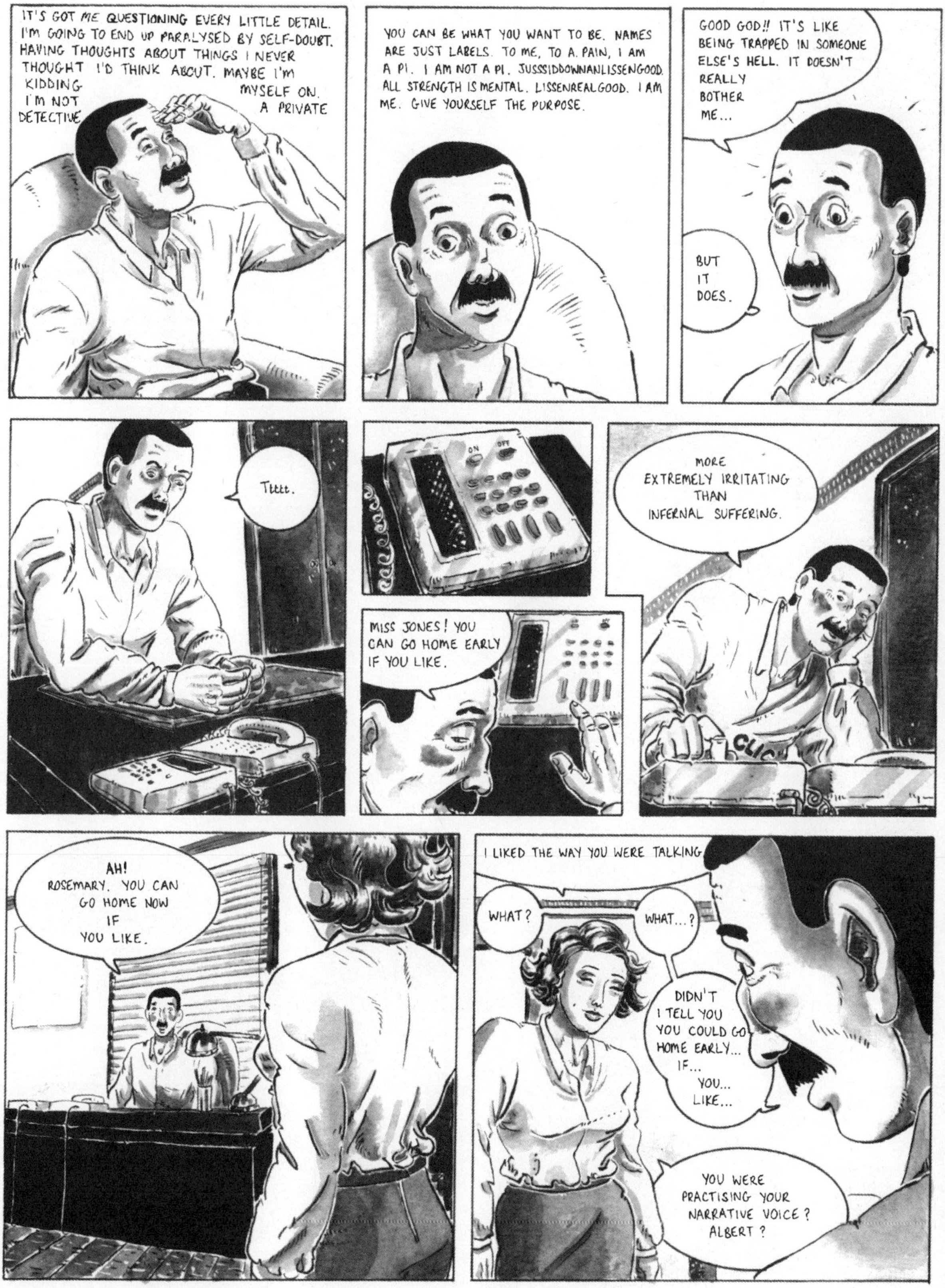
IT'S GOT ME QUESTIONING EVERY LITTLE DETAIL. I'M GOING TO END UP PARALYSED BY SELF-DOUBT. HAVING THOUGHTS ABOUT THINGS I NEVER THOUGHT I'D THINK ABOUT. MAYBE I'M KIDDING MYSELF ON. I'M NOT A PRIVATE DETECTIVE
YOU CAN BE WHAT YOU WANT TO BE. NAMES ARE JUST LABELS. TO ME, TO A. PAIN, I AM A PI. I AM NOT A PI. JUSSSIDDOWNANLISSENGOOD. ALL STRENGTH IS MENTAL. LISSENREALGOOD. I AM ME. GIVE YOURSELF THE PURPOSE.
GOOD GOD!! IT'S LIKE BEING TRAPPED IN SOMEONE ELSE'S HELL. IT DOESN'T REALLY BOTHER ME...
BUT IT DOES.
Ttttt.
ON OFF
MORE EXTREMELY IRRITATING THAN INFERNAL SUFFERING.
MISS JONES! YOU CAN GO HOME EARLY IF YOU LIKE.
CLIC
AH! ROSEMARY. YOU CAN GO HOME NOW IF YOU LIKE.
I LIKED THE WAY YOU WERE TALKING.
WHAT?
WHAT...?
DIDN'T I TELL YOU YOU COULD GO HOME EARLY... IF... YOU... LIKE...
YOU WERE PRACTISING YOUR NARRATIVE VOICE? ALBERT?

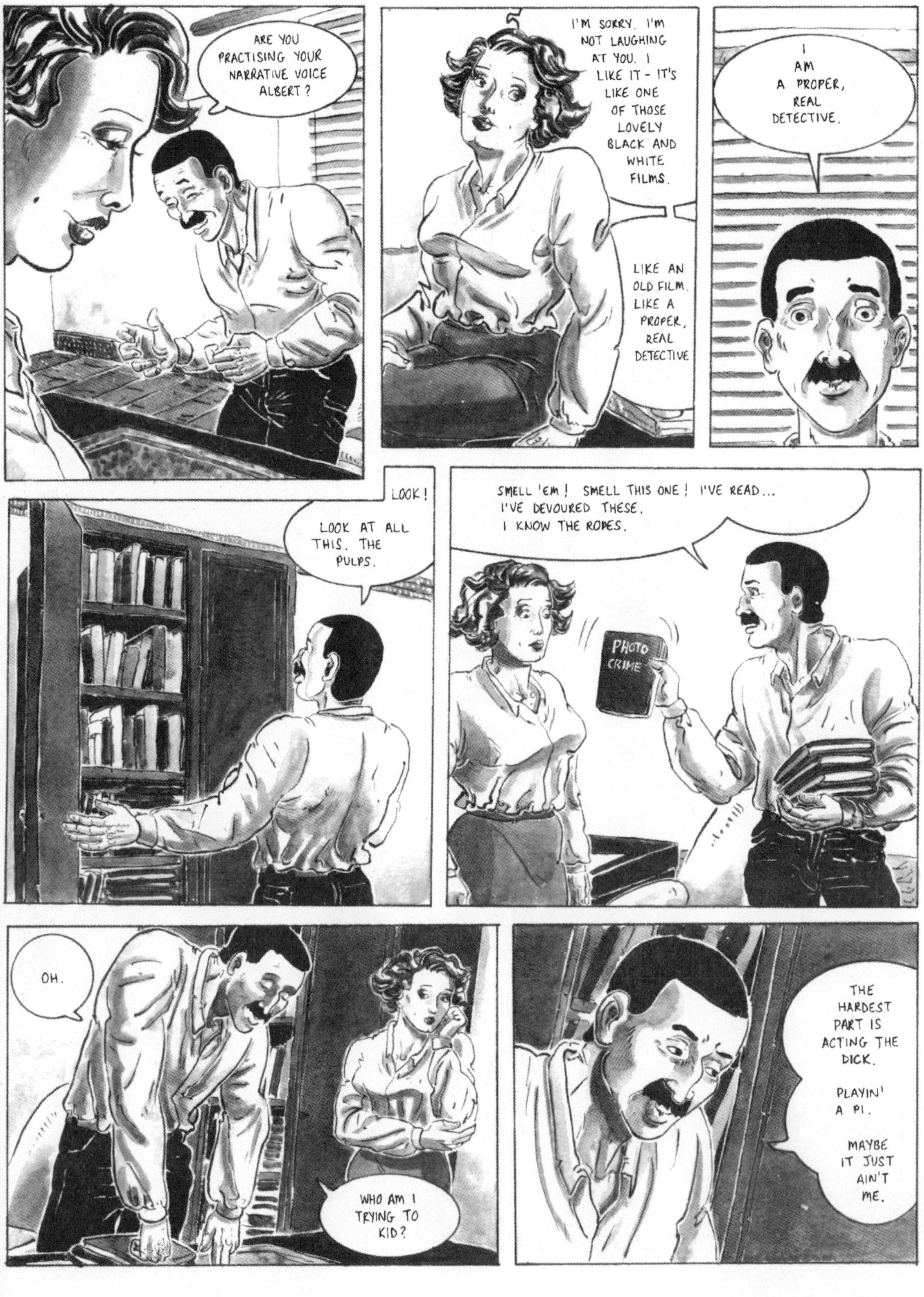
ARE YOU PRACTISING YOUR NARRATIVE VOICE ALBERT?
I'M SORRY. I'M NOT LAUGHING AT YOU. I LIKE IT - IT'S LIKE ONE OF THOSE LOVELY BLACK AND WHITE FILMS.
LIKE AN OLD FILM. LIKE A PROPER, REAL DETECTIVE
I AM A PROPER, REAL DETECTIVE.
LOOK!
LOOK AT ALL THIS. THE PULPS.
SMELL 'EM! SMELL THIS ONE! I'VE READ... I'VE DEVOURED THESE. I KNOW THE ROPES.
PHOTO CRIME
OH.
WHO AM I TRYING TO KID?
THE HARDEST PART IS ACTING THE DICK.
PLAYIN' A PI.
MAYBE IT JUST AIN'T ME.

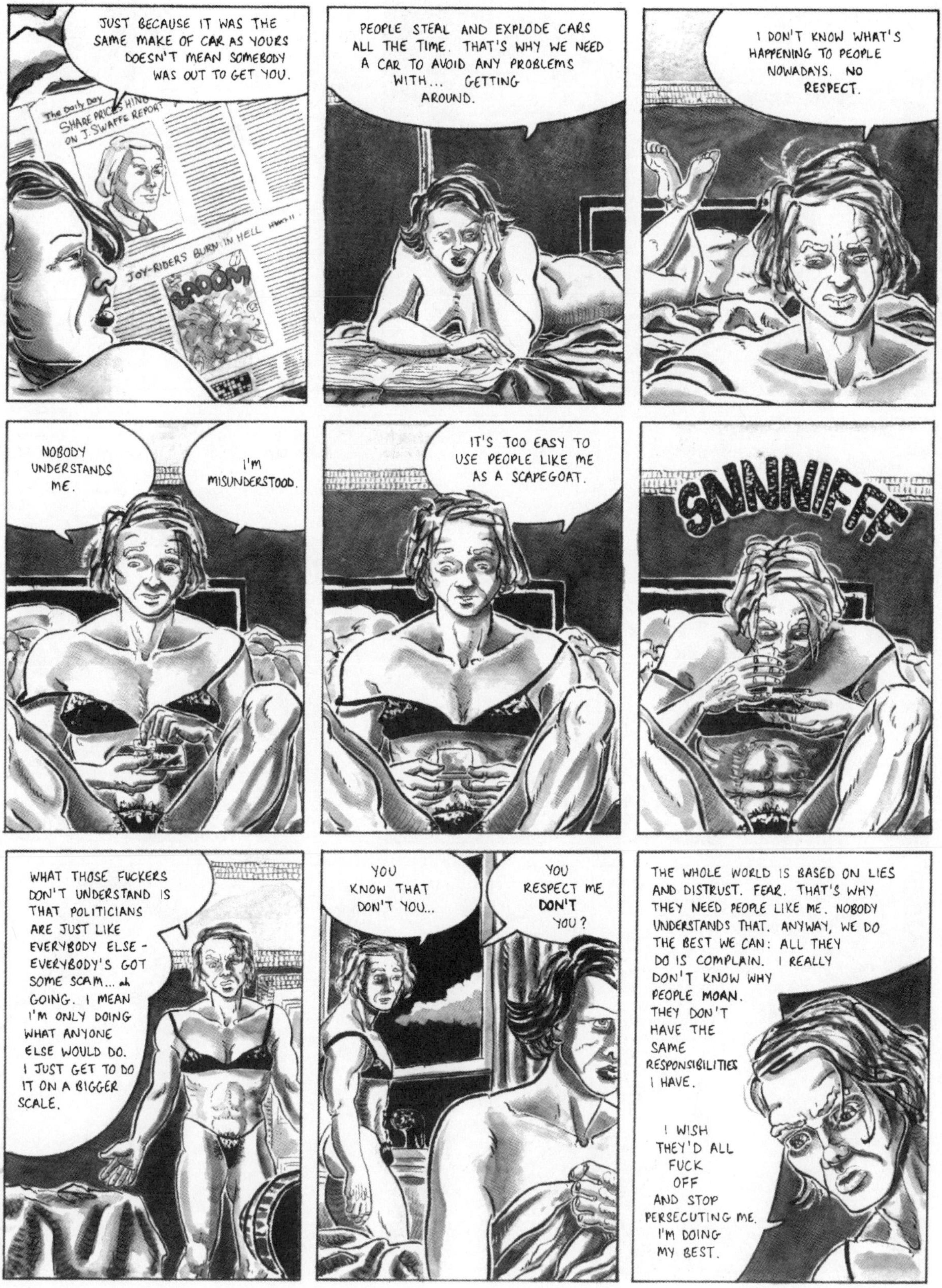

JUST BECAUSE IT WAS THE SAME MAKE OF CAR AS YOURS DOESN'T MEAN SOMEBODY WAS OUT TO GET YOU.
The Daily Day
SHARE PRICES HIND
ON J. SWAFFE REPORT
JOY-RIDERS BURN IN HELL
BADOOM
PEOPLE STEAL AND EXPLODE CARS ALL THE TIME. THAT'S WHY WE NEED A CAR TO AVOID ANY PROBLEMS WITH... GETTING AROUND.
I DON'T KNOW WHAT'S HAPPENING TO PEOPLE NOWADAYS. NO RESPECT.
NOBODY UNDERSTANDS ME.
I'M MISUNDERSTOOD.
IT'S TOO EASY TO USE PEOPLE LIKE ME AS A SCAPEGOAT.
SNNNIFFF
WHAT THOSE FUCKERS DON'T UNDERSTAND IS THAT POLITICIANS ARE JUST LIKE EVERYBODY ELSE - EVERYBODY'S GOT SOME SCAM... ah GOING. I MEAN I'M ONLY DOING WHAT ANYONE ELSE WOULD DO. I JUST GET TO DO IT ON A BIGGER SCALE.
YOU KNOW THAT DON'T YOU...
YOU RESPECT ME **DON'T** YOU?
THE WHOLE WORLD IS BASED ON LIES AND DISTRUST. FEAR. THAT'S WHY THEY NEED PEOPLE LIKE ME. NOBODY UNDERSTANDS THAT. ANYWAY, WE DO THE BEST WE CAN: ALL THEY DO IS COMPLAIN. I REALLY DON'T KNOW WHY PEOPLE **MOAN**. THEY DON'T HAVE THE SAME RESPONSIBILITIES I HAVE.
I WISH THEY'D ALL FUCK OFF AND STOP PERSECUTING ME. I'M DOING MY BEST.

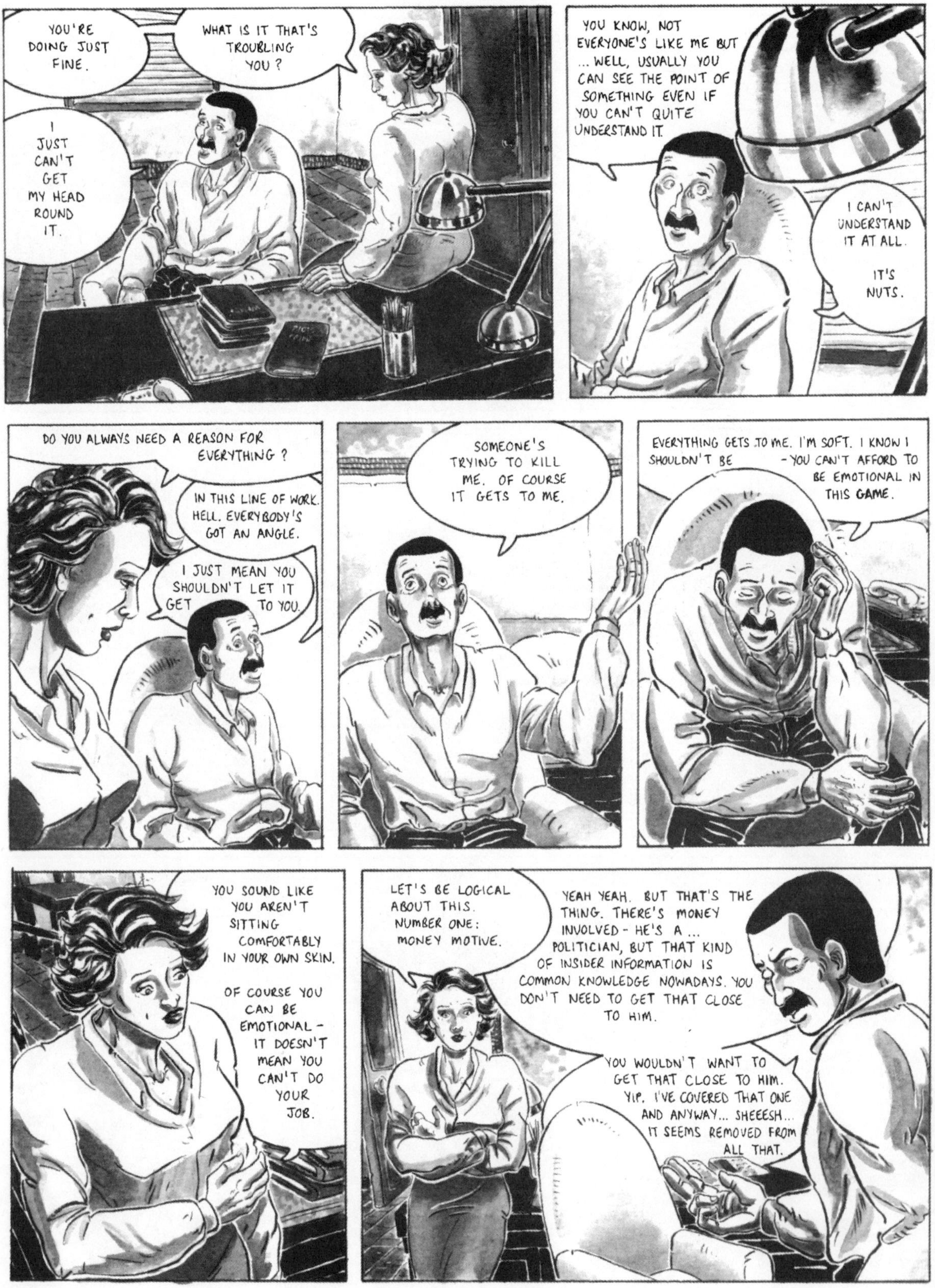
YOU'RE DOING JUST FINE.
WHAT IS IT THAT'S TROUBLING YOU?
I JUST CAN'T GET MY HEAD ROUND IT.
YOU KNOW, NOT EVERYONE'S LIKE ME BUT ... WELL, USUALLY YOU CAN SEE THE POINT OF SOMETHING EVEN IF YOU CAN'T QUITE UNDERSTAND IT.
I CAN'T UNDERSTAND IT AT ALL.
IT'S NUTS.
DO YOU ALWAYS NEED A REASON FOR EVERYTHING?
IN THIS LINE OF WORK. HELL. EVERYBODY'S GOT AN ANGLE.
I JUST MEAN YOU SHOULDN'T LET IT GET TO YOU.
SOMEONE'S TRYING TO KILL ME. OF COURSE IT GETS TO ME.
EVERYTHING GETS TO ME. I'M SOFT. I KNOW I SHOULDN'T BE - YOU CAN'T AFFORD TO BE EMOTIONAL IN THIS GAME.
YOU SOUND LIKE YOU AREN'T SITTING COMFORTABLY IN YOUR OWN SKIN.
OF COURSE YOU CAN BE EMOTIONAL - IT DOESN'T MEAN YOU CAN'T DO YOUR JOB.
LET'S BE LOGICAL ABOUT THIS. NUMBER ONE: MONEY MOTIVE.
YEAH YEAH. BUT THAT'S THE THING. THERE'S MONEY INVOLVED - HE'S A ... POLITICIAN, BUT THAT KIND OF INSIDER INFORMATION IS COMMON KNOWLEDGE NOWADAYS. YOU DON'T NEED TO GET THAT CLOSE TO HIM.
YOU WOULDN'T WANT TO GET THAT CLOSE TO HIM. YIP. I'VE COVERED THAT ONE AND ANYWAY... SHEEESH... IT SEEMS REMOVED FROM ALL THAT.

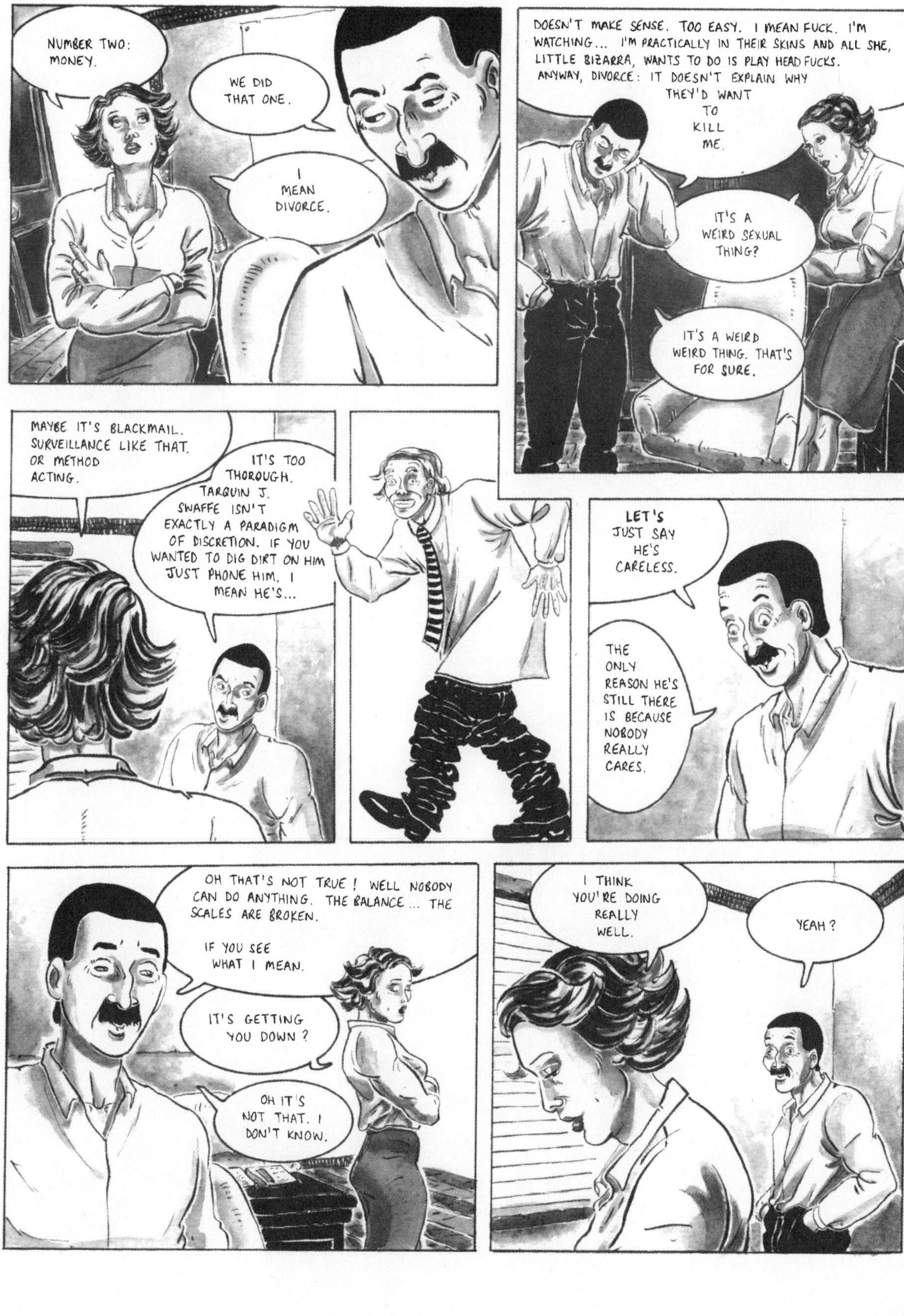
NUMBER TWO: MONEY.
WE DID THAT ONE.
I MEAN DIVORCE.
DOESN'T MAKE SENSE. TOO EASY. I MEAN FUCK. I'M WATCHING... I'M PRACTICALLY IN THEIR SKINS AND ALL SHE, LITTLE BIZARRA, WANTS TO DO IS PLAY HEAD FUCKS. ANYWAY, DIVORCE: IT DOESN'T EXPLAIN WHY THEY'D WANT TO KILL ME.
IT'S A WEIRD SEXUAL THING?
IT'S A WEIRD WEIRD THING. THAT'S FOR SURE.
MAYBE IT'S BLACKMAIL. SURVEILLANCE LIKE THAT. OR METHOD ACTING.
IT'S TOO THOROUGH. TARQUIN J. SWAFFE ISN'T EXACTLY A PARADIGM OF DISCRETION. IF YOU WANTED TO DIG DIRT ON HIM JUST PHONE HIM. I MEAN HE'S...
LET'S JUST SAY HE'S CARELESS.
THE ONLY REASON HE'S STILL THERE IS BECAUSE NOBODY REALLY CARES.
OH THAT'S NOT TRUE! WELL NOBODY CAN DO ANYTHING. THE BALANCE... THE SCALES ARE BROKEN.
IF YOU SEE WHAT I MEAN.
IT'S GETTING YOU DOWN?
OH IT'S NOT THAT. I DON'T KNOW.
I THINK YOU'RE DOING REALLY WELL.
YEAH?

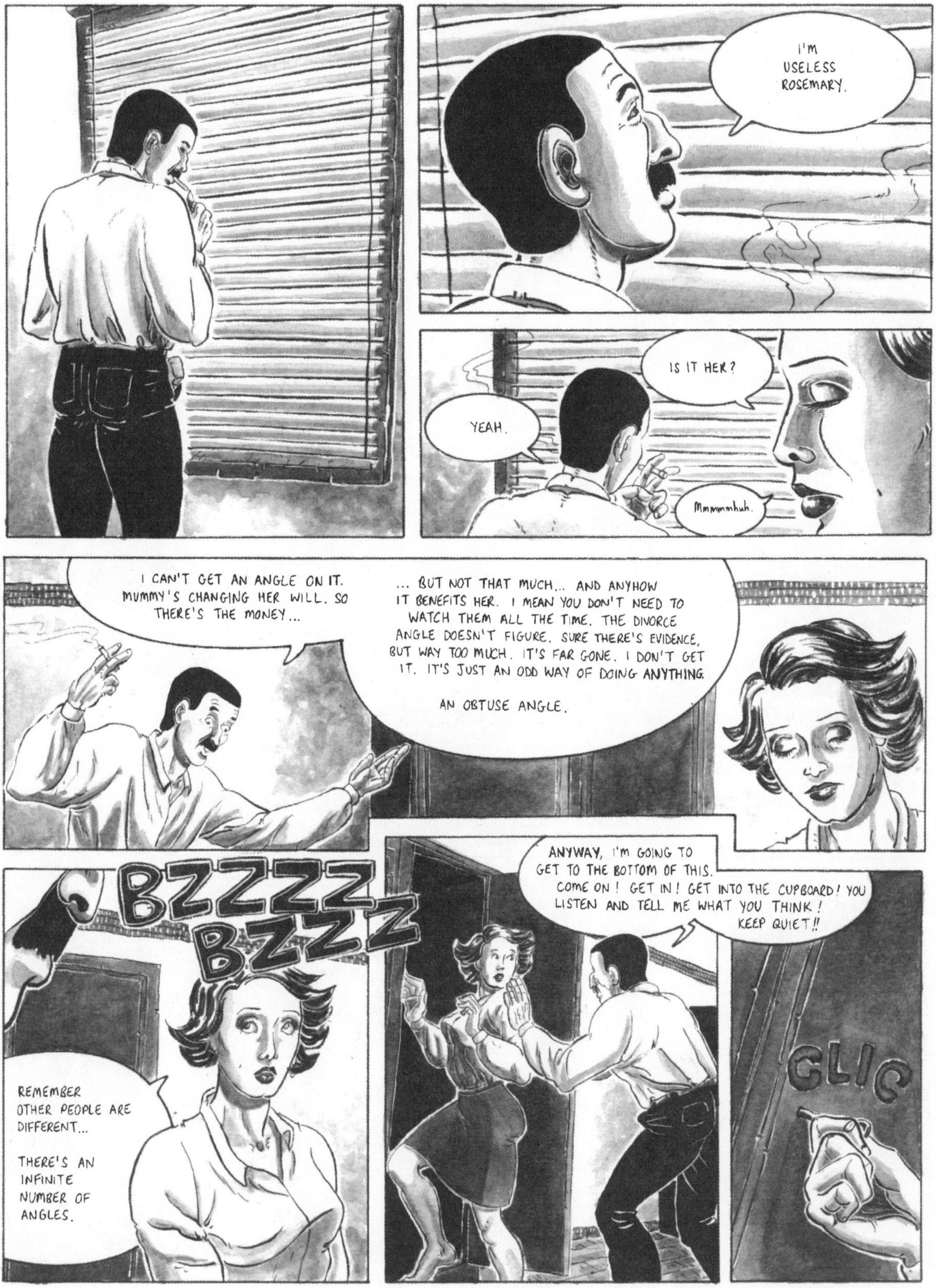
I'M USELESS ROSEMARY.
IS IT HER?
YEAH.
Mmmmmhuh.
I CAN'T GET AN ANGLE ON IT. MUMMY'S CHANGING HER WILL. SO THERE'S THE MONEY...
... BUT NOT THAT MUCH... AND ANYHOW IT BENEFITS HER. I MEAN YOU DON'T NEED TO WATCH THEM ALL THE TIME. THE DIVORCE ANGLE DOESN'T FIGURE. SURE THERE'S EVIDENCE, BUT WAY TOO MUCH. IT'S FAR GONE. I DON'T GET IT. IT'S JUST AN ODD WAY OF DOING ANYTHING.
AN OBTUSE ANGLE.
BZZZZZ BZZZZ
REMEMBER OTHER PEOPLE ARE DIFFERENT...
THERE'S AN INFINITE NUMBER OF ANGLES.
ANYWAY, I'M GOING TO GET TO THE BOTTOM OF THIS. COME ON! GET IN! GET INTO THE CUPBOARD! YOU LISTEN AND TELL ME WHAT YOU THINK! KEEP QUIET!!
CLIC

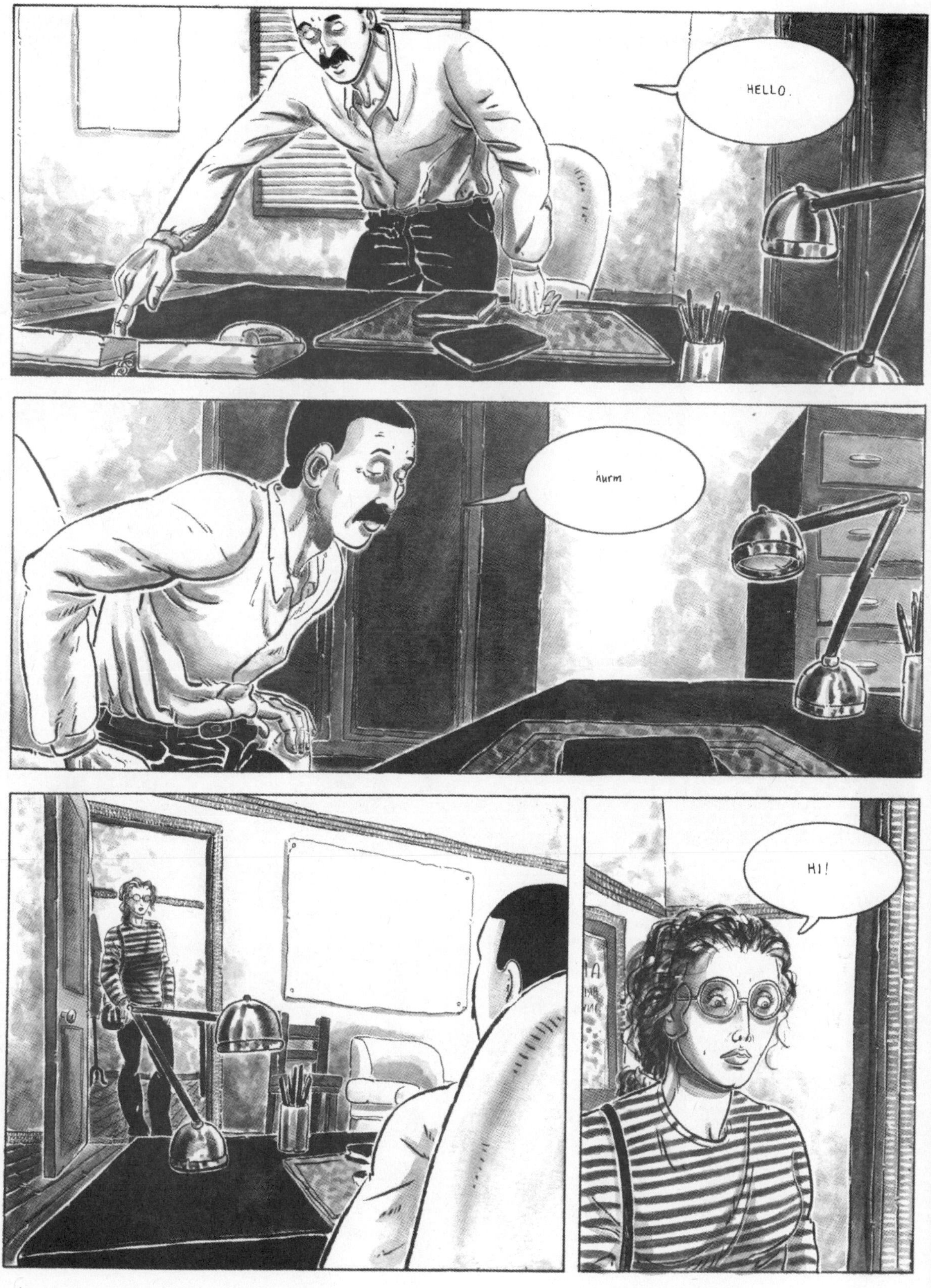
HELLO.
hurm
HI!

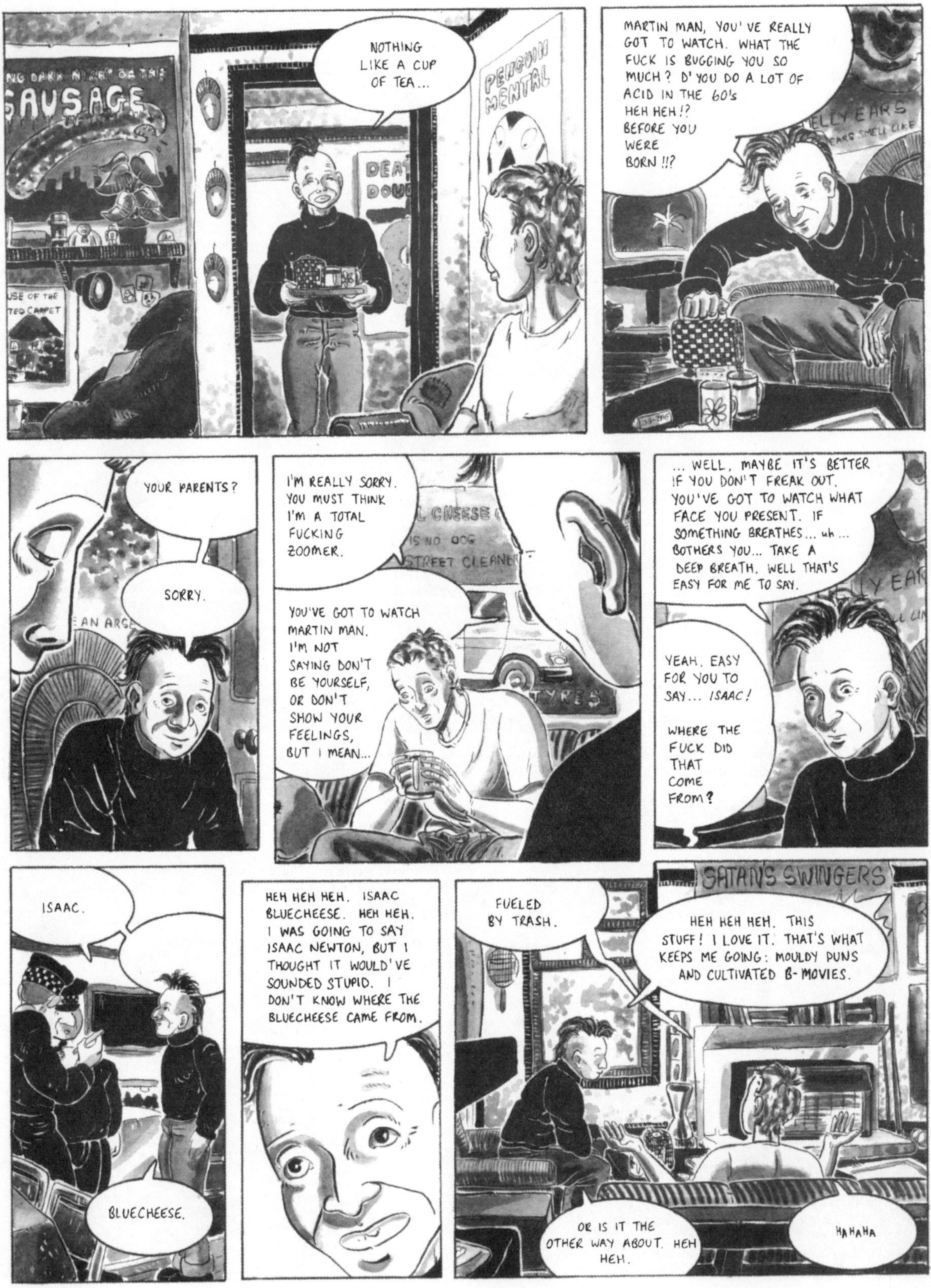
NOTHING LIKE A CUP OF TEA...
MARTIN MAN, YOU'VE REALLY GOT TO WATCH. WHAT THE FUCK IS BUGGING YOU SO MUCH? D'YOU DO A LOT OF ACID IN THE 60's HEH HEH!? BEFORE YOU WERE BORN!!?
YOUR PARENTS?
SORRY.
I'M REALLY SORRY. YOU MUST THINK I'M A TOTAL FUCKING ZOOMER.
YOU'VE GOT TO WATCH MARTIN MAN. I'M NOT SAYING DON'T BE YOURSELF, OR DON'T SHOW YOUR FEELINGS, BUT I MEAN...
... WELL, MAYBE IT'S BETTER IF YOU DON'T FREAK OUT. YOU'VE GOT TO WATCH WHAT FACE YOU PRESENT. IF SOMETHING BREATHES... uh... BOTHERS YOU... TAKE A DEEP BREATH. WELL THAT'S EASY FOR ME TO SAY.
YEAH. EASY FOR YOU TO SAY... ISAAC!
WHERE THE FUCK DID THAT COME FROM?
ISAAC.
BLUECHEESE.
HEH HEH HEH. ISAAC BLUECHEESE. HEH HEH. I WAS GOING TO SAY ISAAC NEWTON, BUT I THOUGHT IT WOULD'VE SOUNDED STUPID. I DON'T KNOW WHERE THE BLUECHEESE CAME FROM.
SATAN'S SWINGERS
FUELED BY TRASH.
HEH HEH HEH. THIS STUFF! I LOVE IT. THAT'S WHAT KEEPS ME GOING: MOULDY PUNS AND CULTIVATED B-MOVIES.
OR IS IT THE OTHER WAY ABOUT. HEH HEH.
HAHAHA

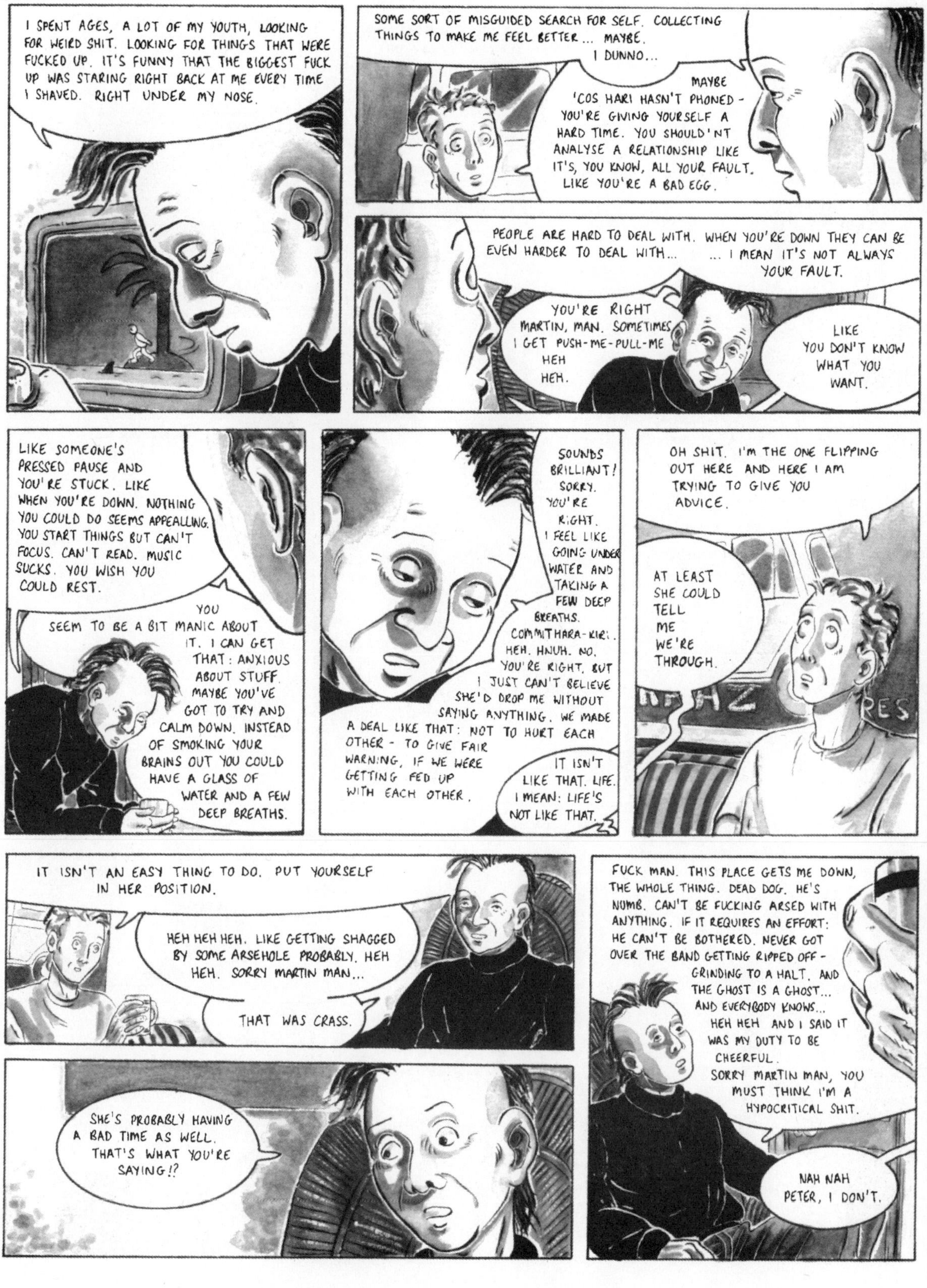
I SPENT AGES, A LOT OF MY YOUTH, LOOKING FOR WEIRD SHIT. LOOKING FOR THINGS THAT WERE FUCKED UP. IT'S FUNNY THAT THE BIGGEST FUCK UP WAS STARING RIGHT BACK AT ME EVERY TIME I SHAVED. RIGHT UNDER MY NOSE.
SOME SORT OF MISGUIDED SEARCH FOR SELF. COLLECTING THINGS TO MAKE ME FEEL BETTER... MAYBE.
I DUNNO...
MAYBE 'COS HARI HASN'T PHONED - YOU'RE GIVING YOURSELF A HARD TIME. YOU SHOULD'NT ANALYSE A RELATIONSHIP LIKE IT'S, YOU KNOW, ALL YOUR FAULT. LIKE YOU'RE A BAD EGG.
PEOPLE ARE HARD TO DEAL WITH. WHEN YOU'RE DOWN THEY CAN BE EVEN HARDER TO DEAL WITH... ... I MEAN IT'S NOT ALWAYS YOUR FAULT.
YOU'RE RIGHT MARTIN, MAN. SOMETIMES I GET PUSH-ME-PULL-ME HEH HEH.
LIKE YOU DON'T KNOW WHAT YOU WANT.
LIKE SOMEONE'S PRESSED PAUSE AND YOU'RE STUCK. LIKE WHEN YOU'RE DOWN. NOTHING YOU COULD DO SEEMS APPEALLING. YOU START THINGS BUT CAN'T FOCUS. CAN'T READ. MUSIC SUCKS. YOU WISH YOU COULD REST.
YOU SEEM TO BE A BIT MANIC ABOUT IT. I CAN GET THAT: ANXIOUS ABOUT STUFF. MAYBE YOU'VE GOT TO TRY AND CALM DOWN. INSTEAD OF SMOKING YOUR BRAINS OUT YOU COULD HAVE A GLASS OF WATER AND A FEW DEEP BREATHS.
SOUNDS BRILLIANT! SORRY. YOU'RE RIGHT. I FEEL LIKE GOING UNDER WATER AND TAKING A FEW DEEP BREATHS. COMMITHARA-KIRI. HEH. HNUH. NO. YOU'RE RIGHT, BUT I JUST CAN'T BELIEVE SHE'D DROP ME WITHOUT SAYING ANYTHING. WE MADE A DEAL LIKE THAT: NOT TO HURT EACH OTHER - TO GIVE FAIR WARNING, IF WE WERE GETTING FED UP WITH EACH OTHER.
IT ISN'T LIKE THAT. LIFE. I MEAN: LIFE'S NOT LIKE THAT.
OH SHIT. I'M THE ONE FLIPPING OUT HERE AND HERE I AM TRYING TO GIVE YOU ADVICE.
AT LEAST SHE COULD TELL ME WE'RE THROUGH.
IT ISN'T AN EASY THING TO DO. PUT YOURSELF IN HER POSITION.
HEH HEH HEH. LIKE GETTING SHAGGED BY SOME ARSEHOLE PROBABLY. HEH HEH. SORRY MARTIN MAN...
THAT WAS CRASS.
SHE'S PROBABLY HAVING A BAD TIME AS WELL. THAT'S WHAT YOU'RE SAYING!?
FUCK MAN. THIS PLACE GETS ME DOWN, THE WHOLE THING. DEAD DOG. HE'S NUMB. CAN'T BE FUCKING ARSED WITH ANYTHING. IF IT REQUIRES AN EFFORT: HE CAN'T BE BOTHERED. NEVER GOT OVER THE BAND GETTING RIPPED OFF - GRINDING TO A HALT. AND THE GHOST IS A GHOST... AND EVERYBODY KNOWS... HEH HEH AND I SAID IT WAS MY DUTY TO BE CHEERFUL. SORRY MARTIN MAN, YOU MUST THINK I'M A HYPOCRITICAL SHIT.
NAH NAH PETER, I DON'T.

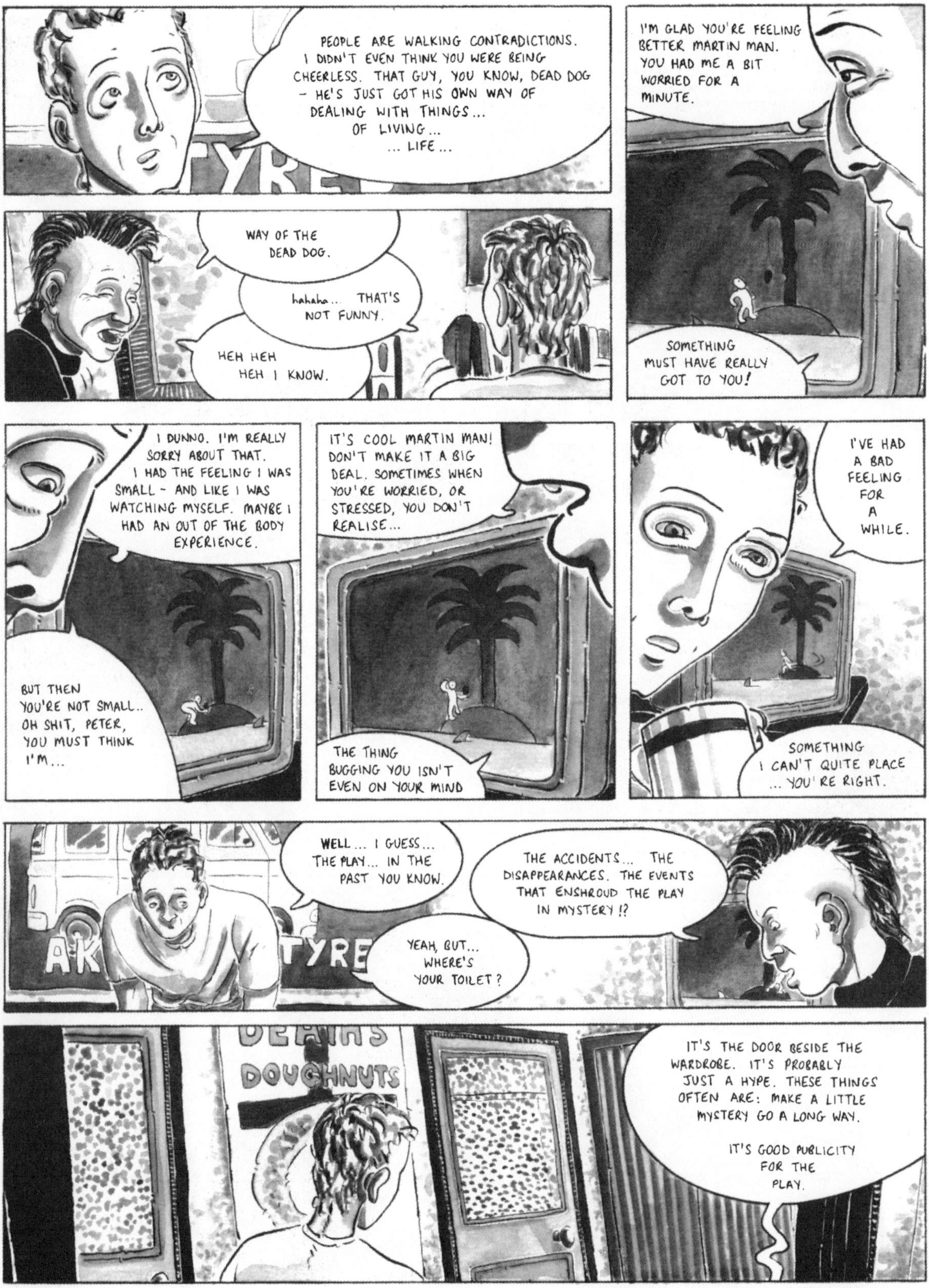
PEOPLE ARE WALKING CONTRADICTIONS. I DIDN'T EVEN THINK YOU WERE BEING CHEERLESS. THAT GUY, YOU KNOW, DEAD DOG - HE'S JUST GOT HIS OWN WAY OF DEALING WITH THINGS... OF LIVING... ...LIFE...
TYRE
I'M GLAD YOU'RE FEELING BETTER MARTIN MAN. YOU HAD ME A BIT WORRIED FOR A MINUTE.
WAY OF THE DEAD DOG.
hahaha... THAT'S NOT FUNNY.
HEH HEH HEH I KNOW.
SOMETHING MUST HAVE REALLY GOT TO YOU!
I DUNNO. I'M REALLY SORRY ABOUT THAT. I HAD THE FEELING I WAS SMALL - AND LIKE I WAS WATCHING MYSELF. MAYBE I HAD AN OUT OF THE BODY EXPERIENCE.
BUT THEN YOU'RE NOT SMALL.. OH SHIT, PETER, YOU MUST THINK I'M...
IT'S COOL MARTIN MAN! DON'T MAKE IT A BIG DEAL. SOMETIMES WHEN YOU'RE WORRIED, OR STRESSED, YOU DON'T REALISE...
THE THING BUGGING YOU ISN'T EVEN ON YOUR MIND
I'VE HAD A BAD FEELING FOR A WHILE.
SOMETHING I CAN'T QUITE PLACE ... YOU'RE RIGHT.
WELL... I GUESS... THE PLAY... IN THE PAST YOU KNOW.
THE ACCIDENTS... THE DISAPPEARANCES. THE EVENTS THAT ENSHROUD THE PLAY IN MYSTERY!?
YEAH, BUT... WHERE'S YOUR TOILET?
TYRE
DOUGHNUTS
IT'S THE DOOR BESIDE THE WARDROBE. IT'S PROBABLY JUST A HYPE. THESE THINGS OFTEN ARE: MAKE A LITTLE MYSTERY GO A LONG WAY.
IT'S GOOD PUBLICITY FOR THE PLAY.

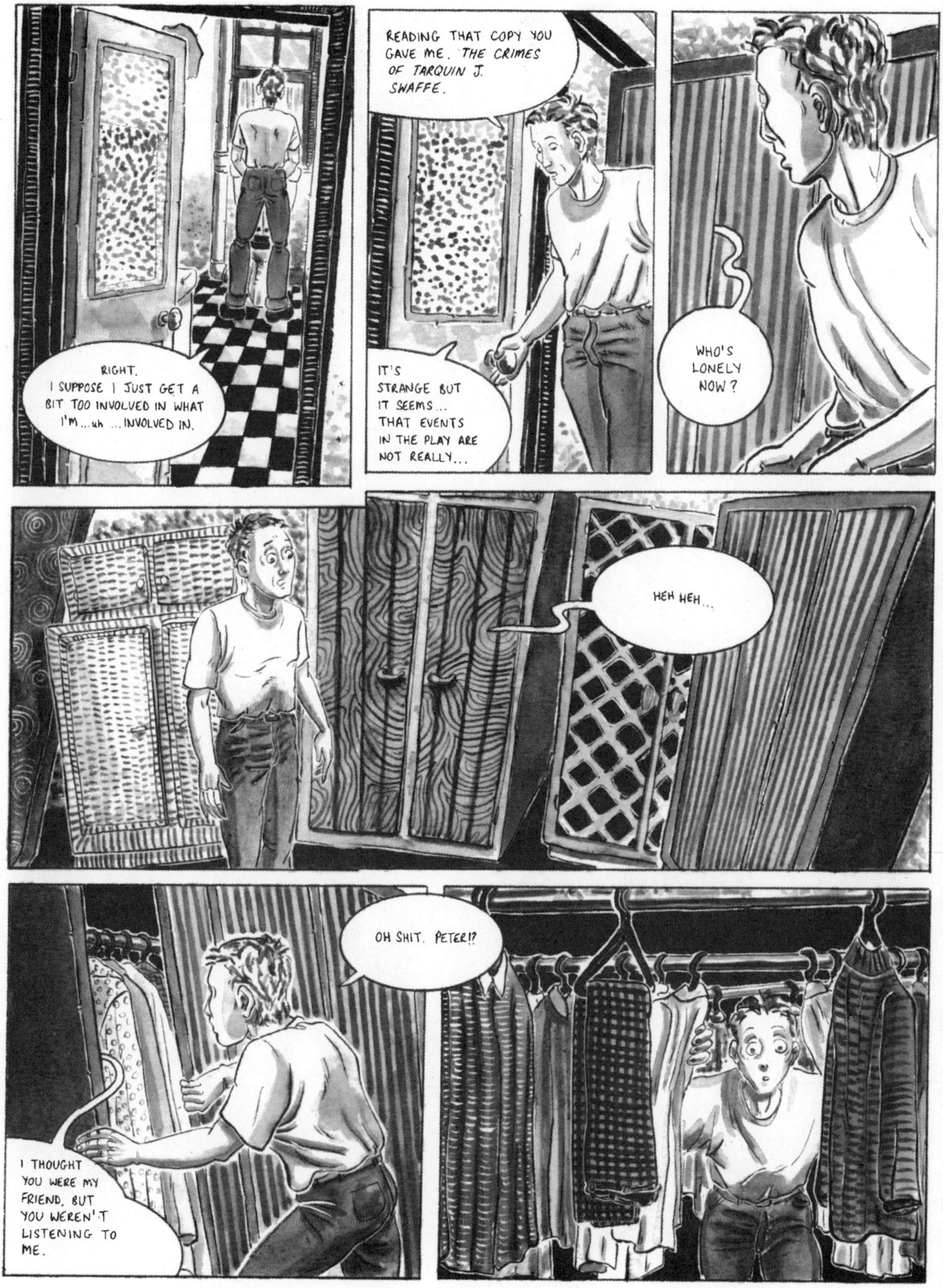

RIGHT.
I SUPPOSE I JUST GET A BIT TOO INVOLVED IN WHAT I'M...uh ...INVOLVED IN.
READING THAT COPY YOU GAVE ME. *THE CRIMES OF TARQUIN J. SWAFFE.*
IT'S STRANGE BUT IT SEEMS... THAT EVENTS IN THE PLAY ARE NOT REALLY...
WHO'S LONELY NOW?
HEH HEH...
OH SHIT. PETER!?
I THOUGHT YOU WERE MY FRIEND, BUT YOU WEREN'T LISTENING TO ME.

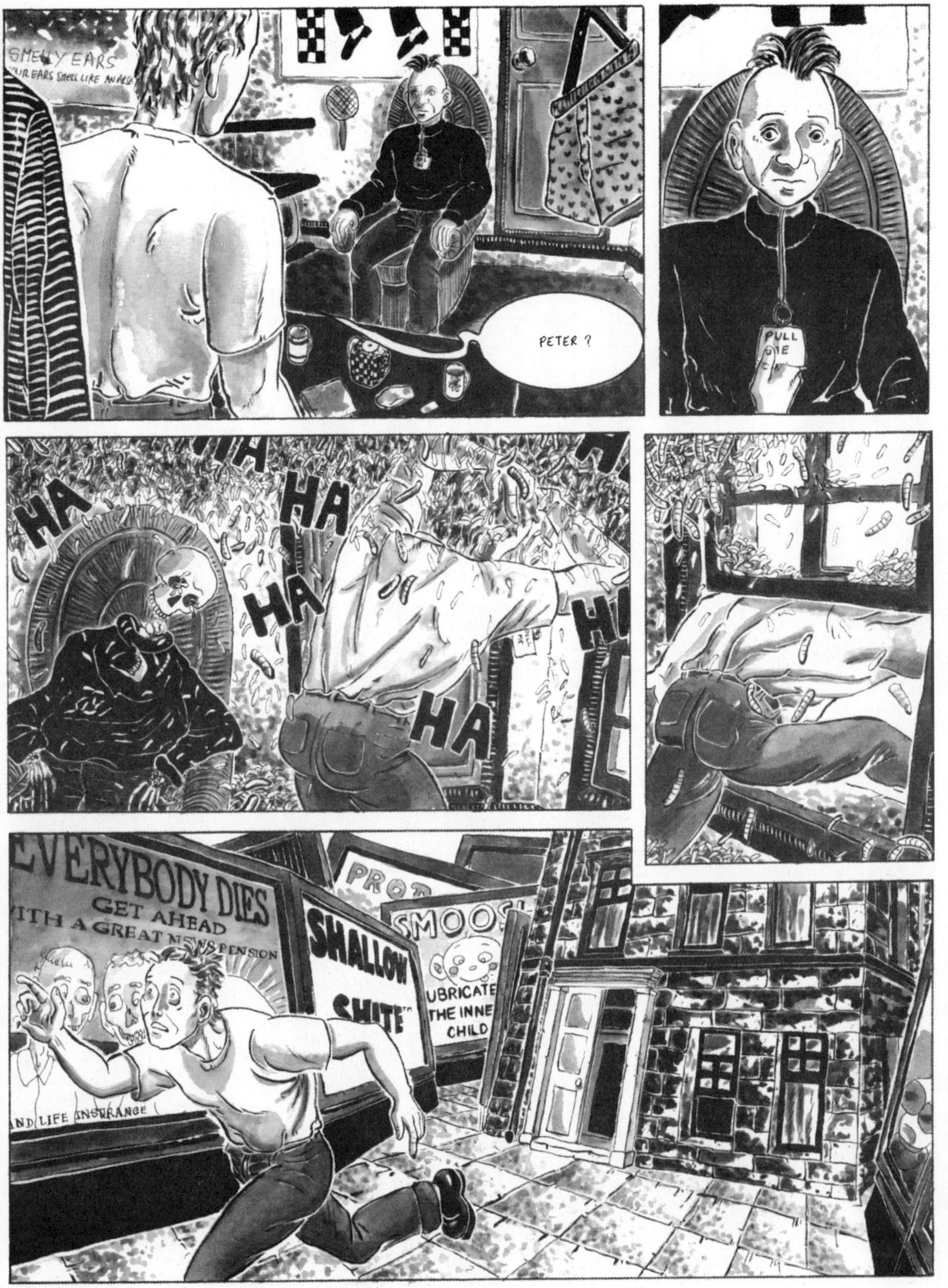
SMELLY EARS
PETER ?
PULL
HA
HA
HA
HA
HA
EVERYBODY DIES
GET AHEAD
WITH A GREAT
PENSION
AND LIFE INSURANCE
SHALLOW
SHITE™
UBRICATE
THE INNE
CHILD

The things you find and their eggs.

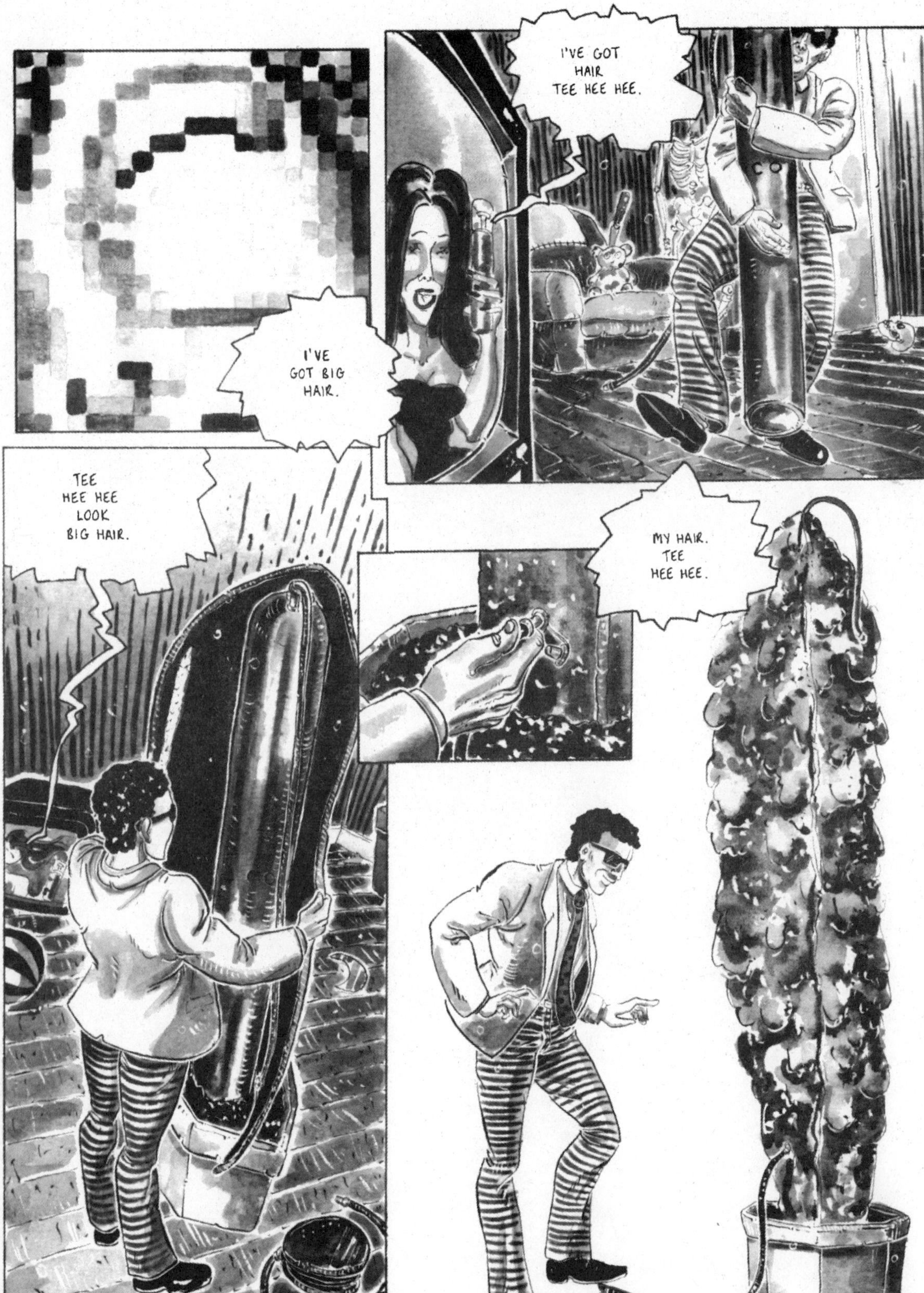
I'VE GOT BIG HAIR.
I'VE GOT HAIR TEE HEE HEE.
TEE HEE HEE LOOK BIG HAIR.
MY HAIR. TEE HEE HEE.

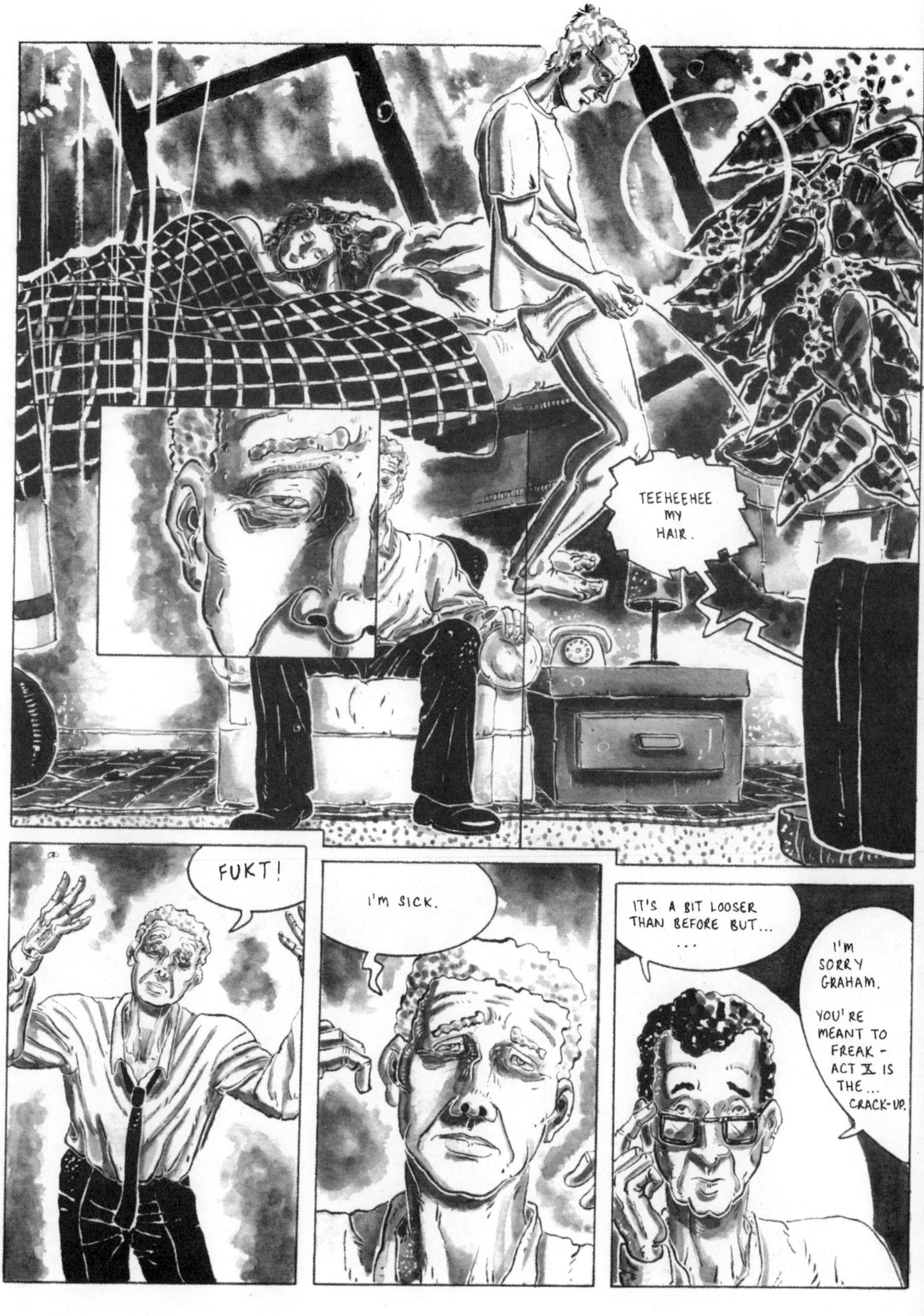
TEEHEEHEE MY HAIR.
FUKT!
I'M SICK.
IT'S A BIT LOOSER THAN BEFORE BUT... ...
I'M SORRY GRAHAM.
YOU'RE MEANT TO FREAK - ACT X IS THE... CRACK-UP.

I'VE GOT AN IDEA. DON'T ACT. JUST BE YOURSELF. BE AS DERANGED AS YOU CAN GET. IMAGINE YOU'RE ALONE. LET OUT YOUR DEMONS ALL OVER THE STAGE. NO **STRAIT JACKET**. NO SELF-CONSCIOUSNESS, NAKED UGLY; UGLY YOU...

I THINK YOUR IDEA DRIBBLES PISS.

YOUR ARMPITS SMELL LIKE YESTERDAY'S TURNIP.

YOU FEEL HORRIBLE BECAUSE YOU'RE BEING HORRIBLE AND YOU'RE BEING HORRIBLE 'COS YOU FEEL HORRIBLE. YOU REFUSE TO INVEST ANYTHING IN THIS PLAY - YOU'RE JUST LETTING THE OUTSIDE WORLD IMPINGE...

YOU POO!

YEAH?

YEAH.

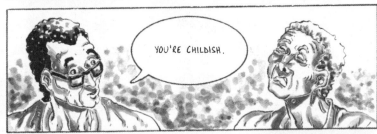

YOU'RE CHILDISH.

HUMMMMMM..... HUMMMMMM HUMMM

I NEED TO STRETCH MY LEGS AND CLEAR MY HEAD. WE'RE GOING TO TAKE A BREAK. LEAVE YOU TWO TO IT. COME ON JUNIPER, WE'LL GO LOOK FOR PETER AND MARTIN... THEY CAN'T HAVE GONE FAR.

WE'LL TRY AND FIND PETER.

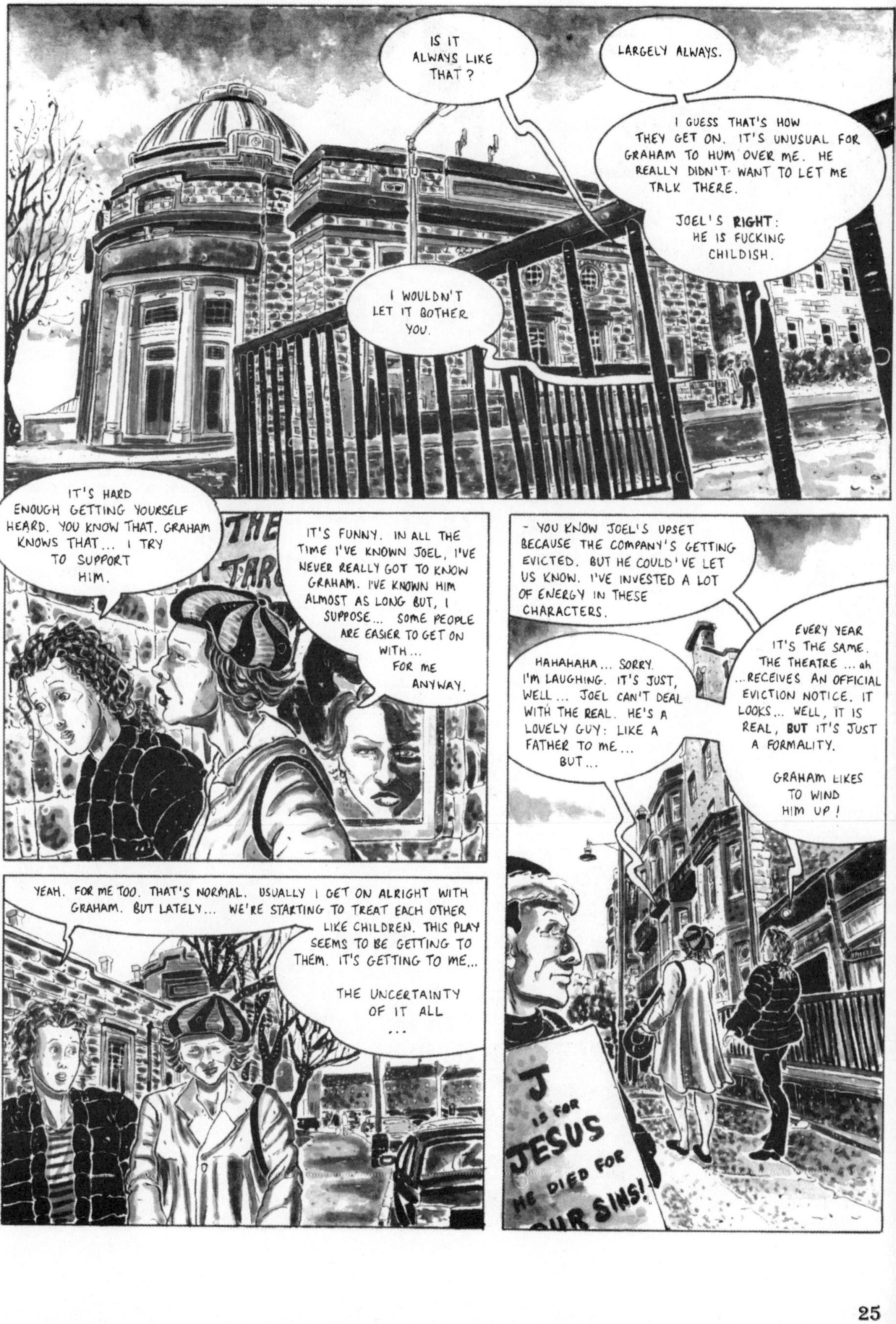
IS IT ALWAYS LIKE THAT?
LARGELY ALWAYS.
I GUESS THAT'S HOW THEY GET ON. IT'S UNUSUAL FOR GRAHAM TO HUM OVER ME. HE REALLY DIDN'T WANT TO LET ME TALK THERE.
JOEL'S **RIGHT**: HE IS FUCKING CHILDISH.
I WOULDN'T LET IT BOTHER YOU.
IT'S HARD ENOUGH GETTING YOURSELF HEARD. YOU KNOW THAT. GRAHAM KNOWS THAT... I TRY TO SUPPORT HIM.
IT'S FUNNY. IN ALL THE TIME I'VE KNOWN JOEL, I'VE NEVER REALLY GOT TO KNOW GRAHAM. I'VE KNOWN HIM ALMOST AS LONG BUT, I SUPPOSE... SOME PEOPLE ARE EASIER TO GET ON WITH... FOR ME ANYWAY.
YEAH. FOR ME TOO. THAT'S NORMAL. USUALLY I GET ON ALRIGHT WITH GRAHAM. BUT LATELY... WE'RE STARTING TO TREAT EACH OTHER LIKE CHILDREN. THIS PLAY SEEMS TO BE GETTING TO THEM. IT'S GETTING TO ME...
THE UNCERTAINTY OF IT ALL ...
- YOU KNOW JOEL'S UPSET BECAUSE THE COMPANY'S GETTING EVICTED. BUT HE COULD'VE LET US KNOW. I'VE INVESTED A LOT OF ENERGY IN THESE CHARACTERS.
HAHAHAHA... SORRY. I'M LAUGHING. IT'S JUST, WELL... JOEL CAN'T DEAL WITH THE REAL. HE'S A LOVELY GUY: LIKE A FATHER TO ME... BUT...
EVERY YEAR IT'S THE SAME. THE THEATRE ... ah ...RECEIVES AN OFFICIAL EVICTION NOTICE. IT LOOKS... WELL, IT IS REAL, **BUT** IT'S JUST A FORMALITY.
GRAHAM LIKES TO WIND HIM UP!
J IS FOR JESUS HE DIED FOR OUR SINS!

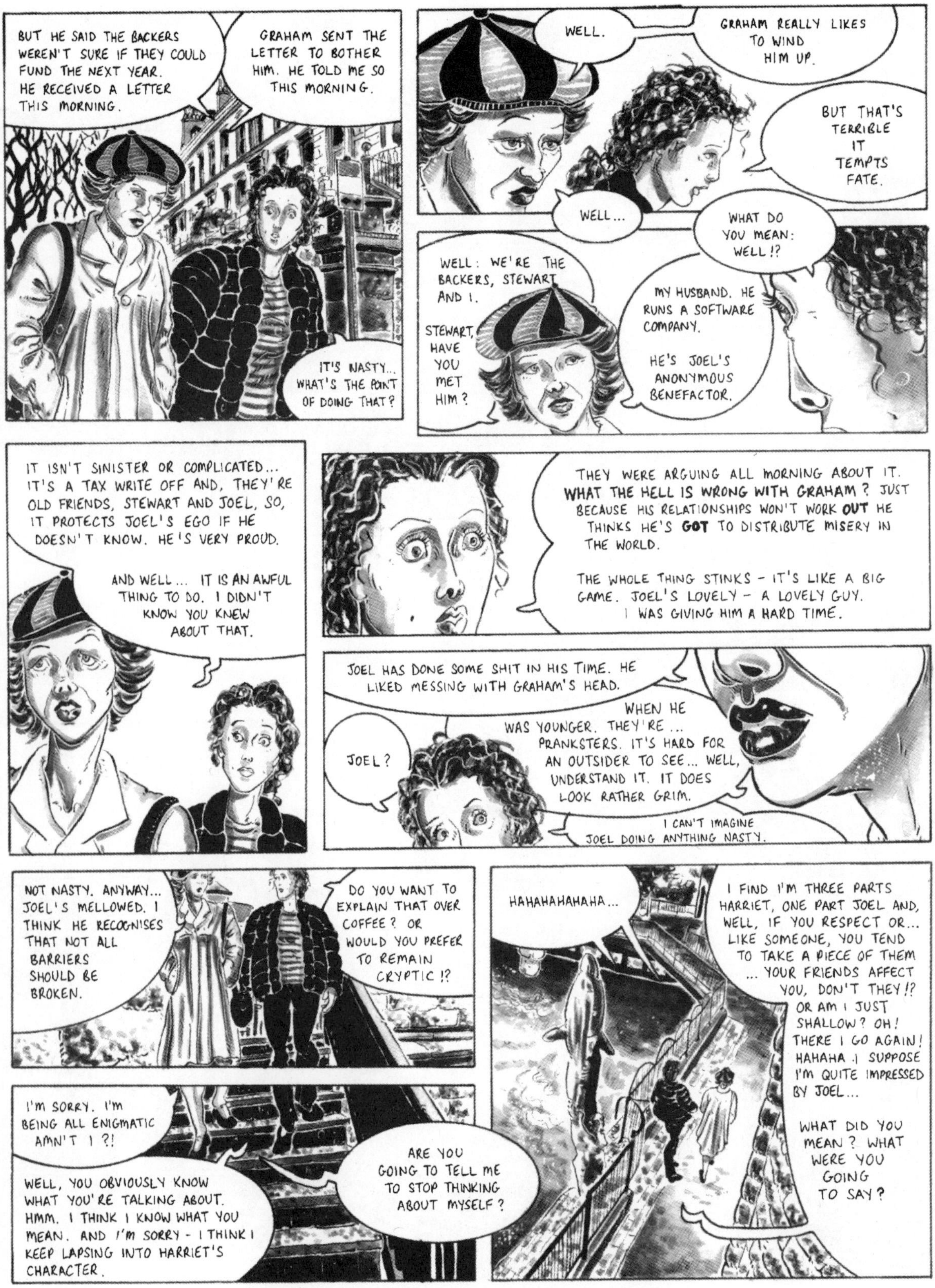
BUT HE SAID THE BACKERS WEREN'T SURE IF THEY COULD FUND THE NEXT YEAR. HE RECEIVED A LETTER THIS MORNING.
GRAHAM SENT THE LETTER TO BOTHER HIM. HE TOLD ME SO THIS MORNING.
IT'S NASTY... WHAT'S THE POINT OF DOING THAT?
WELL.
GRAHAM REALLY LIKES TO WIND HIM UP.
BUT THAT'S TERRIBLE IT TEMPTS FATE.
WELL...
WHAT DO YOU MEAN: WELL !?
WELL: WE'RE THE BACKERS, STEWART AND I.
STEWART, HAVE YOU MET HIM?
MY HUSBAND. HE RUNS A SOFTWARE COMPANY.
HE'S JOEL'S ANONYMOUS BENEFACTOR.
IT ISN'T SINISTER OR COMPLICATED... IT'S A TAX WRITE OFF AND, THEY'RE OLD FRIENDS, STEWART AND JOEL, SO, IT PROTECTS JOEL'S EGO IF HE DOESN'T KNOW. HE'S VERY PROUD.
AND WELL... IT IS AN AWFUL THING TO DO. I DIDN'T KNOW YOU KNEW ABOUT THAT.
THEY WERE ARGUING ALL MORNING ABOUT IT. **WHAT THE HELL IS WRONG WITH GRAHAM?** JUST BECAUSE HIS RELATIONSHIPS WON'T WORK **OUT** HE THINKS HE'S **GOT** TO DISTRIBUTE MISERY IN THE WORLD.
THE WHOLE THING STINKS - IT'S LIKE A BIG GAME. JOEL'S LOVELY - A LOVELY GUY. I WAS GIVING HIM A HARD TIME.
JOEL HAS DONE SOME SHIT IN HIS TIME. HE LIKED MESSING WITH GRAHAM'S HEAD.
JOEL?
WHEN HE WAS YOUNGER. THEY'RE ... PRANKSTERS. IT'S HARD FOR AN OUTSIDER TO SEE... WELL, UNDERSTAND IT. IT DOES LOOK RATHER GRIM.
I CAN'T IMAGINE JOEL DOING ANYTHING NASTY.
NOT NASTY. ANYWAY... JOEL'S MELLOWED. I THINK HE RECOGNISES THAT NOT ALL BARRIERS SHOULD BE BROKEN.
DO YOU WANT TO EXPLAIN THAT OVER COFFEE? OR WOULD YOU PREFER TO REMAIN CRYPTIC !?
I'M SORRY. I'M BEING ALL ENIGMATIC AMN'T I ?!
WELL, YOU OBVIOUSLY KNOW WHAT YOU'RE TALKING ABOUT. HMM. I THINK I KNOW WHAT YOU MEAN. AND I'M SORRY - I THINK I KEEP LAPSING INTO HARRIET'S CHARACTER.
ARE YOU GOING TO TELL ME TO STOP THINKING ABOUT MYSELF?
HAHAHAHAHAHA...
I FIND I'M THREE PARTS HARRIET, ONE PART JOEL AND, WELL, IF YOU RESPECT OR... LIKE SOMEONE, YOU TEND TO TAKE A PIECE OF THEM ... YOUR FRIENDS AFFECT YOU, DON'T THEY !? OR AM I JUST SHALLOW? OH! THERE I GO AGAIN! HAHAHA. I SUPPOSE I'M QUITE IMPRESSED BY JOEL...
WHAT DID YOU MEAN? WHAT WERE YOU GOING TO SAY?

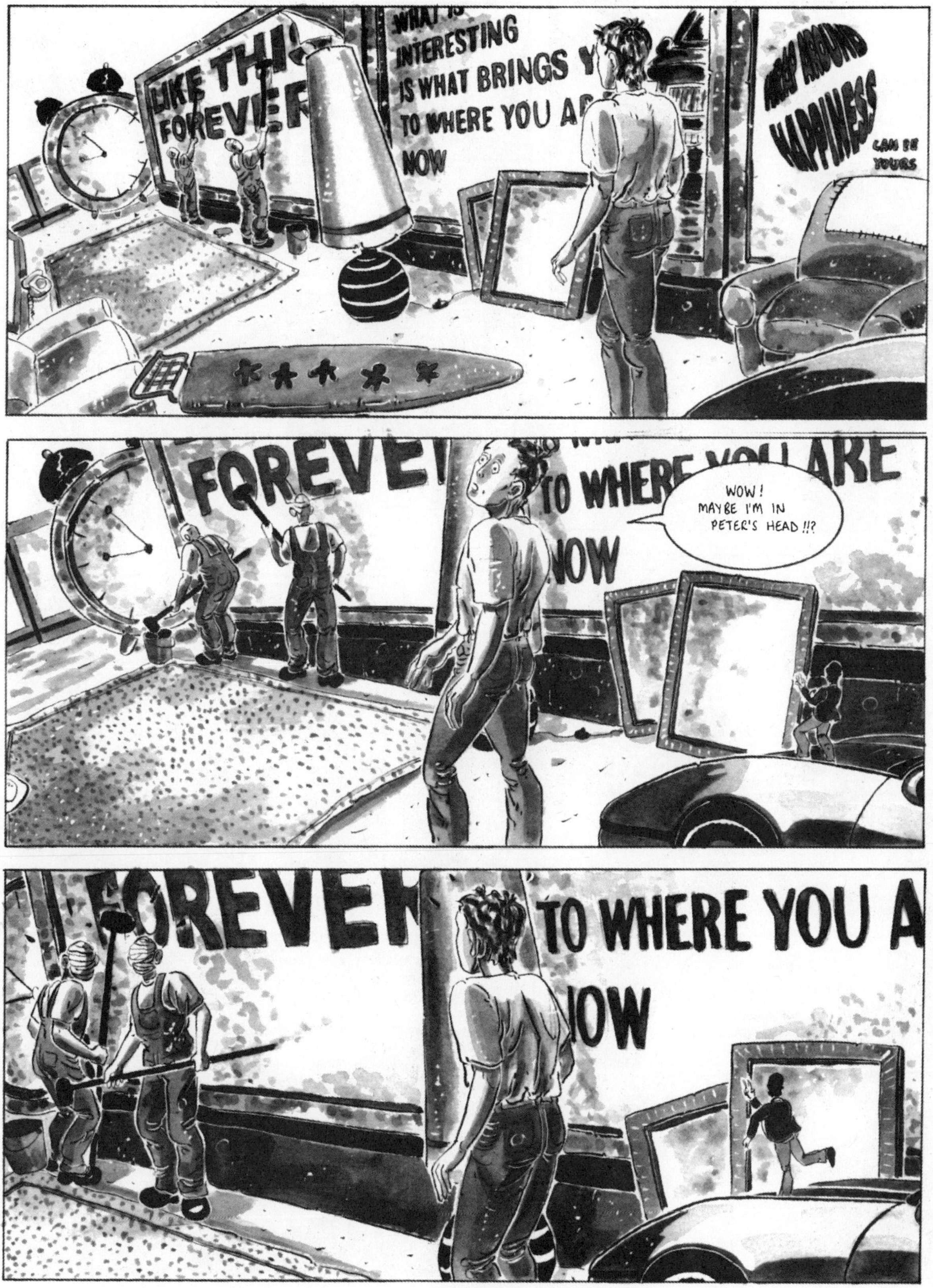
LIKE THI
FOREVE
WHAT IS
INTERESTING
IS WHAT BRINGS Y
TO WHERE YOU A
NOW
WRAP AROUND
HAPPINESS
CAN BE
YOURS
FOREVE
TO WHERE YOU ARE
NOW
WOW! MAYBE I'M IN PETER'S HEAD !!?
FOREVE
TO WHERE YOU A
NOW

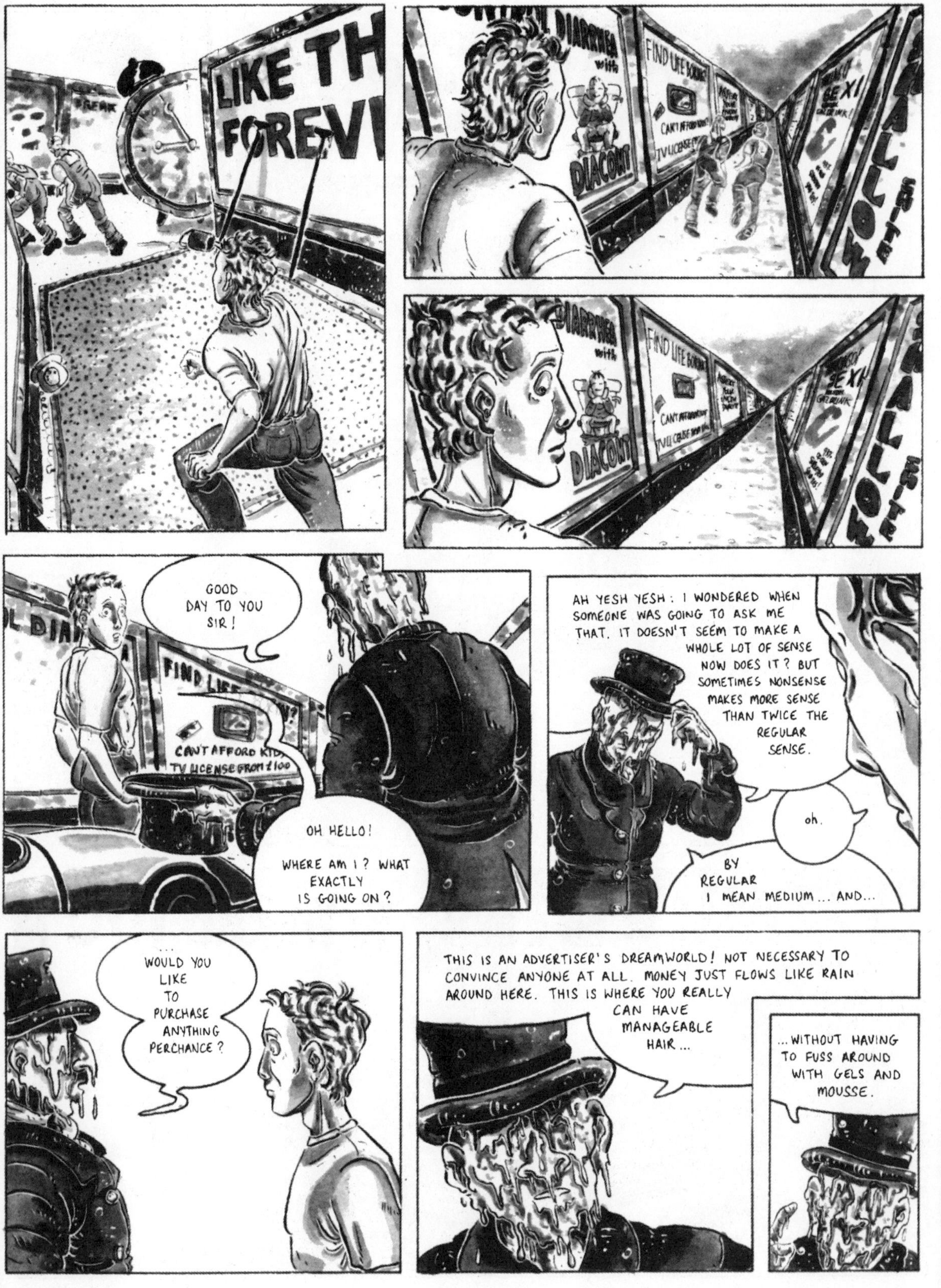
LIKE TH
FOREV
DIARRHEA
with
FIND LIFE BORING?
DIACONT
CAN'T AFFORD KIDS?
TV LICENSE FROM £100
GOOD DAY TO YOU SIR!
OH HELLO!
WHERE AM I? WHAT EXACTLY IS GOING ON?
AH YESH YESH: I WONDERED WHEN SOMEONE WAS GOING TO ASK ME THAT. IT DOESN'T SEEM TO MAKE A WHOLE LOT OF SENSE NOW DOES IT? BUT SOMETIMES NONSENSE MAKES MORE SENSE THAN TWICE THE REGULAR SENSE.
oh.
BY REGULAR I MEAN MEDIUM ... AND...
... WOULD YOU LIKE TO PURCHASE ANYTHING PERCHANCE?
THIS IS AN ADVERTISER'S DREAMWORLD! NOT NECESSARY TO CONVINCE ANYONE AT ALL. MONEY JUST FLOWS LIKE RAIN AROUND HERE. THIS IS WHERE YOU REALLY CAN HAVE MANAGEABLE HAIR...
... WITHOUT HAVING TO FUSS AROUND WITH GELS AND MOUSSE.

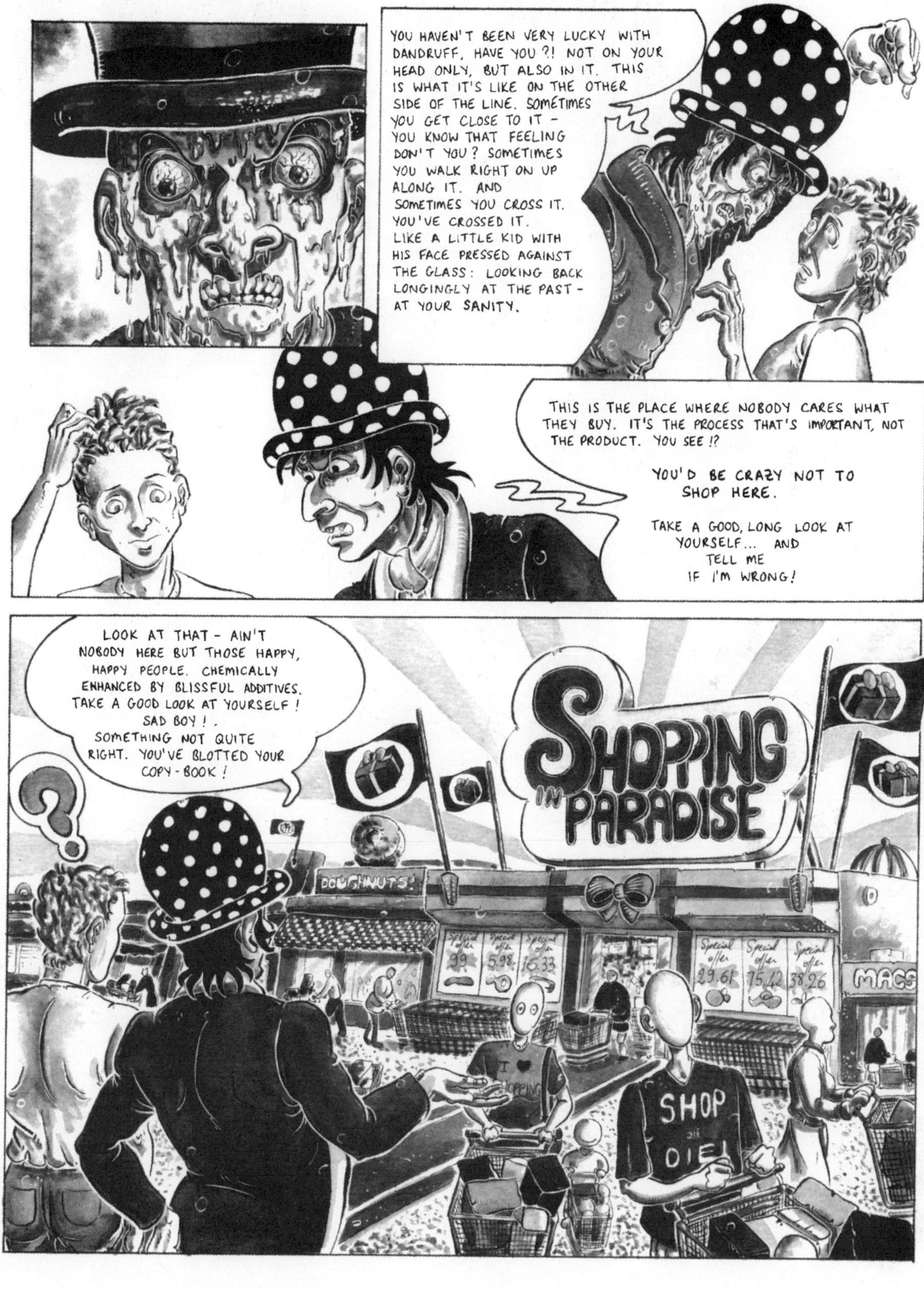

YOU HAVEN'T BEEN VERY LUCKY WITH DANDRUFF, HAVE YOU ?! NOT ON YOUR HEAD ONLY, BUT ALSO IN IT. THIS IS WHAT IT'S LIKE ON THE OTHER SIDE OF THE LINE. SOMETIMES YOU GET CLOSE TO IT - YOU KNOW THAT FEELING DON'T YOU? SOMETIMES YOU WALK RIGHT ON UP ALONG IT. AND SOMETIMES YOU CROSS IT. YOU'VE CROSSED IT. LIKE A LITTLE KID WITH HIS FACE PRESSED AGAINST THE GLASS: LOOKING BACK LONGINGLY AT THE PAST - AT YOUR SANITY.
THIS IS THE PLACE WHERE NOBODY CARES WHAT THEY BUY. IT'S THE PROCESS THAT'S IMPORTANT, NOT THE PRODUCT. YOU SEE !?
YOU'D BE CRAZY NOT TO SHOP HERE.
TAKE A GOOD, LONG LOOK AT YOURSELF... AND TELL ME IF I'M WRONG!
LOOK AT THAT - AIN'T NOBODY HERE BUT THOSE HAPPY, HAPPY PEOPLE. CHEMICALLY ENHANCED BY BLISSFUL ADDITIVES. TAKE A GOOD LOOK AT YOURSELF! SAD BOY! . SOMETHING NOT QUITE RIGHT. YOU'VE BLOTTED YOUR COPY-BOOK!
SHOPPING IN PARADISE
DOUGHNUTS!
Special offer 99
Special offer 5.98
Special offer 16.33
Special offer 29.61
Special offer 75.42
Special offer 38.26
MACS
SHOP
DIE!

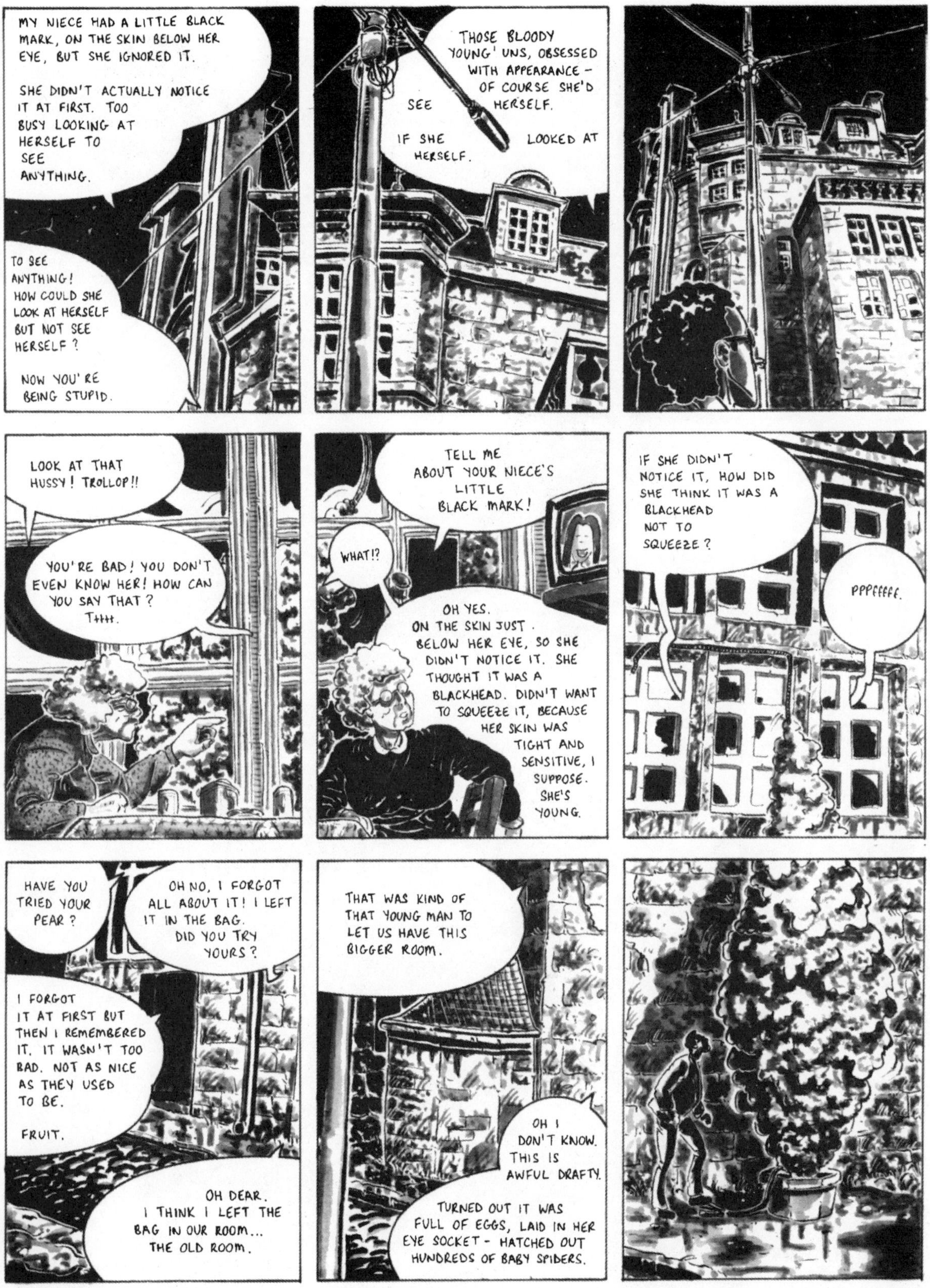
MY NIECE HAD A LITTLE BLACK MARK, ON THE SKIN BELOW HER EYE, BUT SHE IGNORED IT.
SHE DIDN'T ACTUALLY NOTICE IT AT FIRST. TOO BUSY LOOKING AT HERSELF TO SEE ANYTHING.
TO SEE ANYTHING! HOW COULD SHE LOOK AT HERSELF BUT NOT SEE HERSELF?
NOW YOU'RE BEING STUPID.
THOSE BLOODY YOUNG' UNS, OBSESSED WITH APPEARANCE - OF COURSE SHE'D SEE HERSELF.
IF SHE LOOKED AT HERSELF.
LOOK AT THAT HUSSY! TROLLOP!!
YOU'RE BAD! YOU DON'T EVEN KNOW HER! HOW CAN YOU SAY THAT? Ttttt.
TELL ME ABOUT YOUR NIECE'S LITTLE BLACK MARK!
WHAT!?
OH YES. ON THE SKIN JUST BELOW HER EYE, SO SHE DIDN'T NOTICE IT. SHE THOUGHT IT WAS A BLACKHEAD. DIDN'T WANT TO SQUEEZE IT, BECAUSE HER SKIN WAS TIGHT AND SENSITIVE, I SUPPOSE. SHE'S YOUNG.
IF SHE DIDN'T NOTICE IT, HOW DID SHE THINK IT WAS A BLACKHEAD NOT TO SQUEEZE?
PPPFFFFF.
HAVE YOU TRIED YOUR PEAR?
OH NO, I FORGOT ALL ABOUT IT! I LEFT IT IN THE BAG. DID YOU TRY YOURS?
I FORGOT IT AT FIRST BUT THEN I REMEMBERED IT. IT WASN'T TOO BAD. NOT AS NICE AS THEY USED TO BE.
FRUIT.
OH DEAR. I THINK I LEFT THE BAG IN OUR ROOM... THE OLD ROOM.
THAT WAS KIND OF THAT YOUNG MAN TO LET US HAVE THIS BIGGER ROOM.
OH I DON'T KNOW. THIS IS AWFUL DRAFTY.
TURNED OUT IT WAS FULL OF EGGS, LAID IN HER EYE SOCKET - HATCHED OUT HUNDREDS OF BABY SPIDERS.

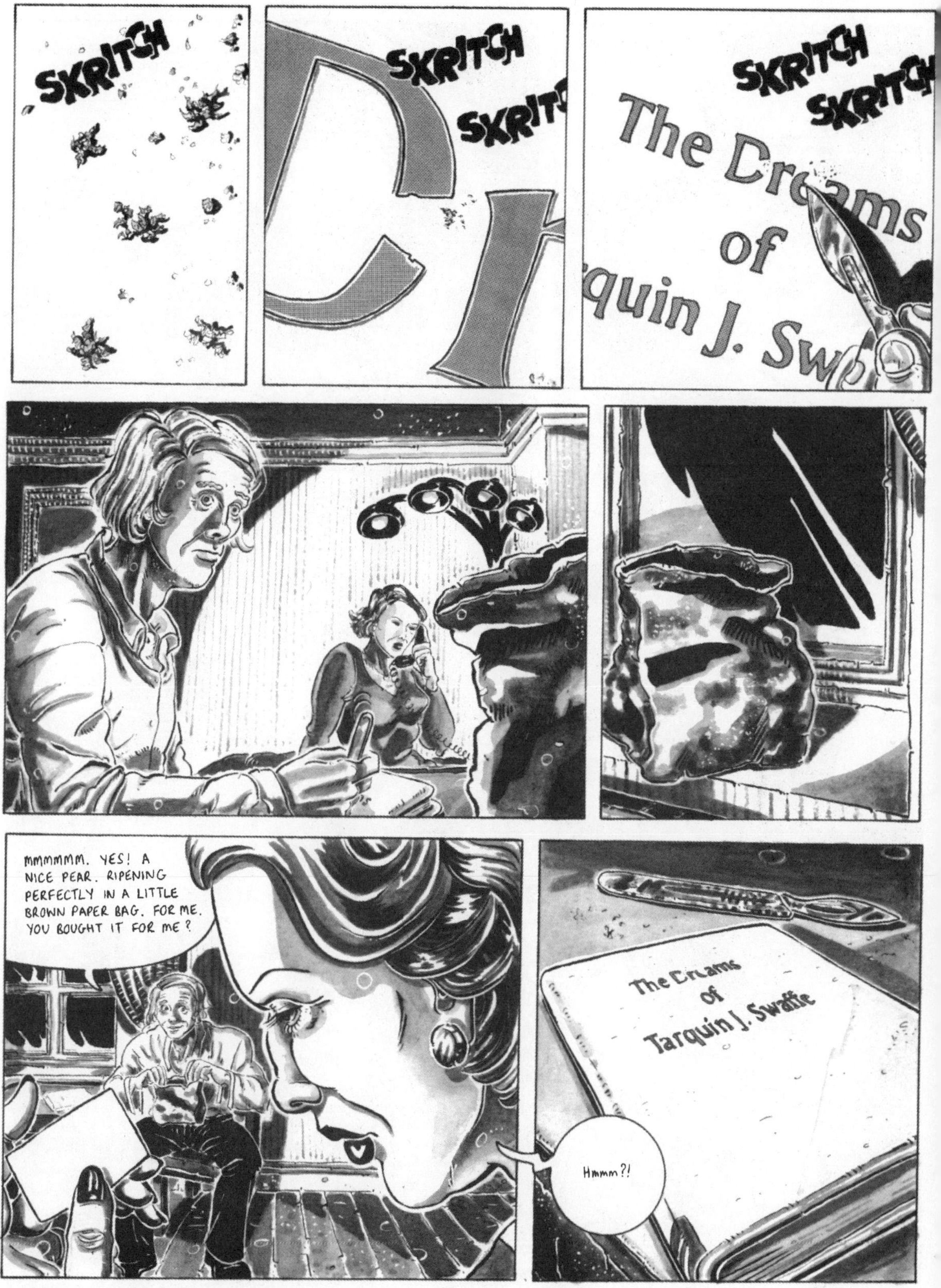
SKRITCH
SKRITCH
SKRITCH
SKRITCH
SKRITCH
The Dreams of
quin J. Sw
MMMMMM. YES! A NICE PEAR. RIPENING PERFECTLY IN A LITTLE BROWN PAPER BAG. FOR ME. YOU BOUGHT IT FOR ME?
The Dreams of Tarquin J. Swaffie
Hmmm?!

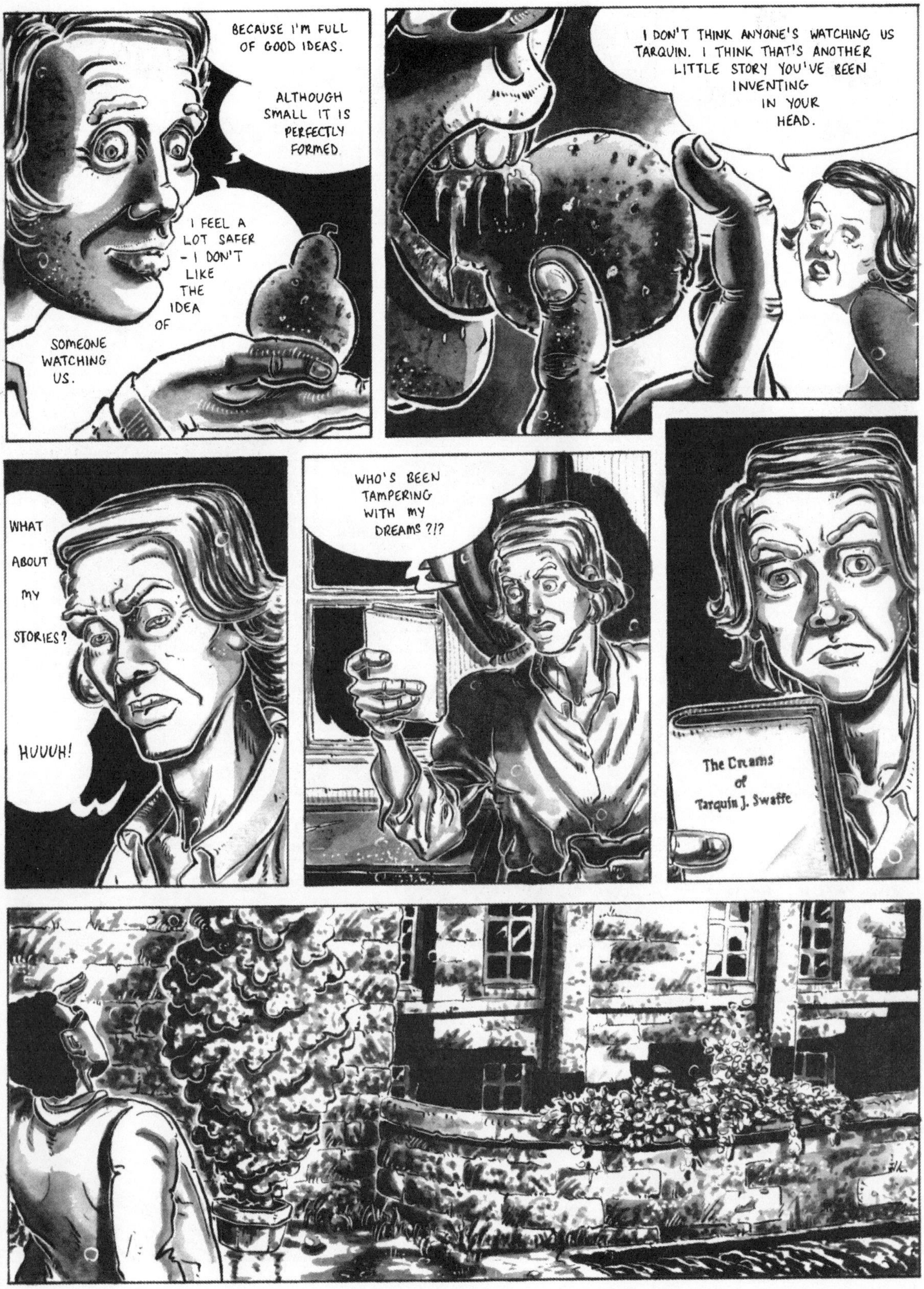
BECAUSE I'M FULL OF GOOD IDEAS.
ALTHOUGH SMALL IT IS PERFECTLY FORMED.
I FEEL A LOT SAFER - I DON'T LIKE THE IDEA OF SOMEONE WATCHING US.
I DON'T THINK ANYONE'S WATCHING US TARQUIN. I THINK THAT'S ANOTHER LITTLE STORY YOU'VE BEEN INVENTING IN YOUR HEAD.
WHAT ABOUT MY STORIES?
HUUUH!
WHO'S BEEN TAMPERING WITH MY DREAMS?!?
The Dreams of Tarquin J. Swaffe

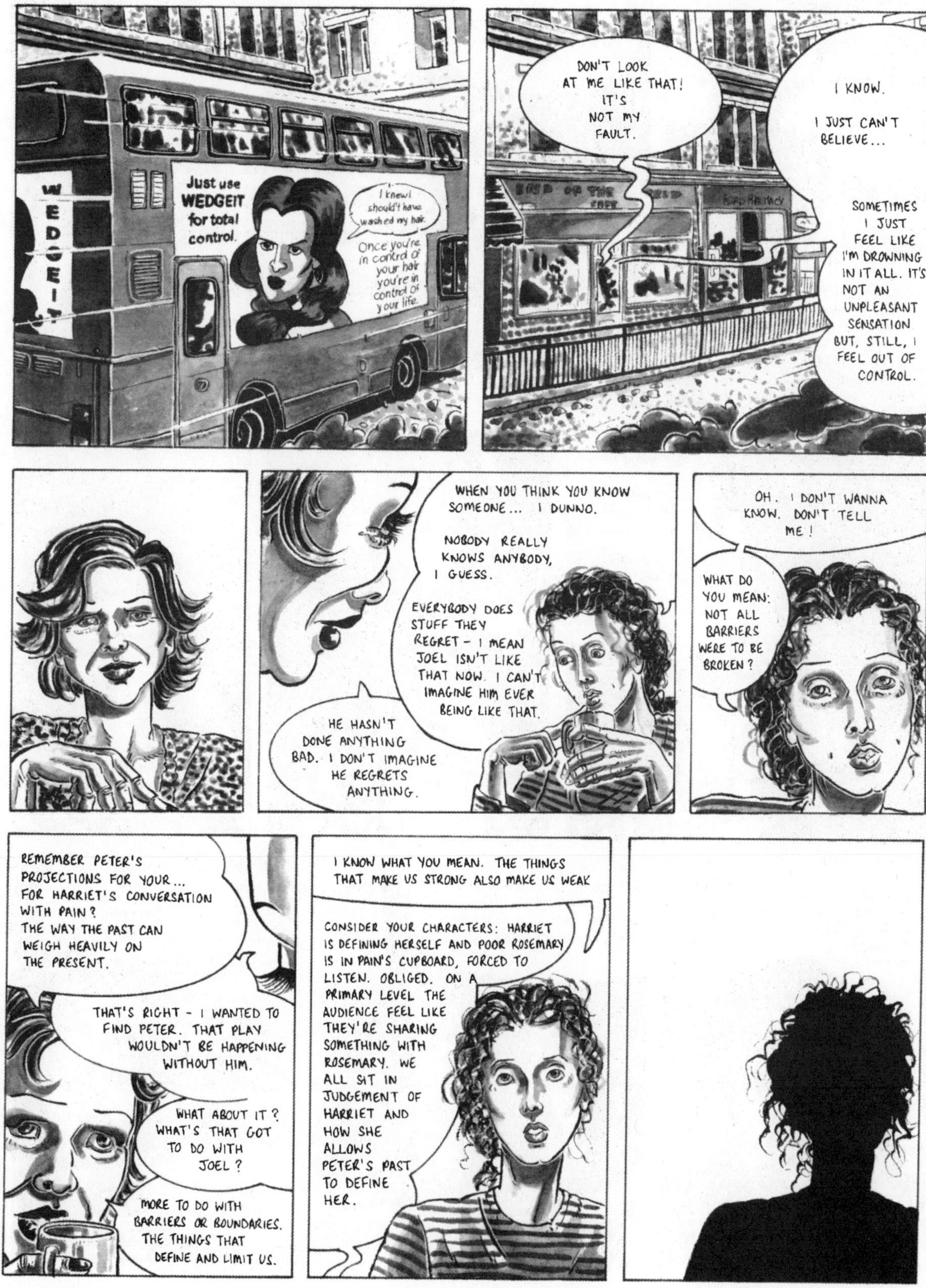

WEDGEIT
Just use WEDGEIT for total control.
I knew! I should've washed my hair.
Once you're in control of your hair you're in control of your life.
DON'T LOOK AT ME LIKE THAT! IT'S NOT MY FAULT.
I KNOW. I JUST CAN'T BELIEVE...
SOMETIMES I JUST FEEL LIKE I'M DROWNING IN IT ALL. IT'S NOT AN UNPLEASANT SENSATION BUT, STILL, I FEEL OUT OF CONTROL.
WHEN YOU THINK YOU KNOW SOMEONE... I DUNNO.
NOBODY REALLY KNOWS ANYBODY, I GUESS.
EVERYBODY DOES STUFF THEY REGRET - I MEAN JOEL ISN'T LIKE THAT NOW. I CAN'T IMAGINE HIM EVER BEING LIKE THAT.
HE HASN'T DONE ANYTHING BAD. I DON'T IMAGINE HE REGRETS ANYTHING.
OH. I DON'T WANNA KNOW. DON'T TELL ME!
WHAT DO YOU MEAN: NOT ALL BARRIERS WERE TO BE BROKEN?
REMEMBER PETER'S PROJECTIONS FOR YOUR... FOR HARRIET'S CONVERSATION WITH PAIN? THE WAY THE PAST CAN WEIGH HEAVILY ON THE PRESENT.
THAT'S RIGHT - I WANTED TO FIND PETER. THAT PLAY WOULDN'T BE HAPPENING WITHOUT HIM.
WHAT ABOUT IT? WHAT'S THAT GOT TO DO WITH JOEL?
MORE TO DO WITH BARRIERS OR BOUNDARIES. THE THINGS THAT DEFINE AND LIMIT US.
I KNOW WHAT YOU MEAN. THE THINGS THAT MAKE US STRONG ALSO MAKE US WEAK
CONSIDER YOUR CHARACTERS: HARRIET IS DEFINING HERSELF AND POOR ROSEMARY IS IN PAIN'S CUPBOARD, FORCED TO LISTEN. OBLIGED. ON A PRIMARY LEVEL THE AUDIENCE FEEL LIKE THEY'RE SHARING SOMETHING WITH ROSEMARY. WE ALL SIT IN JUDGEMENT OF HARRIET AND HOW SHE ALLOWS PETER'S PAST TO DEFINE HER.

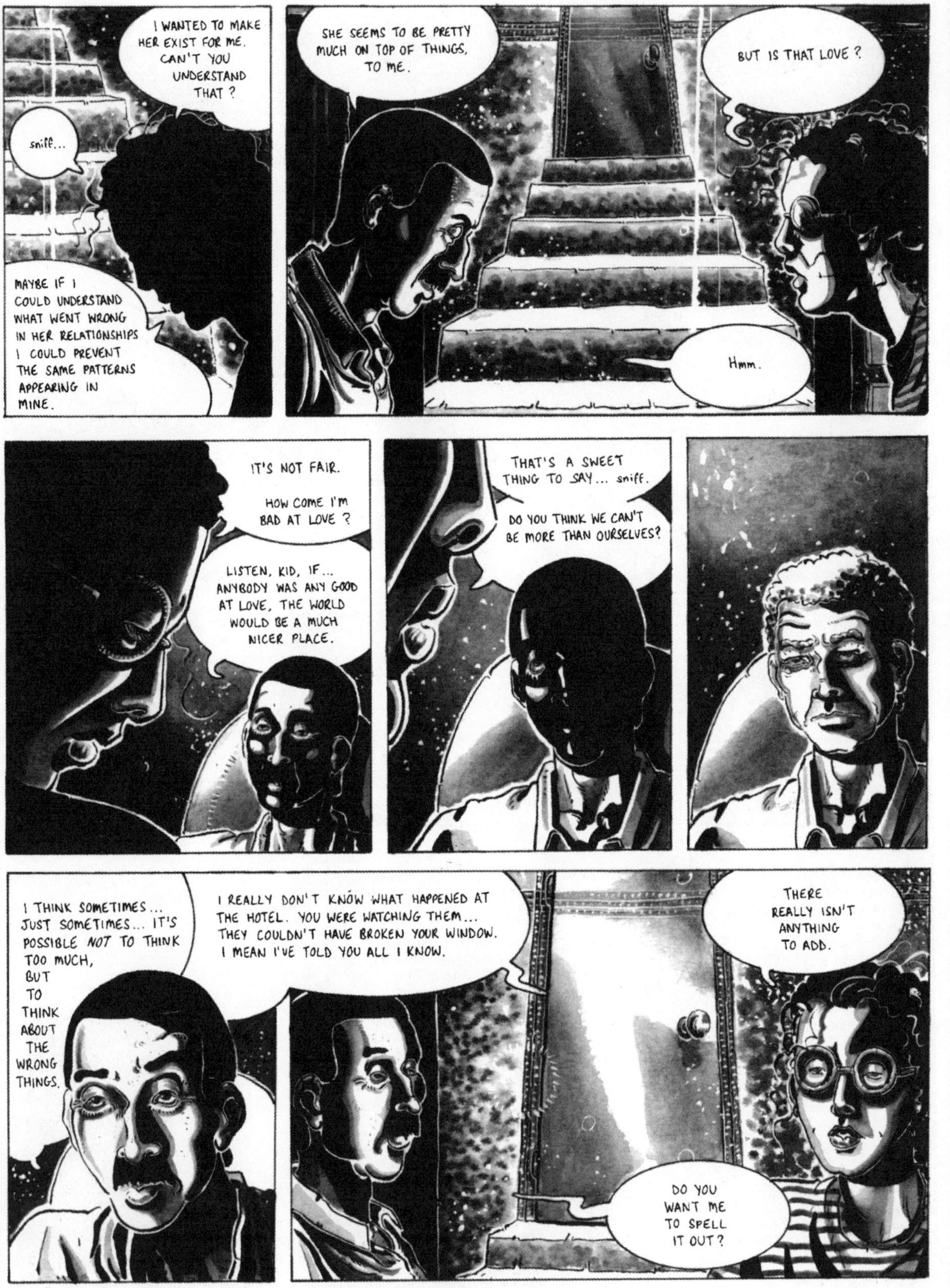

I WANTED TO MAKE HER EXIST FOR ME. CAN'T YOU UNDERSTAND THAT ?
sniff...
MAYBE IF I COULD UNDERSTAND WHAT WENT WRONG IN HER RELATIONSHIPS I COULD PREVENT THE SAME PATTERNS APPEARING IN MINE.
SHE SEEMS TO BE PRETTY MUCH ON TOP OF THINGS, TO ME.
BUT IS THAT LOVE ?
Hmm.
IT'S NOT FAIR.
HOW COME I'M BAD AT LOVE ?
LISTEN, KID, IF... ANYBODY WAS ANY GOOD AT LOVE, THE WORLD WOULD BE A MUCH NICER PLACE.
THAT'S A SWEET THING TO SAY... sniff.
DO YOU THINK WE CAN'T BE MORE THAN OURSELVES?
I THINK SOMETIMES... JUST SOMETIMES... IT'S POSSIBLE NOT TO THINK TOO MUCH, BUT TO THINK ABOUT THE WRONG THINGS.
I REALLY DON'T KNOW WHAT HAPPENED AT THE HOTEL. YOU WERE WATCHING THEM... THEY COULDN'T HAVE BROKEN YOUR WINDOW. I MEAN I'VE TOLD YOU ALL I KNOW.
THERE REALLY ISN'T ANYTHING TO ADD.
DO YOU WANT ME TO SPELL IT OUT?

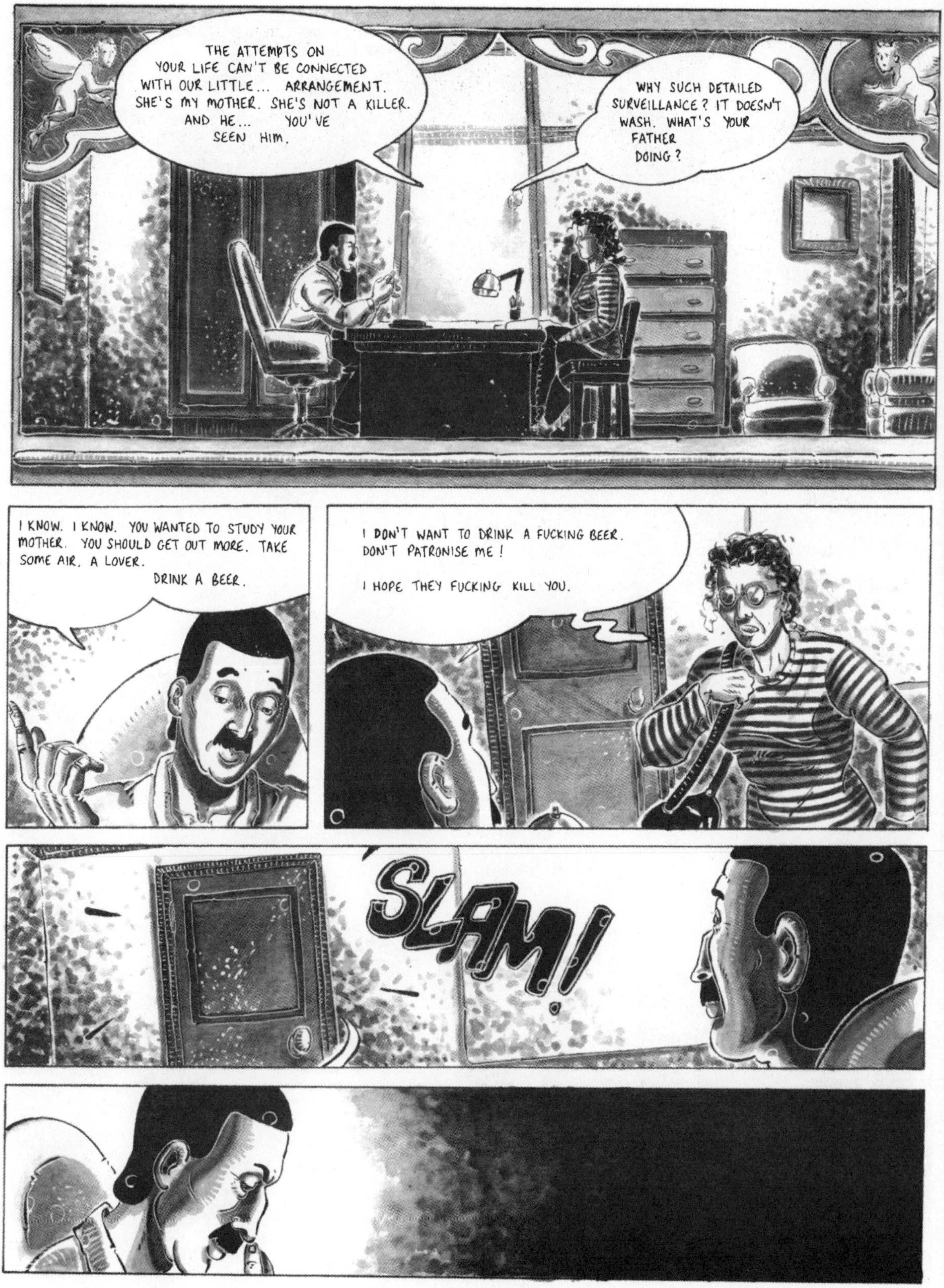
THE ATTEMPTS ON YOUR LIFE CAN'T BE CONNECTED WITH OUR LITTLE... ARRANGEMENT. SHE'S MY MOTHER. SHE'S NOT A KILLER. AND HE... YOU'VE SEEN HIM.
WHY SUCH DETAILED SURVEILLANCE? IT DOESN'T WASH. WHAT'S YOUR FATHER DOING?
I KNOW. I KNOW. YOU WANTED TO STUDY YOUR MOTHER. YOU SHOULD GET OUT MORE. TAKE SOME AIR, A LOVER. DRINK A BEER.
I DON'T WANT TO DRINK A FUCKING BEER. DON'T PATRONISE ME!
I HOPE THEY FUCKING KILL YOU.
SLAM!

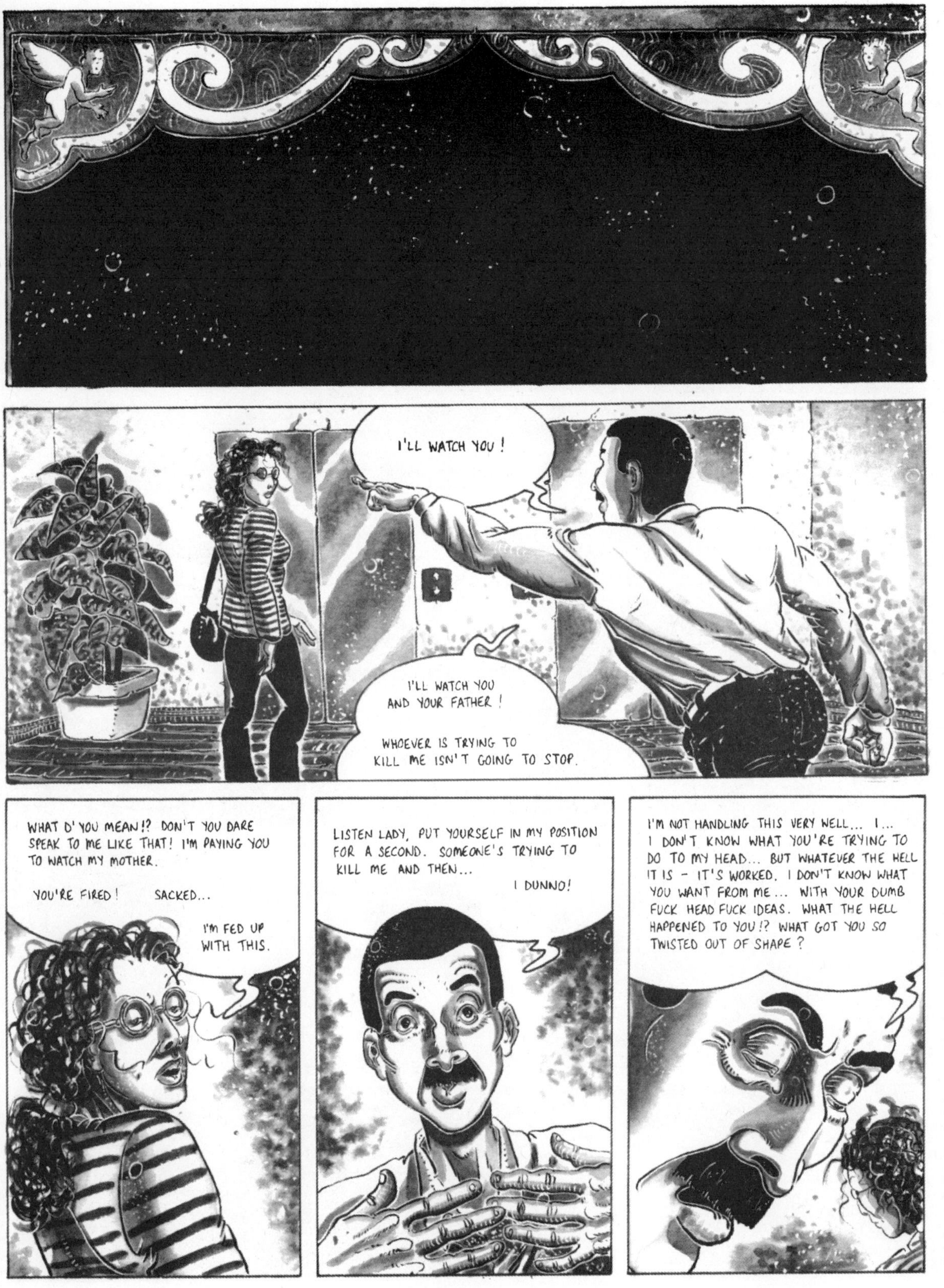

I'LL WATCH YOU !
I'LL WATCH YOU AND YOUR FATHER !
WHOEVER IS TRYING TO KILL ME ISN'T GOING TO STOP.
WHAT D' YOU MEAN !? DON'T YOU DARE SPEAK TO ME LIKE THAT! I'M PAYING YOU TO WATCH MY MOTHER.
YOU'RE FIRED ! SACKED...
I'M FED UP WITH THIS.
LISTEN LADY, PUT YOURSELF IN MY POSITION FOR A SECOND. SOMEONE'S TRYING TO KILL ME AND THEN...
I DUNNO!
I'M NOT HANDLING THIS VERY WELL... I... I DON'T KNOW WHAT YOU'RE TRYING TO DO TO MY HEAD... BUT WHATEVER THE HELL IT IS - IT'S WORKED. I DON'T KNOW WHAT YOU WANT FROM ME... WITH YOUR DUMB FUCK HEAD FUCK IDEAS. WHAT THE HELL HAPPENED TO YOU !? WHAT GOT YOU SO TWISTED OUT OF SHAPE ?

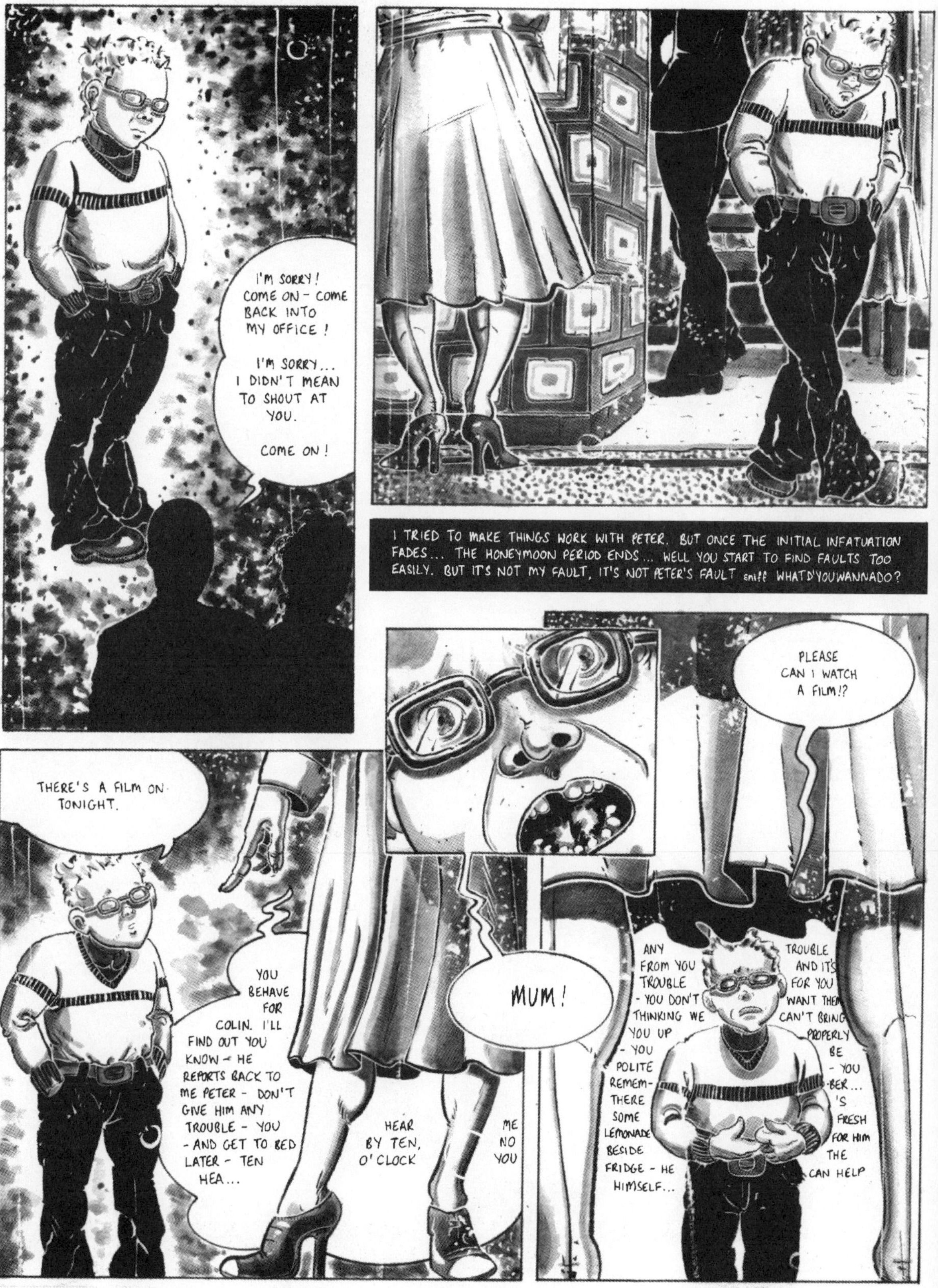
I'M SORRY! COME ON - COME BACK INTO MY OFFICE!
I'M SORRY... I DIDN'T MEAN TO SHOUT AT YOU.
COME ON!
I TRIED TO MAKE THINGS WORK WITH PETER. BUT ONCE THE INITIAL INFATUATION FADES... THE HONEYMOON PERIOD ENDS... WELL YOU START TO FIND FAULTS TOO EASILY. BUT IT'S NOT MY FAULT, IT'S NOT PETER'S FAULT sniff WHAT'D'YOUWANNADO?
PLEASE CAN I WATCH A FILM!?
THERE'S A FILM ON TONIGHT.
MUM!
YOU BEHAVE FOR COLIN. I'LL FIND OUT YOU KNOW - HE REPORTS BACK TO ME PETER - DON'T GIVE HIM ANY TROUBLE - YOU - AND GET TO BED LATER - TEN HEA...
HEAR BY TEN, O'CLOCK
ME NO YOU
ANY FROM YOU TROUBLE - YOU DON'T THINKING WE YOU UP - YOU POLITE REMEM- THERE SOME LEMONADE BESIDE FRIDGE - HE HIMSELF...
TROUBLE AND IT'S FOR YOU WANT THEM CAN'T BRING PROPERLY BE - YOU -BER... 'S FRESH FOR HIM THE CAN HELP

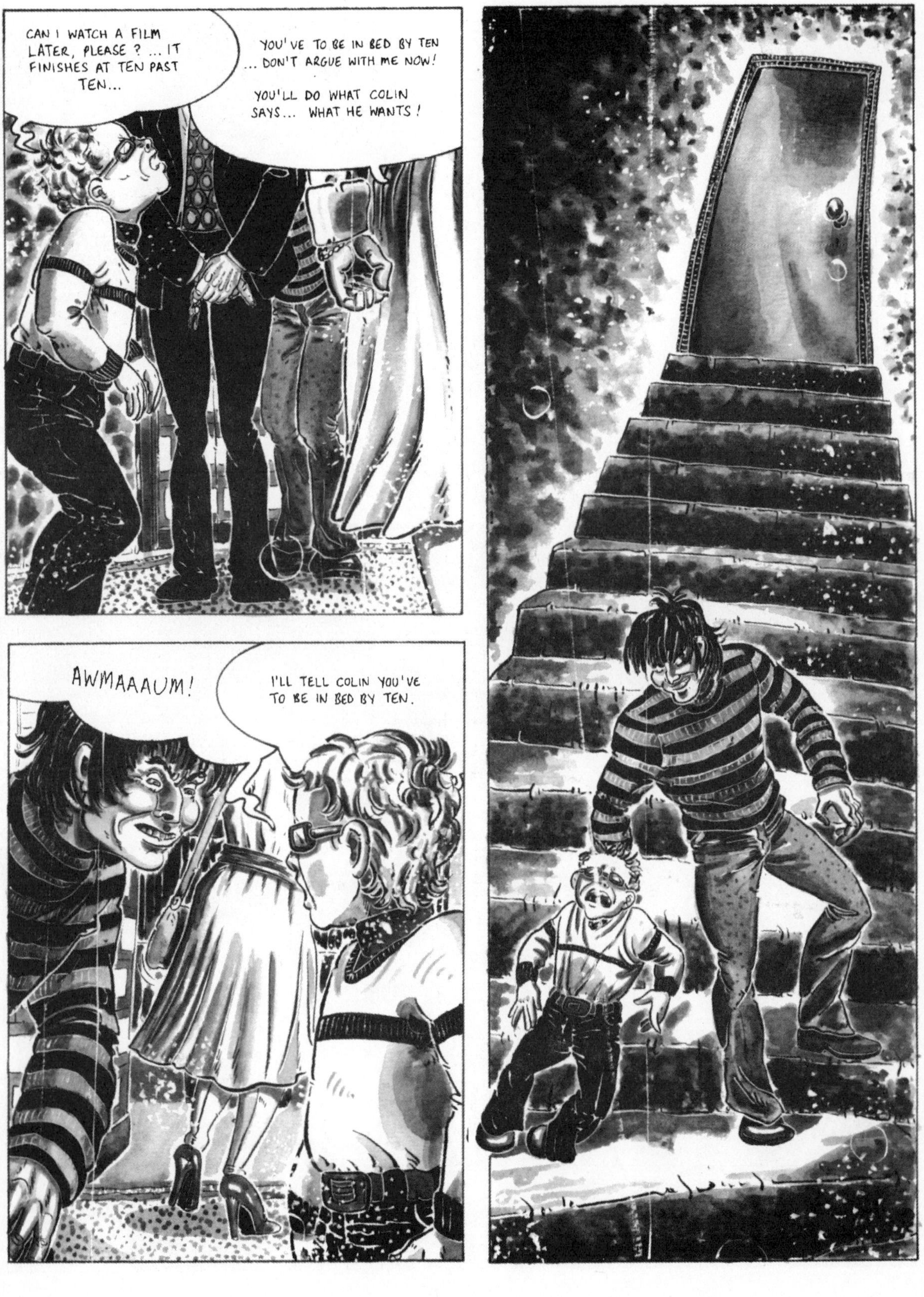
CAN I WATCH A FILM LATER, PLEASE ? ... IT FINISHES AT TEN PAST TEN...
YOU'VE TO BE IN BED BY TEN ... DON'T ARGUE WITH ME NOW!
YOU'LL DO WHAT COLIN SAYS... WHAT HE WANTS !
AWMAAAUM!
I'LL TELL COLIN YOU'VE TO BE IN BED BY TEN.

What would you do
if the things you thought
came true?

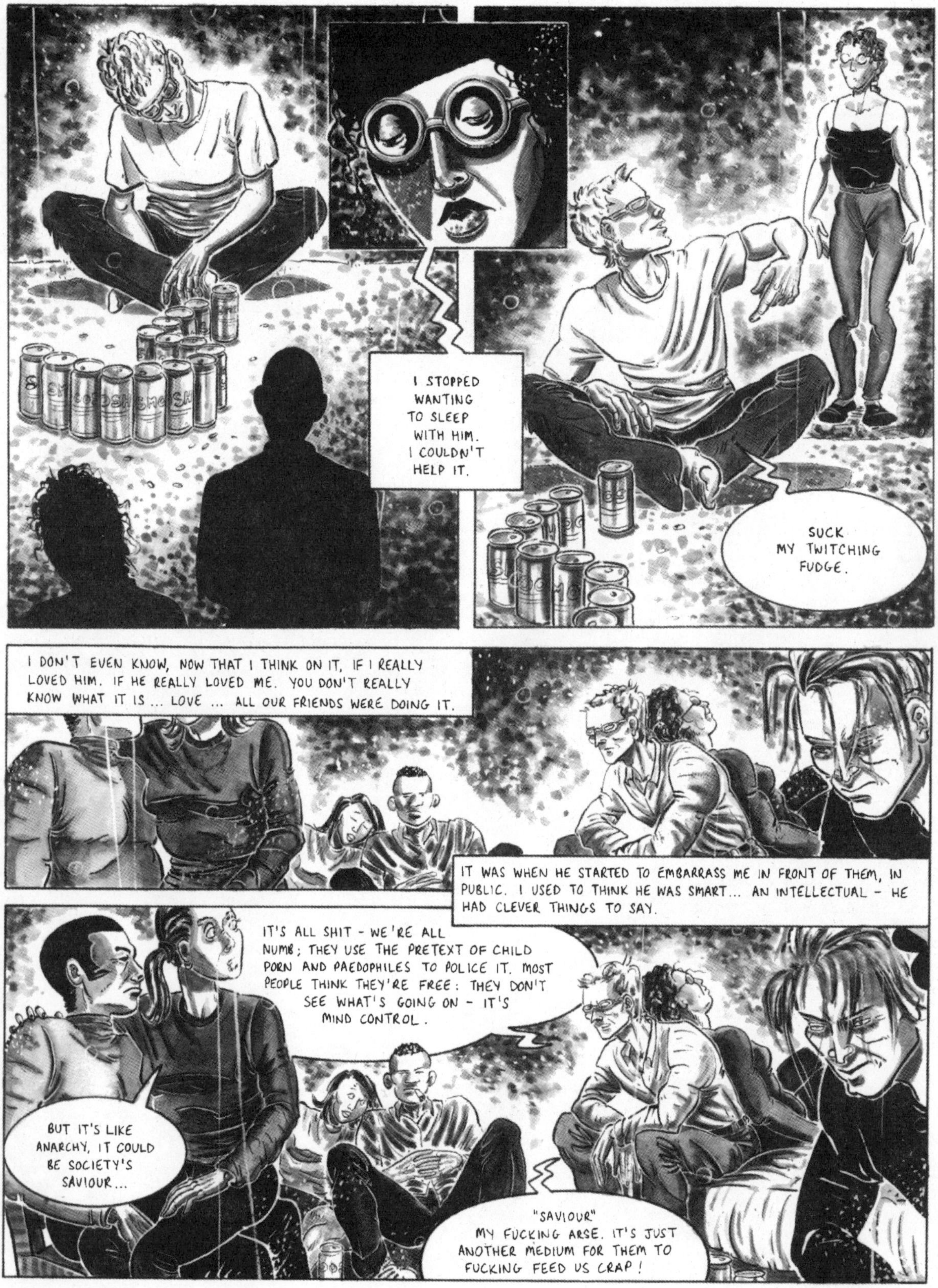

I STOPPED WANTING TO SLEEP WITH HIM. I COULDN'T HELP IT.
SUCK MY TWITCHING FUDGE.
I DON'T EVEN KNOW, NOW THAT I THINK ON IT, IF I REALLY LOVED HIM. IF HE REALLY LOVED ME. YOU DON'T REALLY KNOW WHAT IT IS ... LOVE ... ALL OUR FRIENDS WERE DOING IT.
IT WAS WHEN HE STARTED TO EMBARRASS ME IN FRONT OF THEM, IN PUBLIC. I USED TO THINK HE WAS SMART... AN INTELLECTUAL - HE HAD CLEVER THINGS TO SAY.
IT'S ALL SHIT - WE'RE ALL NUMB; THEY USE THE PRETEXT OF CHILD PORN AND PAEDOPHILES TO POLICE IT. MOST PEOPLE THINK THEY'RE FREE: THEY DON'T SEE WHAT'S GOING ON - IT'S MIND CONTROL.
BUT IT'S LIKE ANARCHY, IT COULD BE SOCIETY'S SAVIOUR...
"SAVIOUR" MY FUCKING ARSE. IT'S JUST ANOTHER MEDIUM FOR THEM TO FUCKING FEED US CRAP!

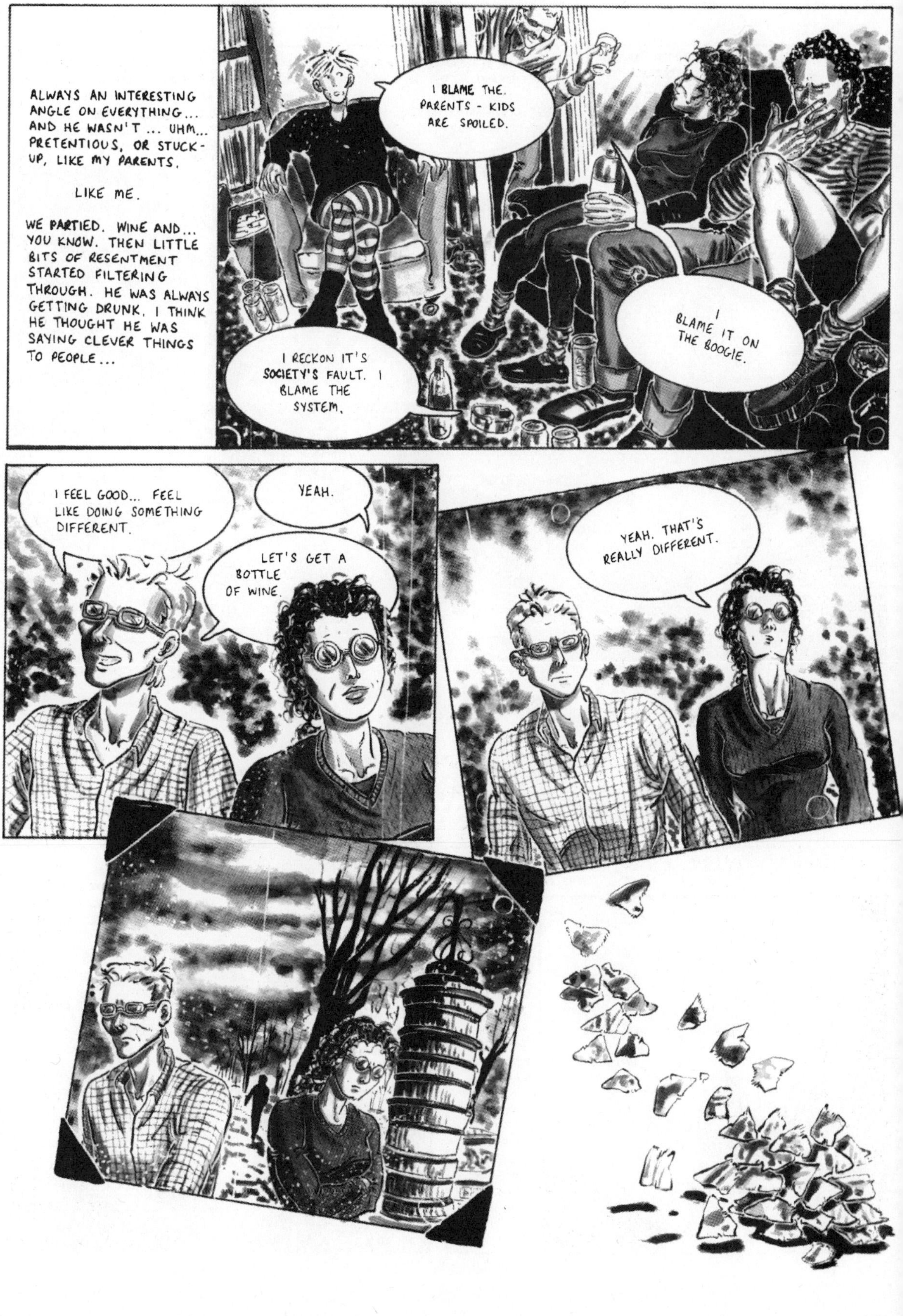
ALWAYS AN INTERESTING ANGLE ON EVERYTHING... AND HE WASN'T ... UHM... PRETENTIOUS, OR STUCK-UP, LIKE MY PARENTS.
LIKE ME.
WE PARTIED. WINE AND... YOU KNOW. THEN LITTLE BITS OF RESENTMENT STARTED FILTERING THROUGH. HE WAS ALWAYS GETTING DRUNK. I THINK HE THOUGHT HE WAS SAYING CLEVER THINGS TO PEOPLE...
I BLAME THE. PARENTS - KIDS ARE SPOILED.
I RECKON IT'S SOCIETY'S FAULT. I BLAME THE SYSTEM.
I BLAME IT ON THE BOOGIE.
I FEEL GOOD... FEEL LIKE DOING SOMETHING DIFFERENT.
YEAH.
LET'S GET A BOTTLE OF WINE.
YEAH. THAT'S REALLY DIFFERENT.

HE TOLD ME ABOUT HIS CHILDHOOD TRAUMAS. THINGS HE DIDN'T THINK, WELL, REALISE, HE HADN'T DEALT WITH. YOU SEE, HE COULDN'T EQUATE IT WITH HIS UNHAPPINESS TWENTY YEARS LATER. HE THINKS HIS DRINKING IS A CELEBRATION OF LIFE. I THINK HE'D RATHER BLAME SOMETHING ELSE RATHER THAN THE BOTTLE. IT SEEMS EASIER SOMEHOW IF IT'S SOMEONE ELSE'S FAULT.

HIS MIND REFUSED TO REMEMBER WHAT HE WAS TRYING TO FORGET.

BUT A FRAGMENT KEPT CREEPING THROUGH.

OH THAT'S NOT FAIR. I'M BEING UNKIND. I TRIED TO HELP PETER. I SUPPOSE YOU... YOU THINK YOU'RE IN LOVE. IF I'D REALLY LOVED HIM... HE'D REALLY LOVED ME... HE WOULDN'T HAVE TO GET FUCKED UP ALL THE TIME.

sniff... I DON'T KNOW HOW TO LOVE.

BUT SURELY YOU HAD SOME FUN!? HE KNEW HOW TO ENJOY HIMSELF, RIGHT? HE WASN'T THAT BAD A GUY... RIGHT?

HE LIKED TO IMPERSONATE POLICEMEN.

SAY: SHOE SNIFF!

LEISURE SQUAD

HE WAS GOOD WITH PEOPLE, HE COULD MAKE THEM LAUGH...

SAY... SHOE SNIFF

SNOOSHIFF.

BUT DEEP DOWN HE WAS SAD. I FOUND THE MOST BEAUTIFUL POETRY. OFTEN, IT'S LIKE THAT, ISN'T IT? THE CLOWN CRYING BEHIND THE SMILE.

Climbing onto the box she was able to clamber onto the wall and obtain a clear view of the garden beyond. It was quite simply not what she expected at all. Losing the mystery of the unknown had made her procrastinate. It had been a difficult decision, certainly, given the gravity of the situation. The mystery, however, had not seemed such a great thing compared with the promised knowledge. A true surprise gasped in wonder at its beauty. Now as she surveyed the garden in all its splendour, hidden now revealed, her eyes... amazement! The garden ...be oscillating in the sunlight. ...has a small shed, set in the centre, ...it came a pale blue glow. ...wondered what was inside.

BUT HE WASN'T ALWAYS SMILING— SOMETIMES HE WOULD RANT.

IT MADE ITS OWN KIND OF SENSE, YOU KNOW.

THEY'VE GOT US FUCKED EVERY WAY. CONSTANTLY MONITORING YOU AND FEEDING YOU SHIT THROUGH THE TUBE. THE CAMERA'S ON YOU MAN— SO YOU'D BETTER SMILE.

BUT IT'S TO PREVENT CRIME PETER MAN. YOU'RE FUCKING PARA.

BUT IT'S THE SAME... GUNS AND CRACK... BOOZE AND SMACK

IT'S THE MODERN WAY: URBAN DECAY!

LIGHTEN UP!

HE EMBARRASSED ME - IN FRONT OF MY FRIENDS.

GET UP PETER! MY FRIENDS ARE HERE.

LOOKS LIKE TURTLE PIZZA.

HAH HAH HAAH

LOOK AT HIM! PATHETIC. HE'S DRUNK.

I COULD PUT UP WITH HIM. JUST ABOUT! BUT THEN IT ALL FELL TO PIECES...

I'VE FOUND A DEEP SLEEP EGG.

I THINK HE FOUND EVERYTHING TOO EASY. I RECKON THAT'S WHY HE ALWAYS GOT SO WRECKED. AND WHAT THE BABY-SITTER DID!

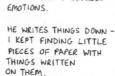

IN THE TOILET. HOLDING HIM UP BY THE EAR. I GUESS OTHER STUFF HAPPENED BUT HIS MIND HAS BLANKED IT.

OR ELSE HE WON'T TALK ABOUT IT.

MY FATHER'S LIKE THAT: CAN'T EXPRESS EMOTIONS.

HE WRITES THINGS DOWN - I KEPT FINDING LITTLE PIECES OF PAPER WITH THINGS WRITTEN ON THEM.

LOOK!

I am voided.

HE FINDS IT HARD SINCE MUM LEFT.

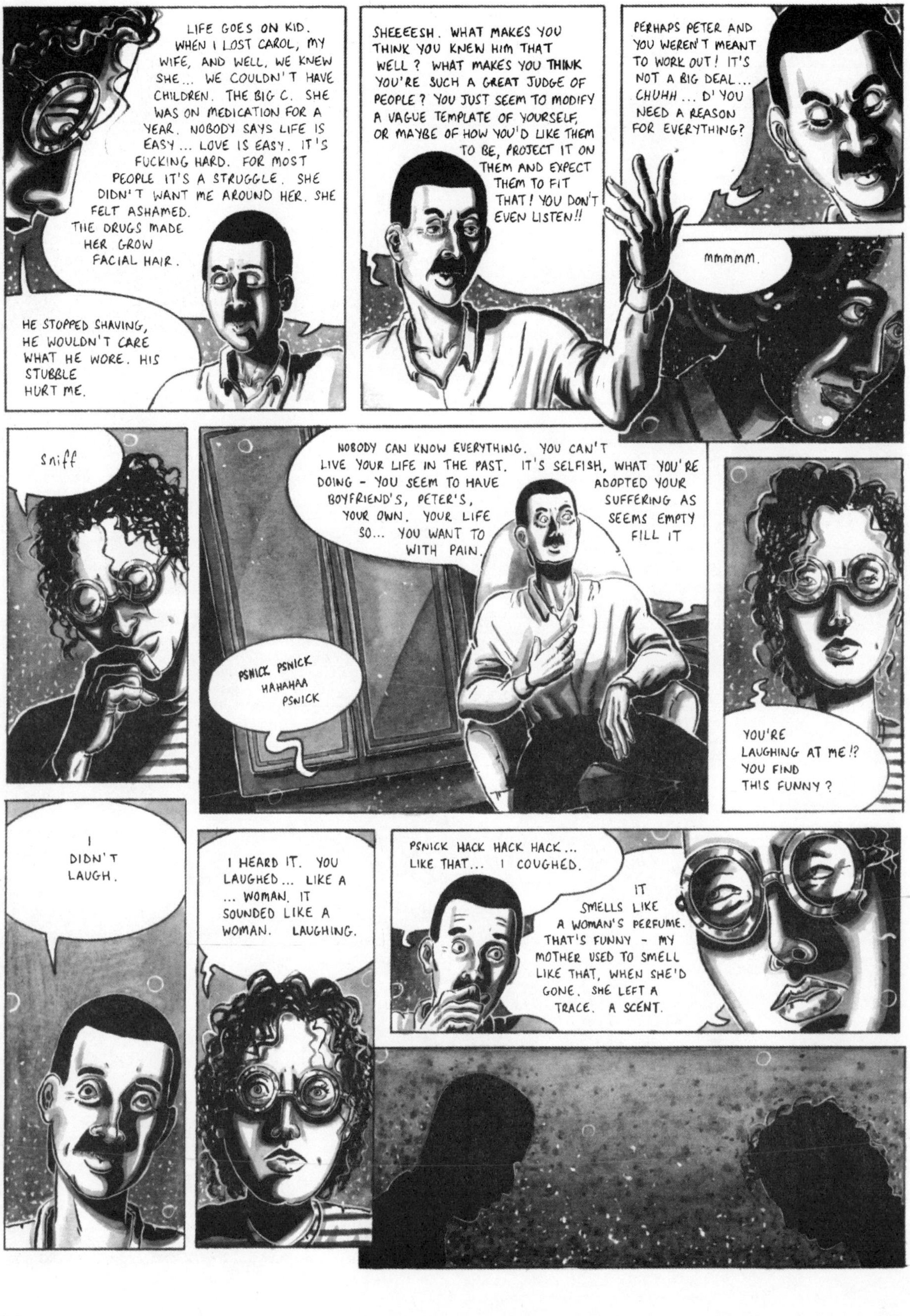
LIFE GOES ON KID. WHEN I LOST CAROL, MY WIFE, AND WELL, WE KNEW SHE... WE COULDN'T HAVE CHILDREN. THE BIG C. SHE WAS ON MEDICATION FOR A YEAR. NOBODY SAYS LIFE IS EASY... LOVE IS EASY. IT'S FUCKING HARD. FOR MOST PEOPLE IT'S A STRUGGLE. SHE DIDN'T WANT ME AROUND HER. SHE FELT ASHAMED. THE DRUGS MADE HER GROW FACIAL HAIR.
HE STOPPED SHAVING, HE WOULDN'T CARE WHAT HE WORE. HIS STUBBLE HURT ME.
SHEEEESH. WHAT MAKES YOU THINK YOU KNEW HIM THAT WELL? WHAT MAKES YOU THINK YOU'RE SUCH A GREAT JUDGE OF PEOPLE? YOU JUST SEEM TO MODIFY A VAGUE TEMPLATE OF YOURSELF, OR MAYBE OF HOW YOU'D LIKE THEM TO BE, PROJECT IT ON THEM AND EXPECT THEM TO FIT THAT! YOU DON'T EVEN LISTEN!!
PERHAPS PETER AND YOU WEREN'T MEANT TO WORK OUT! IT'S NOT A BIG DEAL... CHUHH... D' YOU NEED A REASON FOR EVERYTHING?
mmmmm.
Sniff
NOBODY CAN KNOW EVERYTHING. YOU CAN'T LIVE YOUR LIFE IN THE PAST. IT'S SELFISH, WHAT YOU'RE DOING - YOU SEEM TO HAVE ADOPTED YOUR BOYFRIEND'S, PETER'S, SUFFERING AS YOUR OWN. YOUR LIFE SEEMS EMPTY SO... YOU WANT TO FILL IT WITH PAIN.
PSNICK PSNICK HAHAHAA PSNICK
YOU'RE LAUGHING AT ME!? YOU FIND THIS FUNNY?
I DIDN'T LAUGH.
I HEARD IT. YOU LAUGHED... LIKE A ... WOMAN. IT SOUNDED LIKE A WOMAN. LAUGHING.
PSNICK HACK HACK HACK... LIKE THAT... I COUGHED.
IT SMELLS LIKE A WOMAN'S PERFUME. THAT'S FUNNY - MY MOTHER USED TO SMELL LIKE THAT, WHEN SHE'D GONE. SHE LEFT A TRACE. A SCENT.

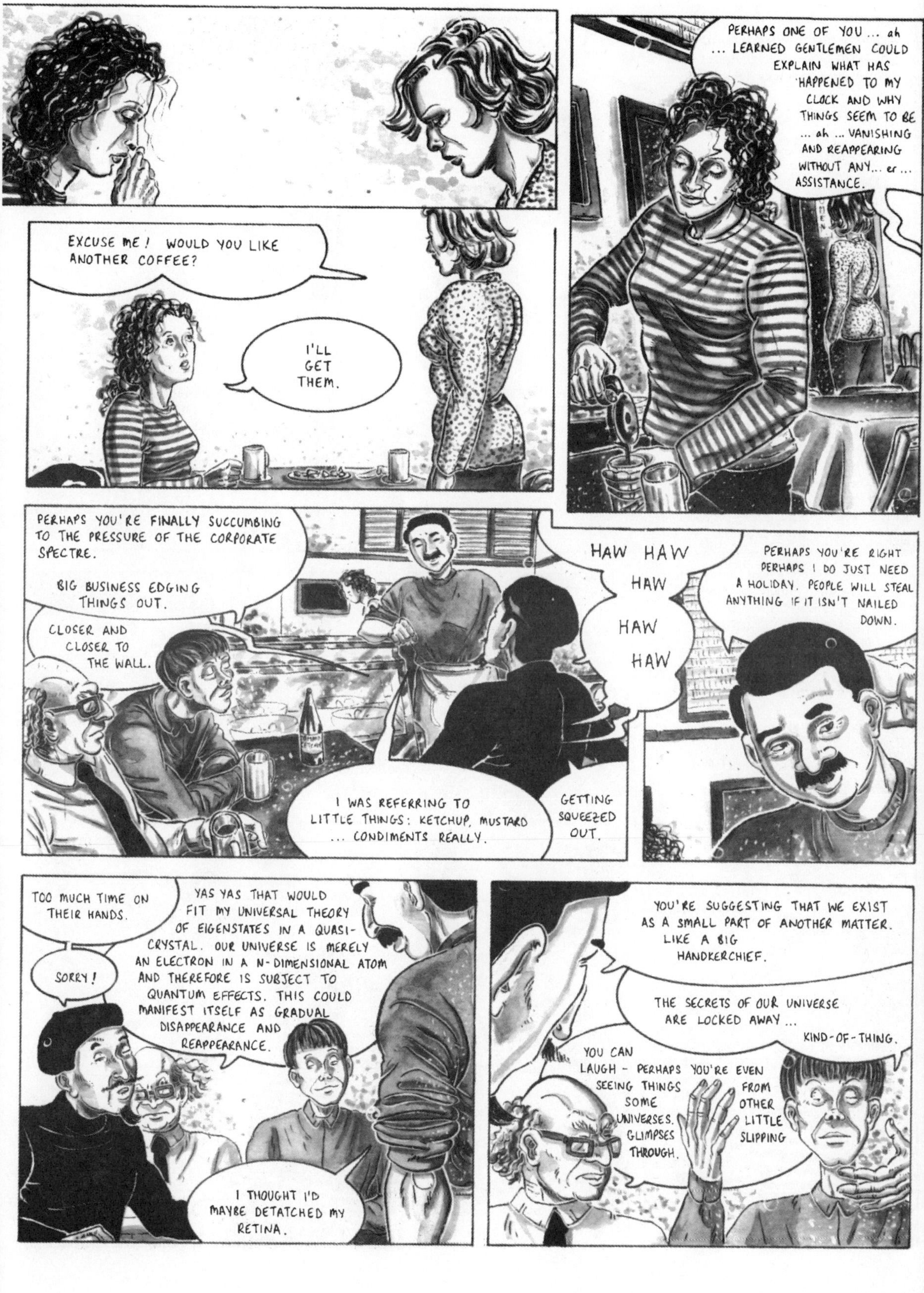
PERHAPS ONE OF YOU ... ah ... LEARNED GENTLEMEN COULD EXPLAIN WHAT HAS HAPPENED TO MY CLOCK AND WHY THINGS SEEM TO BE ... ah ... VANISHING AND REAPPEARING WITHOUT ANY ... er ... ASSISTANCE.
EXCUSE ME! WOULD YOU LIKE ANOTHER COFFEE?
I'LL GET THEM.
PERHAPS YOU'RE FINALLY SUCCUMBING TO THE PRESSURE OF THE CORPORATE SPECTRE.
BIG BUSINESS EDGING THINGS OUT.
CLOSER AND CLOSER TO THE WALL.
I WAS REFERRING TO LITTLE THINGS: KETCHUP, MUSTARD ... CONDIMENTS REALLY.
GETTING SQUEEZED OUT.
HAW HAW HAW HAW HAW
PERHAPS YOU'RE RIGHT PERHAPS I DO JUST NEED A HOLIDAY. PEOPLE WILL STEAL ANYTHING IF IT ISN'T NAILED DOWN.
TOO MUCH TIME ON THEIR HANDS.
SORRY!
YAS YAS THAT WOULD FIT MY UNIVERSAL THEORY OF EIGENSTATES IN A QUASI-CRYSTAL. OUR UNIVERSE IS MERELY AN ELECTRON IN A N-DIMENSIONAL ATOM AND THEREFORE IS SUBJECT TO QUANTUM EFFECTS. THIS COULD MANIFEST ITSELF AS GRADUAL DISAPPEARANCE AND REAPPEARANCE.
I THOUGHT I'D MAYBE DETATCHED MY RETINA.
YOU'RE SUGGESTING THAT WE EXIST AS A SMALL PART OF ANOTHER MATTER. LIKE A BIG HANDKERCHIEF.
THE SECRETS OF OUR UNIVERSE ARE LOCKED AWAY ... KIND-OF-THING.
YOU CAN LAUGH - PERHAPS YOU'RE EVEN SEEING THINGS FROM SOME OTHER UNIVERSES. LITTLE GLIMPSES SLIPPING THROUGH.

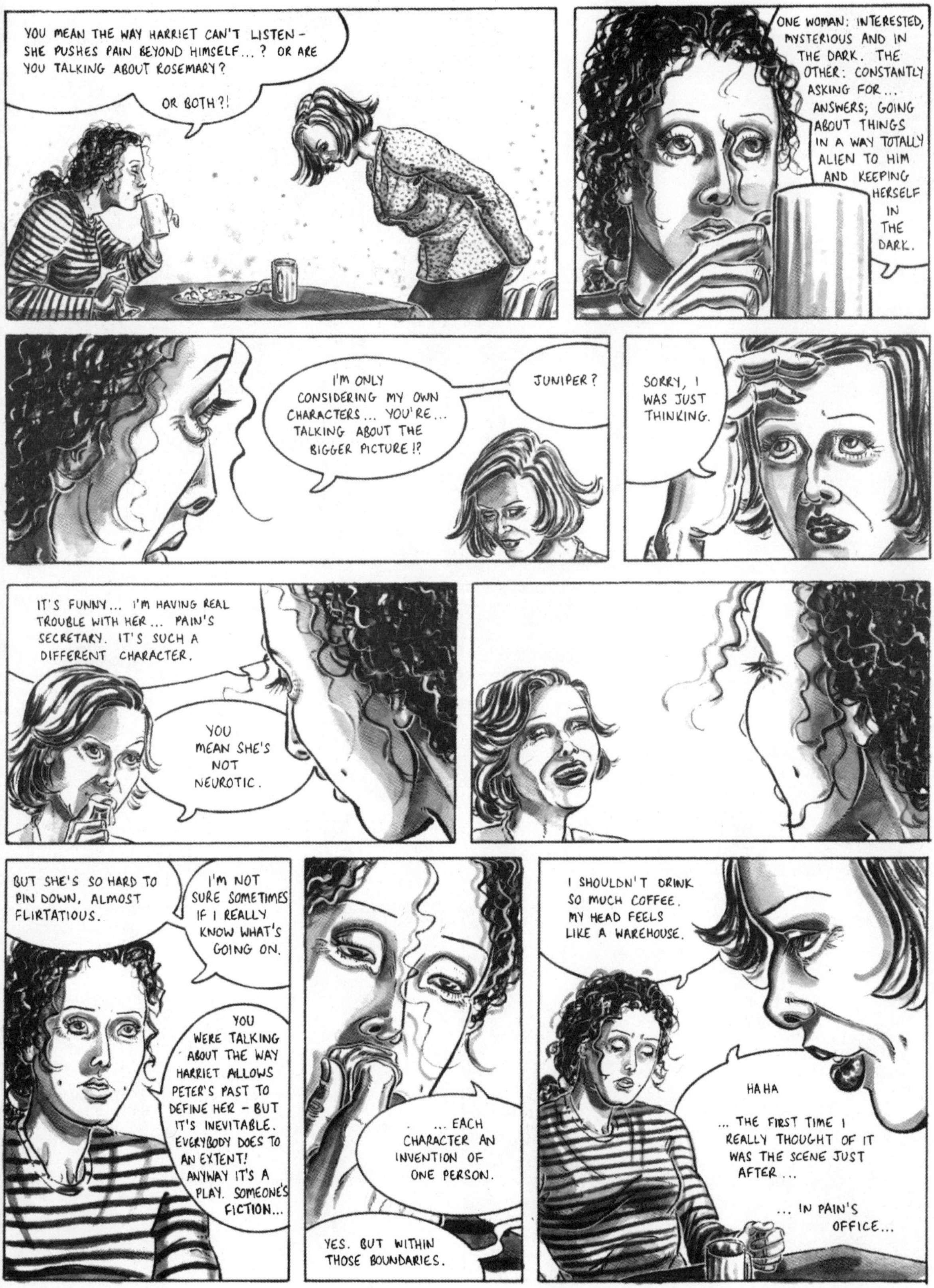
YOU MEAN THE WAY HARRIET CAN'T LISTEN - SHE PUSHES PAIN BEYOND HIMSELF...? OR ARE YOU TALKING ABOUT ROSEMARY?
OR BOTH?!
ONE WOMAN: INTERESTED, MYSTERIOUS AND IN THE DARK. THE OTHER: CONSTANTLY ASKING FOR... ANSWERS; GOING ABOUT THINGS IN A WAY TOTALLY ALIEN TO HIM AND KEEPING HERSELF IN THE DARK.
JUNIPER?
I'M ONLY CONSIDERING MY OWN CHARACTERS... YOU'RE... TALKING ABOUT THE BIGGER PICTURE!?
SORRY, I WAS JUST THINKING.
IT'S FUNNY... I'M HAVING REAL TROUBLE WITH HER... PAIN'S SECRETARY. IT'S SUCH A DIFFERENT CHARACTER.
YOU MEAN SHE'S NOT NEUROTIC.
BUT SHE'S SO HARD TO PIN DOWN, ALMOST FLIRTATIOUS.
I'M NOT SURE SOMETIMES IF I REALLY KNOW WHAT'S GOING ON.
YOU WERE TALKING ABOUT THE WAY HARRIET ALLOWS PETER'S PAST TO DEFINE HER - BUT IT'S INEVITABLE. EVERYBODY DOES TO AN EXTENT! ANYWAY IT'S A PLAY. SOMEONE'S FICTION...
... EACH CHARACTER AN INVENTION OF ONE PERSON.
YES. BUT WITHIN THOSE BOUNDARIES.
I SHOULDN'T DRINK SO MUCH COFFEE. MY HEAD FEELS LIKE A WAREHOUSE.
HA HA
... THE FIRST TIME I REALLY THOUGHT OF IT WAS THE SCENE JUST AFTER...
... IN PAIN'S OFFICE...

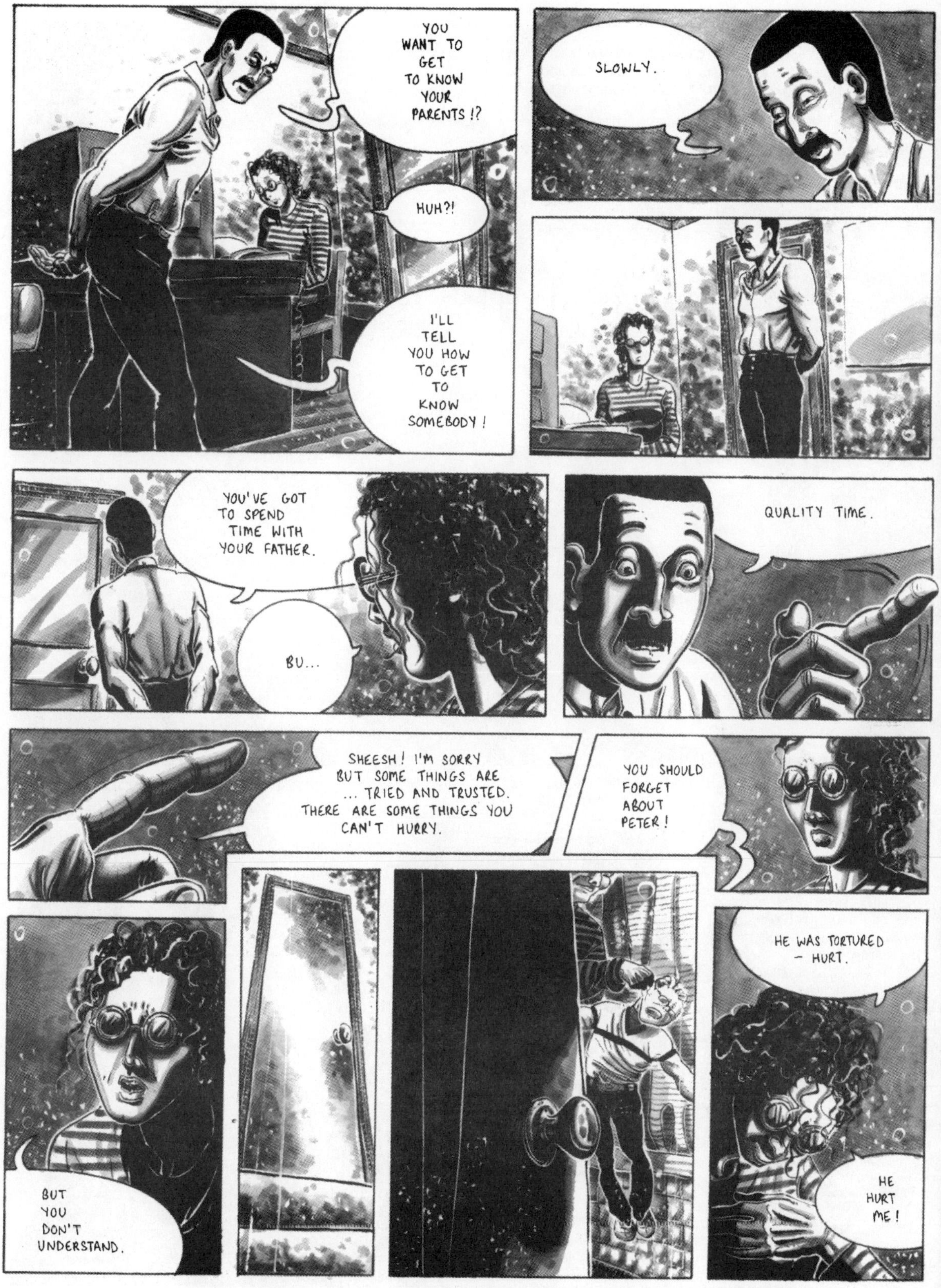
YOU WANT TO GET TO KNOW YOUR PARENTS !?
HUH?!
I'LL TELL YOU HOW TO GET TO KNOW SOMEBODY !
SLOWLY.
YOU'VE GOT TO SPEND TIME WITH YOUR FATHER.
BU...
QUALITY TIME.
SHEESH! I'M SORRY BUT SOME THINGS ARE ... TRIED AND TRUSTED. THERE ARE SOME THINGS YOU CAN'T HURRY.
YOU SHOULD FORGET ABOUT PETER!
BUT YOU DON'T UNDERSTAND.
HE WAS TORTURED - HURT.
HE HURT ME!

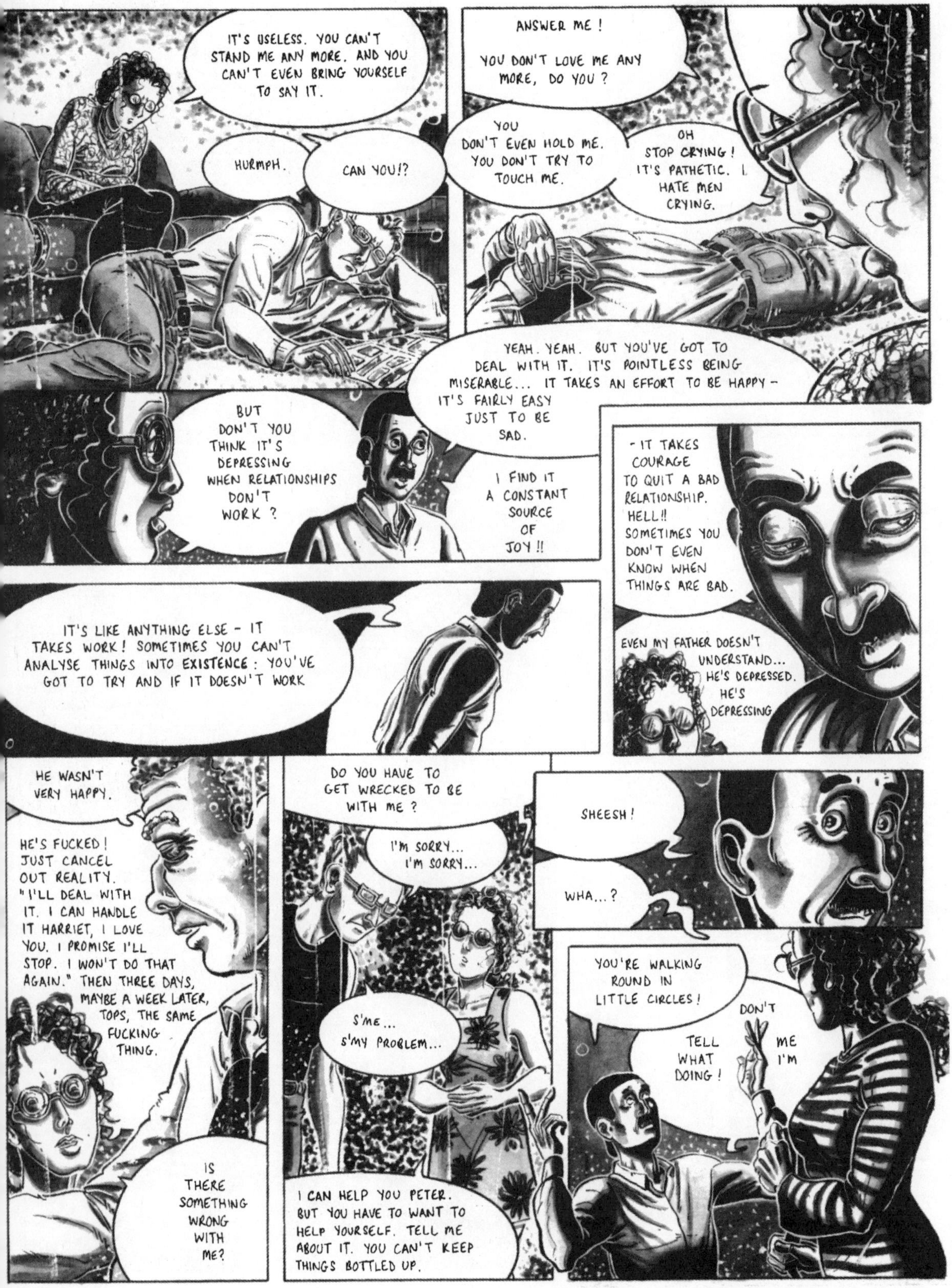
IT'S USELESS. YOU CAN'T STAND ME ANY MORE. AND YOU CAN'T EVEN BRING YOURSELF TO SAY IT.
HURMPH.
CAN YOU!?
ANSWER ME!
YOU DON'T LOVE ME ANY MORE, DO YOU?
YOU DON'T EVEN HOLD ME. YOU DON'T TRY TO TOUCH ME.
OH STOP CRYING! IT'S PATHETIC. I HATE MEN CRYING.
YEAH. YEAH. BUT YOU'VE GOT TO DEAL WITH IT. IT'S POINTLESS BEING MISERABLE... IT TAKES AN EFFORT TO BE HAPPY - IT'S FAIRLY EASY JUST TO BE SAD.
BUT DON'T YOU THINK IT'S DEPRESSING WHEN RELATIONSHIPS DON'T WORK?
I FIND IT A CONSTANT SOURCE OF JOY!!
- IT TAKES COURAGE TO QUIT A BAD RELATIONSHIP. HELL!! SOMETIMES YOU DON'T EVEN KNOW WHEN THINGS ARE BAD.
IT'S LIKE ANYTHING ELSE - IT TAKES WORK! SOMETIMES YOU CAN'T ANALYSE THINGS INTO EXISTENCE: YOU'VE GOT TO TRY AND IF IT DOESN'T WORK
EVEN MY FATHER DOESN'T UNDERSTAND... HE'S DEPRESSED. HE'S DEPRESSING
HE WASN'T VERY HAPPY.
HE'S FUCKED! JUST CANCEL OUT REALITY. "I'LL DEAL WITH IT. I CAN HANDLE IT HARRIET, I LOVE YOU. I PROMISE I'LL STOP. I WON'T DO THAT AGAIN." THEN THREE DAYS, MAYBE A WEEK LATER, TOPS, THE SAME FUCKING THING.
IS THERE SOMETHING WRONG WITH ME?
DO YOU HAVE TO GET WRECKED TO BE WITH ME?
I'M SORRY... I'M SORRY...
S'ME... S'MY PROBLEM...
I CAN HELP YOU PETER. BUT YOU HAVE TO WANT TO HELP YOURSELF. TELL ME ABOUT IT. YOU CAN'T KEEP THINGS BOTTLED UP.
SHEESH!
WHA...?
YOU'RE WALKING ROUND IN LITTLE CIRCLES!
DON'T TELL ME WHAT I'M DOING!

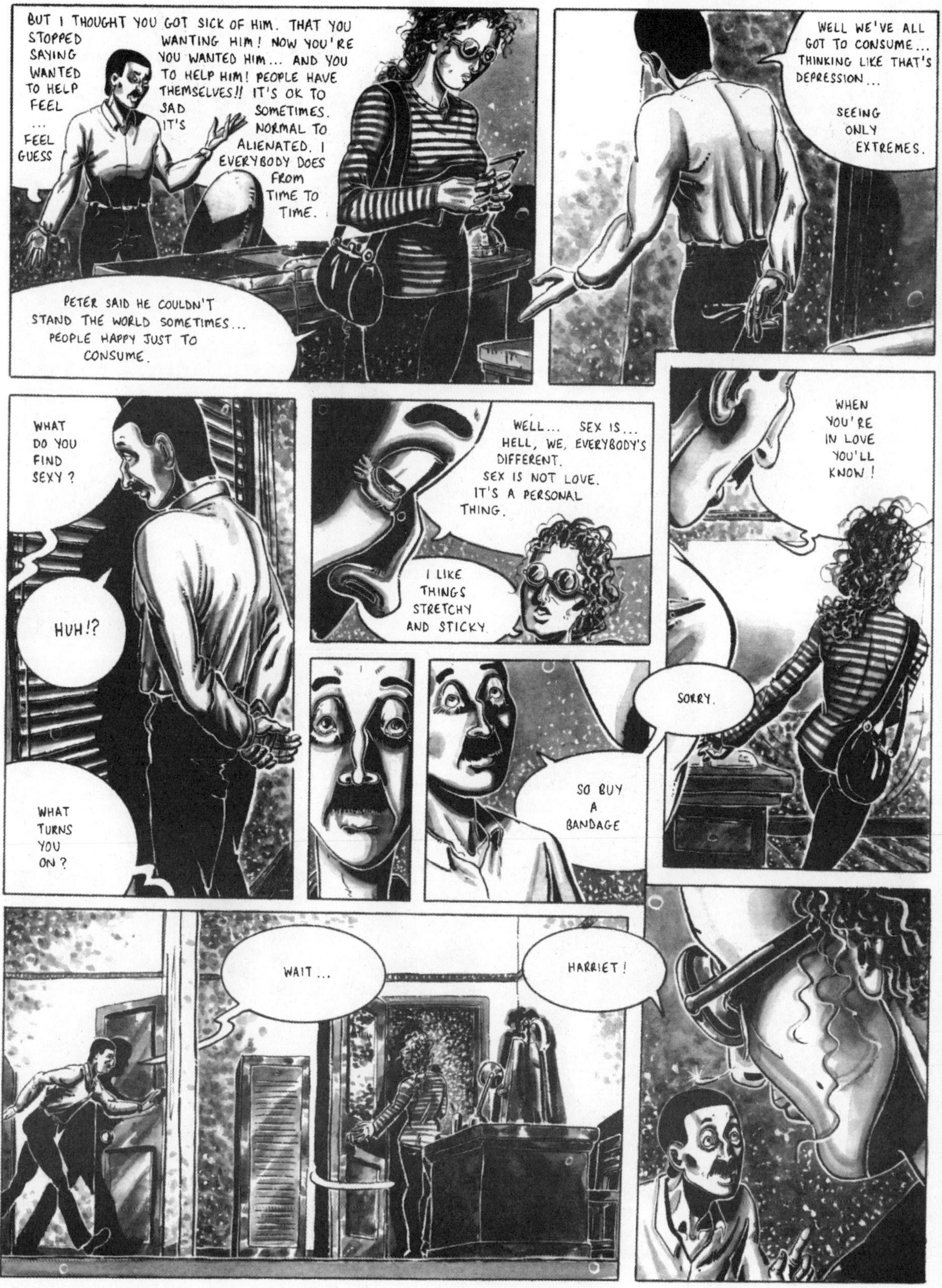

BUT I THOUGHT YOU GOT SICK OF HIM. THAT YOU STOPPED WANTING HIM! NOW YOU'RE SAYING YOU WANTED HIM... AND YOU WANTED TO HELP HIM! PEOPLE HAVE TO HELP THEMSELVES!! IT'S OK TO FEEL SAD SOMETIMES. ... IT'S NORMAL TO FEEL ALIENATED. I GUESS EVERYBODY DOES FROM TIME TO TIME.
PETER SAID HE COULDN'T STAND THE WORLD SOMETIMES... PEOPLE HAPPY JUST TO CONSUME.
WELL WE'VE ALL GOT TO CONSUME... THINKING LIKE THAT'S DEPRESSION...
SEEING ONLY EXTREMES.
WHAT DO YOU FIND SEXY?
HUH!?
WHAT TURNS YOU ON?
WELL... SEX IS... HELL, WE, EVERYBODY'S DIFFERENT. SEX IS NOT LOVE. IT'S A PERSONAL THING.
I LIKE THINGS STRETCHY AND STICKY.
SO BUY A BANDAGE
WHEN YOU'RE IN LOVE YOU'LL KNOW!
SORRY.
WAIT...
HARRIET!

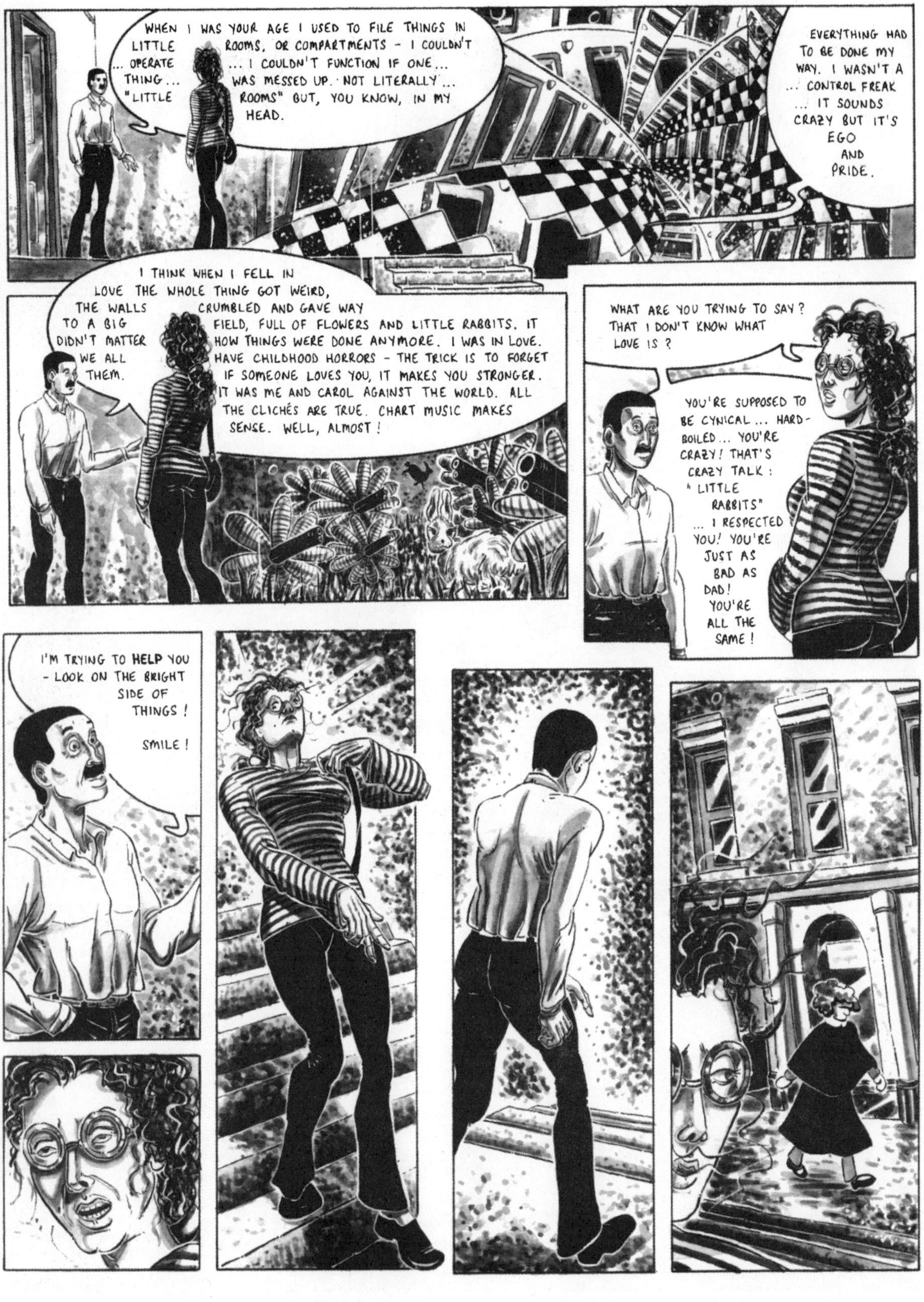
WHEN I WAS YOUR AGE I USED TO FILE THINGS IN LITTLE ROOMS, OR COMPARTMENTS - I COULDN'T ... OPERATE ... I COULDN'T FUNCTION IF ONE ... THING ... WAS MESSED UP. NOT LITERALLY ... "LITTLE ROOMS" BUT, YOU KNOW, IN MY HEAD.
EVERYTHING HAD TO BE DONE MY WAY. I WASN'T A ... CONTROL FREAK ... IT SOUNDS CRAZY BUT IT'S EGO AND PRIDE.
I THINK WHEN I FELL IN LOVE THE WHOLE THING GOT WEIRD, THE WALLS CRUMBLED AND GAVE WAY TO A BIG FIELD, FULL OF FLOWERS AND LITTLE RABBITS. IT DIDN'T MATTER HOW THINGS WERE DONE ANYMORE. I WAS IN LOVE. WE ALL HAVE CHILDHOOD HORRORS - THE TRICK IS TO FORGET THEM. IF SOMEONE LOVES YOU, IT MAKES YOU STRONGER. IT WAS ME AND CAROL AGAINST THE WORLD. ALL THE CLICHÉS ARE TRUE. CHART MUSIC MAKES SENSE. WELL, ALMOST!
WHAT ARE YOU TRYING TO SAY? THAT I DON'T KNOW WHAT LOVE IS?
YOU'RE SUPPOSED TO BE CYNICAL ... HARD-BOILED ... YOU'RE CRAZY! THAT'S CRAZY TALK: "LITTLE RABBITS" ... I RESPECTED YOU! YOU'RE JUST AS BAD AS DAD! YOU'RE ALL THE SAME!
I'M TRYING TO HELP YOU - LOOK ON THE BRIGHT SIDE OF THINGS!
SMILE!

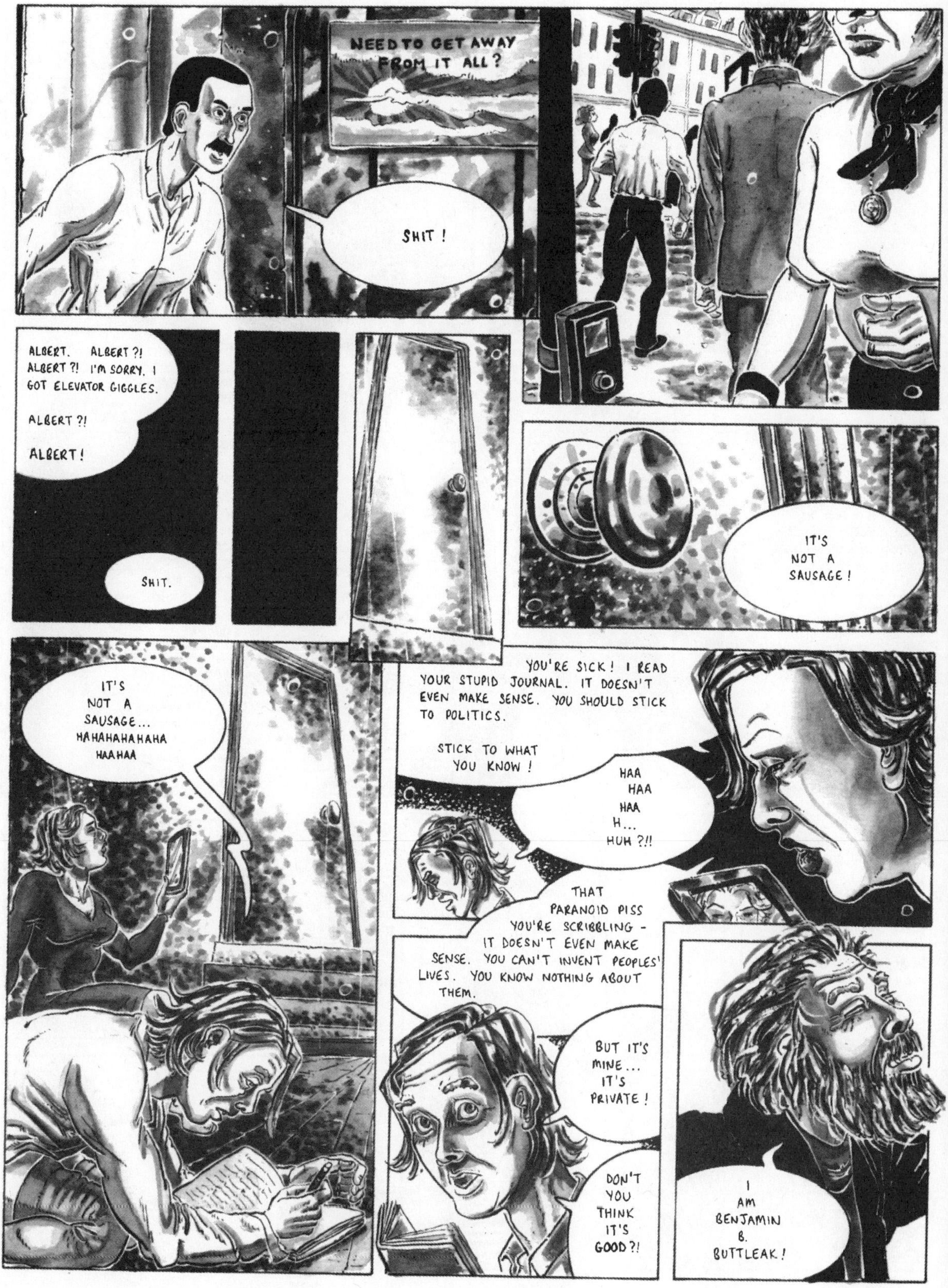
NEED TO GET AWAY FROM IT ALL?
SHIT!
ALBERT. ALBERT?! ALBERT?! I'M SORRY. I GOT ELEVATOR GIGGLES.
ALBERT?!
ALBERT!
SHIT.
IT'S NOT A SAUSAGE!
IT'S NOT A SAUSAGE... HAHAHAHAHAHA HAAHAA
YOU'RE SICK! I READ YOUR STUPID JOURNAL. IT DOESN'T EVEN MAKE SENSE. YOU SHOULD STICK TO POLITICS.
STICK TO WHAT YOU KNOW!
HAA HAA HAA H... HUH?!!
THAT PARANOID PISS YOU'RE SCRIBBLING - IT DOESN'T EVEN MAKE SENSE. YOU CAN'T INVENT PEOPLES' LIVES. YOU KNOW NOTHING ABOUT THEM.
BUT IT'S MINE... IT'S PRIVATE!
DON'T YOU THINK IT'S GOOD?!
I AM BENJAMIN B. BUTTLEAK!

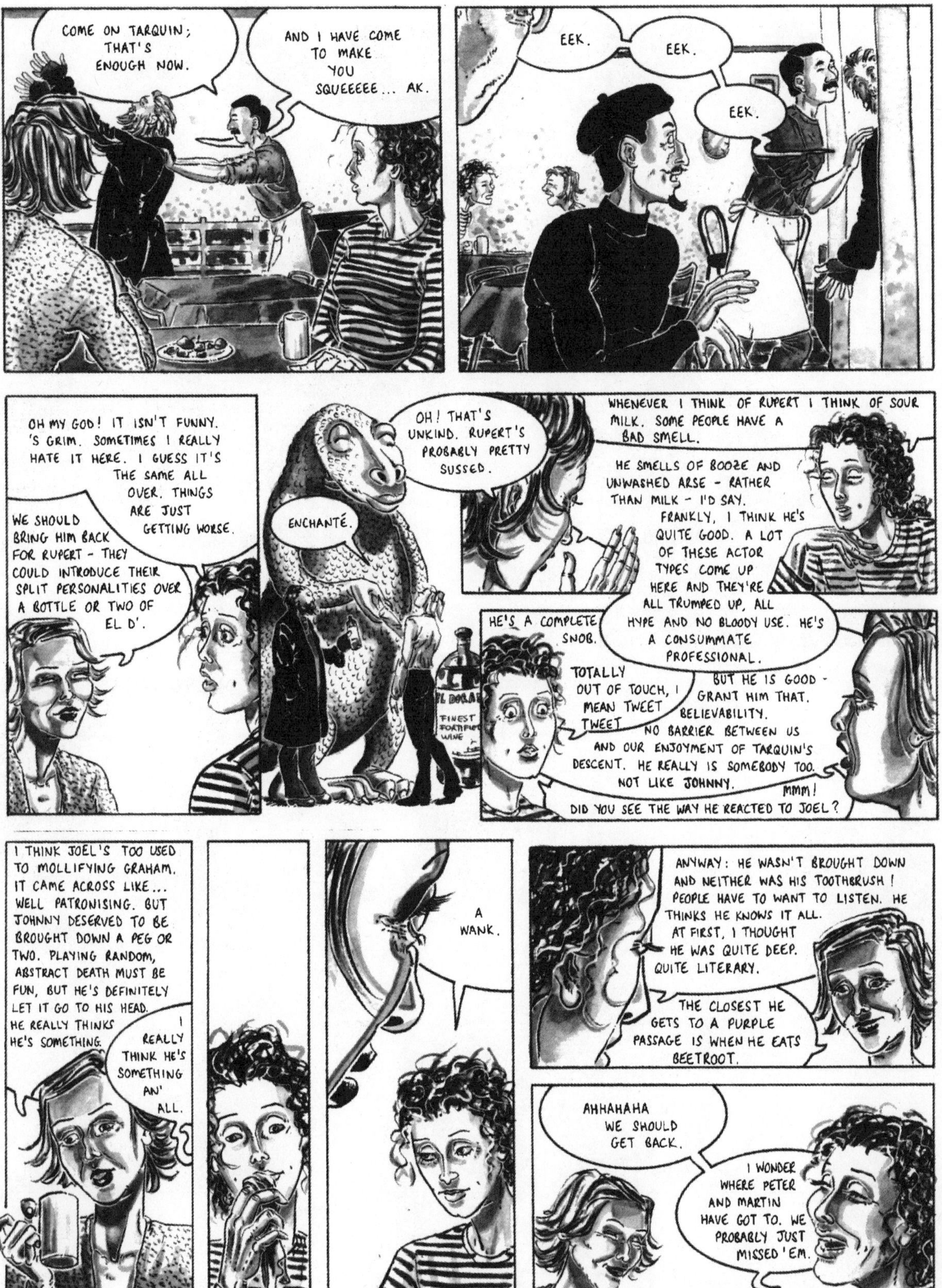
COME ON TARQUIN; THAT'S ENOUGH NOW.
AND I HAVE COME TO MAKE YOU SQUEEEEE... AK.
EEK.
EEK.
EEK.
OH MY GOD! IT ISN'T FUNNY. 'S GRIM. SOMETIMES I REALLY HATE IT HERE. I GUESS IT'S THE SAME ALL OVER. THINGS ARE JUST GETTING WORSE.
WE SHOULD BRING HIM BACK FOR RUPERT - THEY COULD INTRODUCE THEIR SPLIT PERSONALITIES OVER A BOTTLE OR TWO OF EL D'.
OH! THAT'S UNKIND. RUPERT'S PROBABLY PRETTY SUSSED.
ENCHANTÉ.
FINEST FORTIFIED WINE
WHENEVER I THINK OF RUPERT I THINK OF SOUR MILK. SOME PEOPLE HAVE A BAD SMELL.
HE SMELLS OF BOOZE AND UNWASHED ARSE - RATHER THAN MILK - I'D SAY.
FRANKLY, I THINK HE'S QUITE GOOD. A LOT OF THESE ACTOR TYPES COME UP HERE AND THEY'RE ALL TRUMPED UP, ALL HYPE AND NO BLOODY USE. HE'S A CONSUMMATE PROFESSIONAL.
HE'S A COMPLETE SNOB.
TOTALLY OUT OF TOUCH, I MEAN TWEET TWEET
BUT HE IS GOOD - GRANT HIM THAT. BELIEVABILITY.
NO BARRIER BETWEEN US AND OUR ENJOYMENT OF TARQUIN'S DESCENT. HE REALLY IS SOMEBODY TOO. NOT LIKE JOHNNY.
MMM!
DID YOU SEE THE WAY HE REACTED TO JOEL?
I THINK JOEL'S TOO USED TO MOLLIFYING GRAHAM. IT CAME ACROSS LIKE... WELL PATRONISING. BUT JOHNNY DESERVED TO BE BROUGHT DOWN A PEG OR TWO. PLAYING RANDOM, ABSTRACT DEATH MUST BE FUN, BUT HE'S DEFINITELY LET IT GO TO HIS HEAD. HE REALLY THINKS HE'S SOMETHING.
I REALLY THINK HE'S SOMETHING AN' ALL.
A WANK.
ANYWAY: HE WASN'T BROUGHT DOWN AND NEITHER WAS HIS TOOTHBRUSH! PEOPLE HAVE TO WANT TO LISTEN. HE THINKS HE KNOWS IT ALL.
AT FIRST, I THOUGHT HE WAS QUITE DEEP. QUITE LITERARY.
THE CLOSEST HE GETS TO A PURPLE PASSAGE IS WHEN HE EATS BEETROOT.
AHHAHAHA WE SHOULD GET BACK.
I WONDER WHERE PETER AND MARTIN HAVE GOT TO. WE PROBABLY JUST MISSED 'EM.

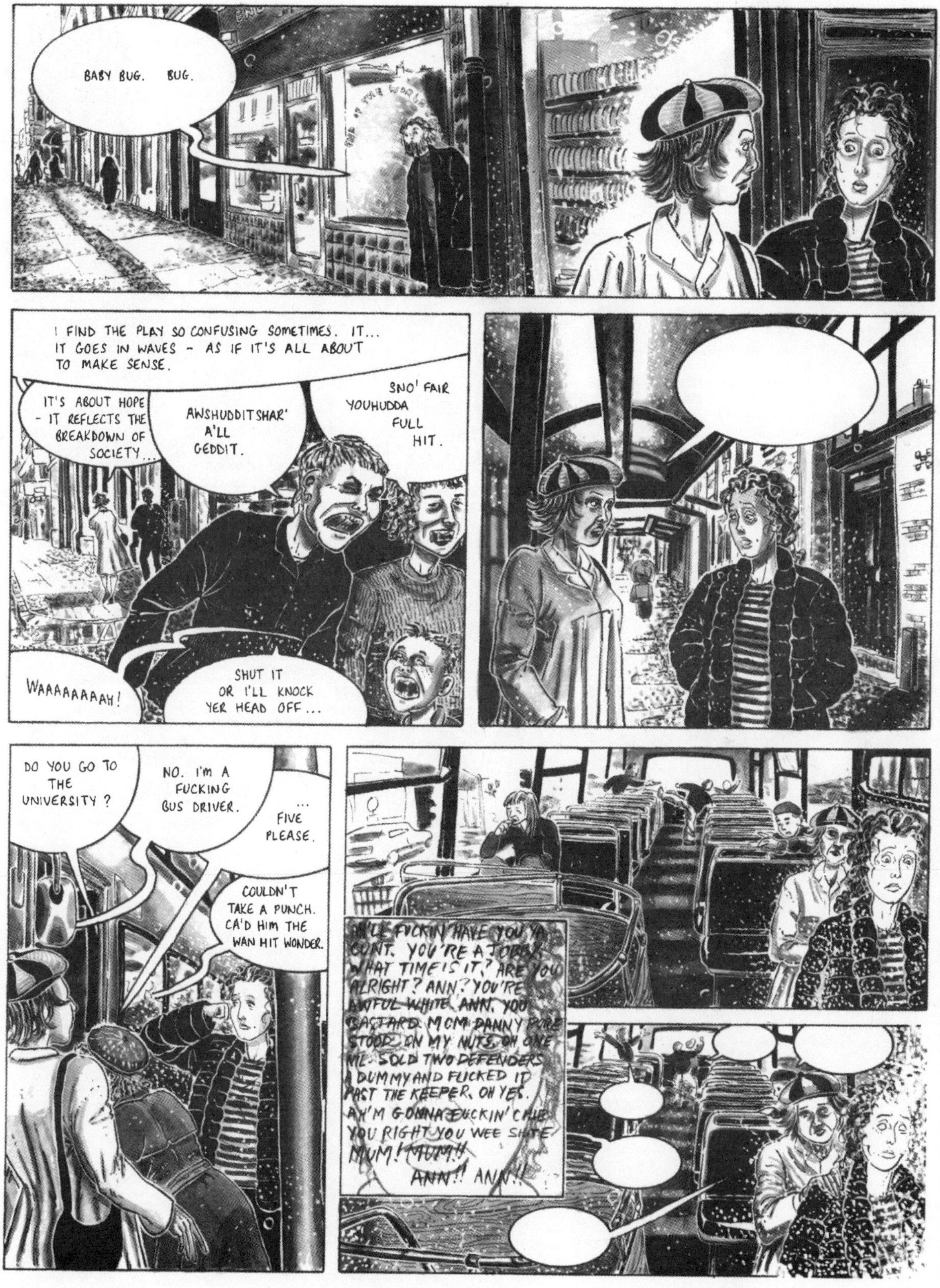
BABY BUG. BUG.
I FIND THE PLAY SO CONFUSING SOMETIMES. IT... IT GOES IN WAVES - AS IF IT'S ALL ABOUT TO MAKE SENSE.
IT'S ABOUT HOPE - IT REFLECTS THE BREAKDOWN OF SOCIETY...
AWSHUDDITSHAR' A'LL GEDDIT.
SNO' FAIR YOUHUDDA FULL HIT.
WAAAAAAAAH!
SHUT IT OR I'LL KNOCK YER HEAD OFF...
DO YOU GO TO THE UNIVERSITY?
NO. I'M A FUCKING BUS DRIVER.
... FIVE PLEASE.
COULDN'T TAKE A PUNCH. CA'D HIM THE WAN HIT WONDER.
AH'LL FUCKIN HAVE YOU YA CUNT. YOU'RE A JOBBY. WHAT TIME IS IT? ARE YOU ALRIGHT? ANN? YOU'RE AWFUL WHITE ANN. YOU BASTARD MOM DANNY PURE STOOD ON MY NUTS. OH ONE NIL. SOLD TWO DEFENDERS A DUMMY AND FLICKED IT PAST THE KEEPER. OH YES. AH'M GONNA FUCKIN' CHIB YOU RIGHT YOU WEE SHITE MUM! MUM!!
ANN!! ANN!!

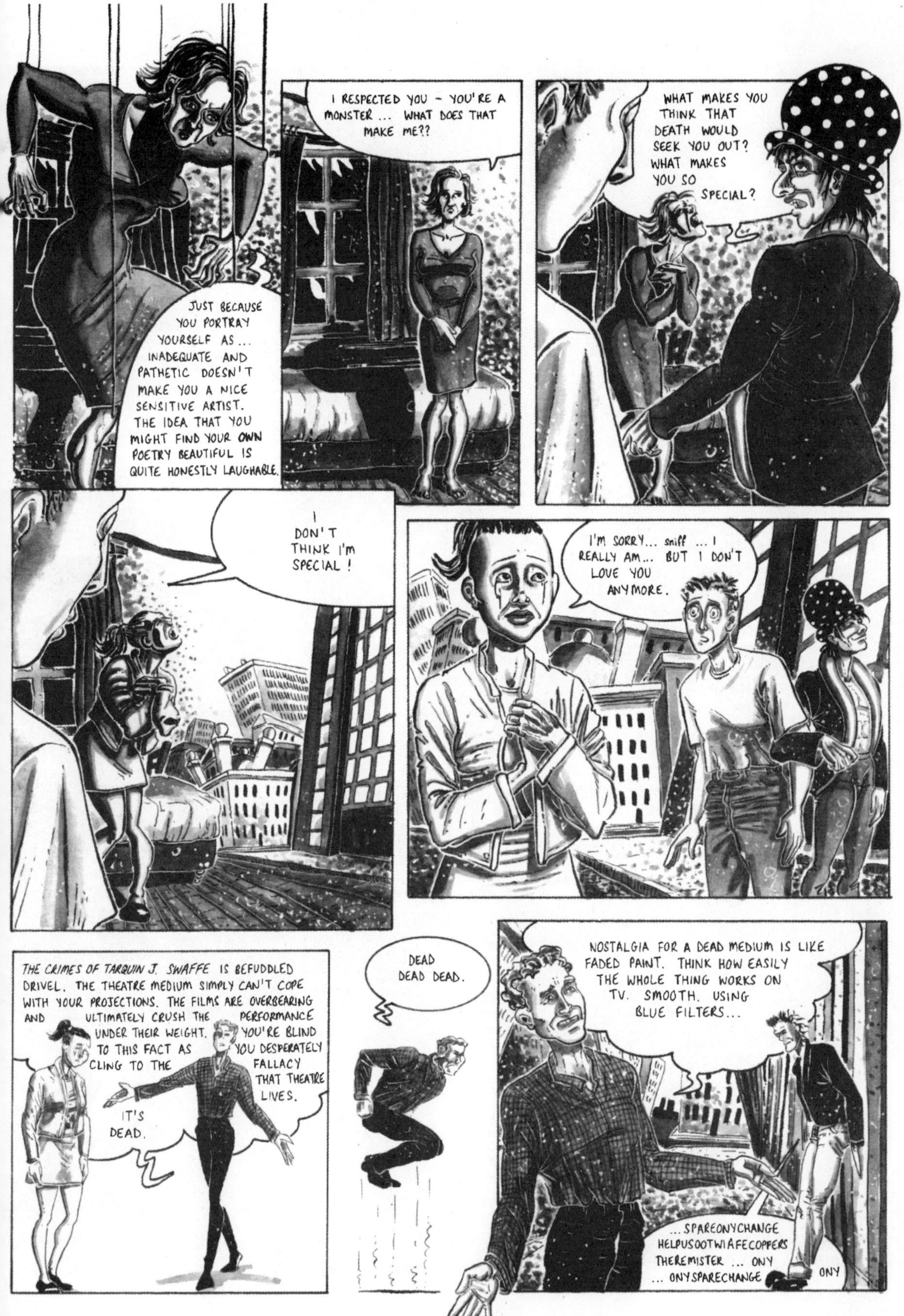
JUST BECAUSE YOU PORTRAY YOURSELF AS... INADEQUATE AND PATHETIC DOESN'T MAKE YOU A NICE SENSITIVE ARTIST. THE IDEA THAT YOU MIGHT FIND YOUR OWN POETRY BEAUTIFUL IS QUITE HONESTLY LAUGHABLE.
I RESPECTED YOU - YOU'RE A MONSTER... WHAT DOES THAT MAKE ME??
WHAT MAKES YOU THINK THAT DEATH WOULD SEEK YOU OUT? WHAT MAKES YOU SO SPECIAL?
I DON'T THINK I'M SPECIAL!
I'M SORRY... sniff ... I REALLY AM... BUT I DON'T LOVE YOU ANYMORE.
THE CRIMES OF TARQUIN J. SWAFFE IS BEFUDDLED DRIVEL. THE THEATRE MEDIUM SIMPLY CAN'T COPE WITH YOUR PROJECTIONS. THE FILMS ARE OVERBEARING AND ULTIMATELY CRUSH THE PERFORMANCE UNDER THEIR WEIGHT. YOU'RE BLIND TO THIS FACT AS YOU DESPERATELY CLING TO THE FALLACY THAT THEATRE LIVES.
IT'S DEAD.
DEAD DEAD DEAD.
NOSTALGIA FOR A DEAD MEDIUM IS LIKE FADED PAINT. THINK HOW EASILY THE WHOLE THING WORKS ON TV. SMOOTH. USING BLUE FILTERS...
...SPAREONYCHANGE HELPUSOOTWIAFECOPPERS THEREMISTER ... ONY ... ONYSPARECHANGE
ONY

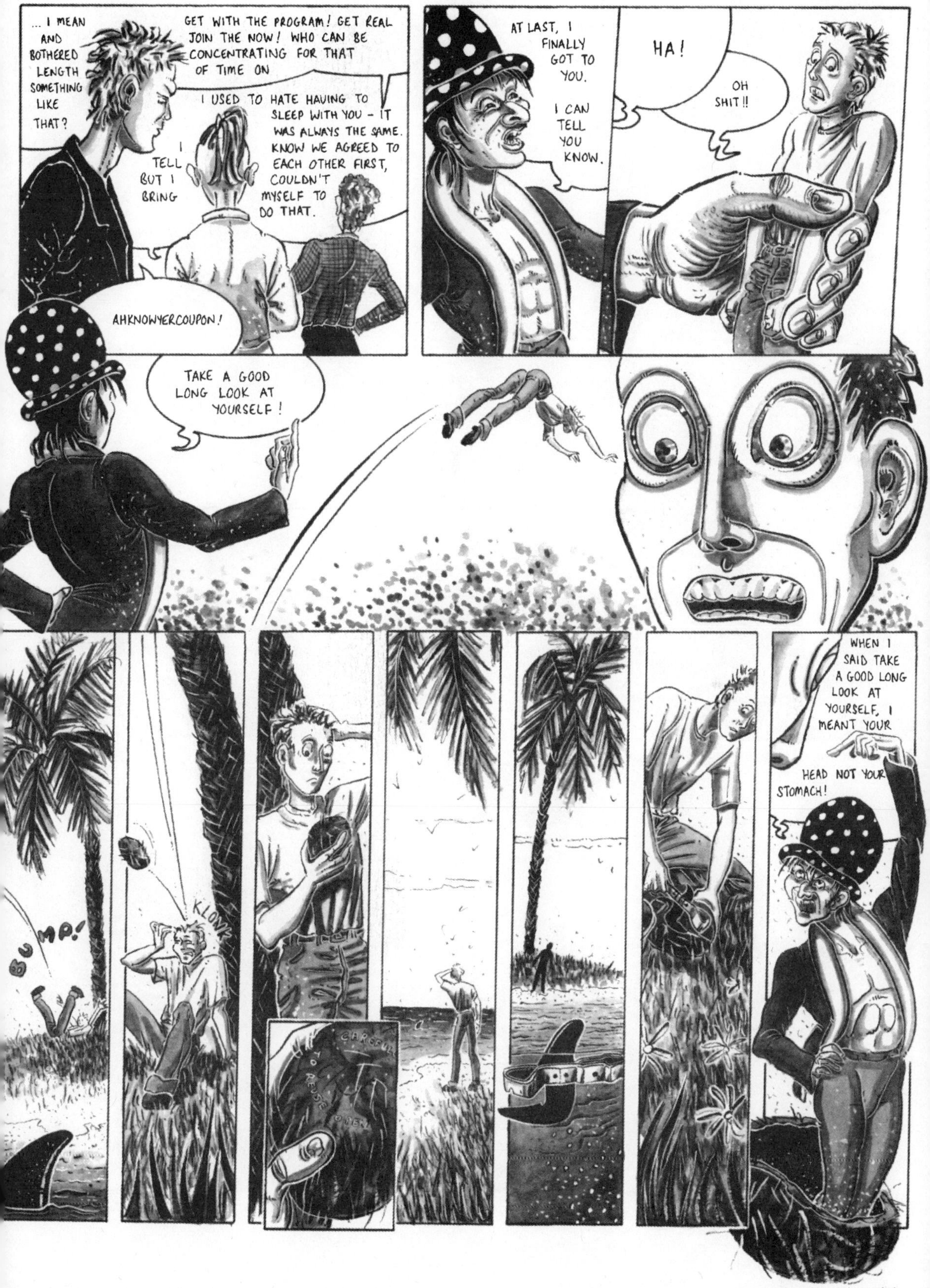

... I MEAN AND BOTHERED LENGTH SOMETHING LIKE THAT?
GET WITH THE PROGRAM! GET REAL JOIN THE NOW! WHO CAN BE CONCENTRATING FOR THAT OF TIME ON
I USED TO HATE HAVING TO SLEEP WITH YOU - IT WAS ALWAYS THE SAME. KNOW WE AGREED TO EACH OTHER FIRST, COULDN'T MYSELF TO DO THAT.
I TELL BUT I BRING
AHKNOWYERCOUPON!
AT LAST, I FINALLY GOT TO YOU. I CAN TELL YOU KNOW.
HA!
OH SHIT!!
TAKE A GOOD LONG LOOK AT YOURSELF!
BUMP!
KLONK
WHEN I SAID TAKE A GOOD LONG LOOK AT YOURSELF, I MEANT YOUR HEAD NOT YOUR STOMACH!

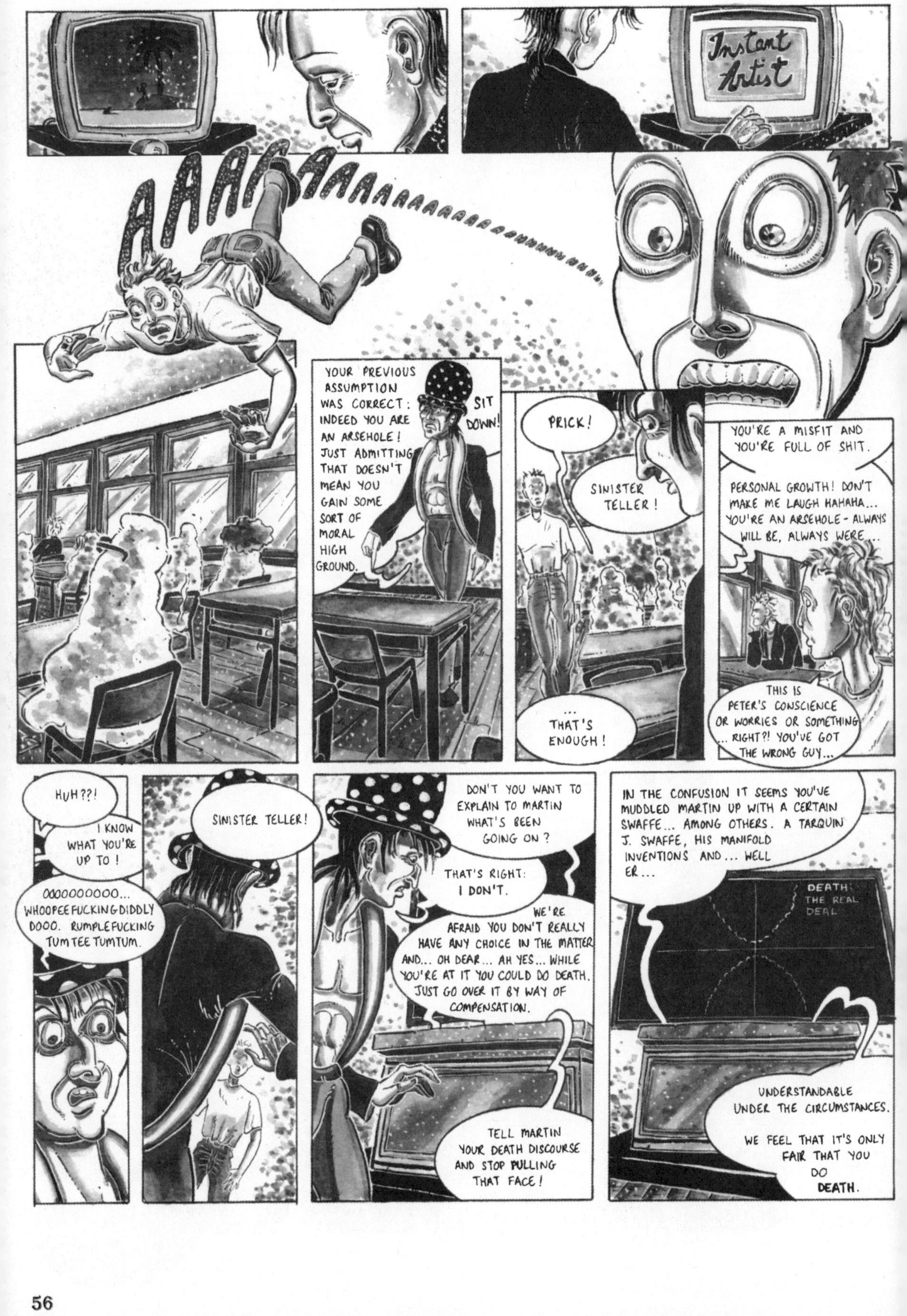
Instant Artist
AAAAAAAAAAAAAAAAAAAAAAAAAAAAAAA
YOUR PREVIOUS ASSUMPTION WAS CORRECT: INDEED YOU ARE AN ARSEHOLE! JUST ADMITTING THAT DOESN'T MEAN YOU GAIN SOME SORT OF MORAL HIGH GROUND.
SIT DOWN!
PRICK!
SINISTER TELLER!
... THAT'S ENOUGH!
YOU'RE A MISFIT AND YOU'RE FULL OF SHIT.
PERSONAL GROWTH! DON'T MAKE ME LAUGH HAHAHA... YOU'RE AN ARSEHOLE - ALWAYS WILL BE, ALWAYS WERE...
THIS IS PETER'S CONSCIENCE OR WORRIES OR SOMETHING ... RIGHT?! YOU'VE GOT THE WRONG GUY...
HUH??!
I KNOW WHAT YOU'RE UP TO!
OOOOOOOOOO... WHOOPEEFUCKINGDIDDLY DOOO. RUMPLEFUCKING TUMTEE TUMTUM.
SINISTER TELLER!
DON'T YOU WANT TO EXPLAIN TO MARTIN WHAT'S BEEN GOING ON?
THAT'S RIGHT: I DON'T.
WE'RE AFRAID YOU DON'T REALLY HAVE ANY CHOICE IN THE MATTER AND... OH DEAR... AH YES... WHILE YOU'RE AT IT YOU COULD DO DEATH. JUST GO OVER IT BY WAY OF COMPENSATION.
TELL MARTIN YOUR DEATH DISCOURSE AND STOP PULLING THAT FACE!
IN THE CONFUSION IT SEEMS YOU'VE MUDDLED MARTIN UP WITH A CERTAIN SWAFFE... AMONG OTHERS. A TARQUIN J. SWAFFE, HIS MANIFOLD INVENTIONS AND... WELL ER...
DEATH: THE REAL DEAL
UNDERSTANDABLE UNDER THE CIRCUMSTANCES.
WE FEEL THAT IT'S ONLY FAIR THAT YOU DO DEATH.

The darkness was like a lump.

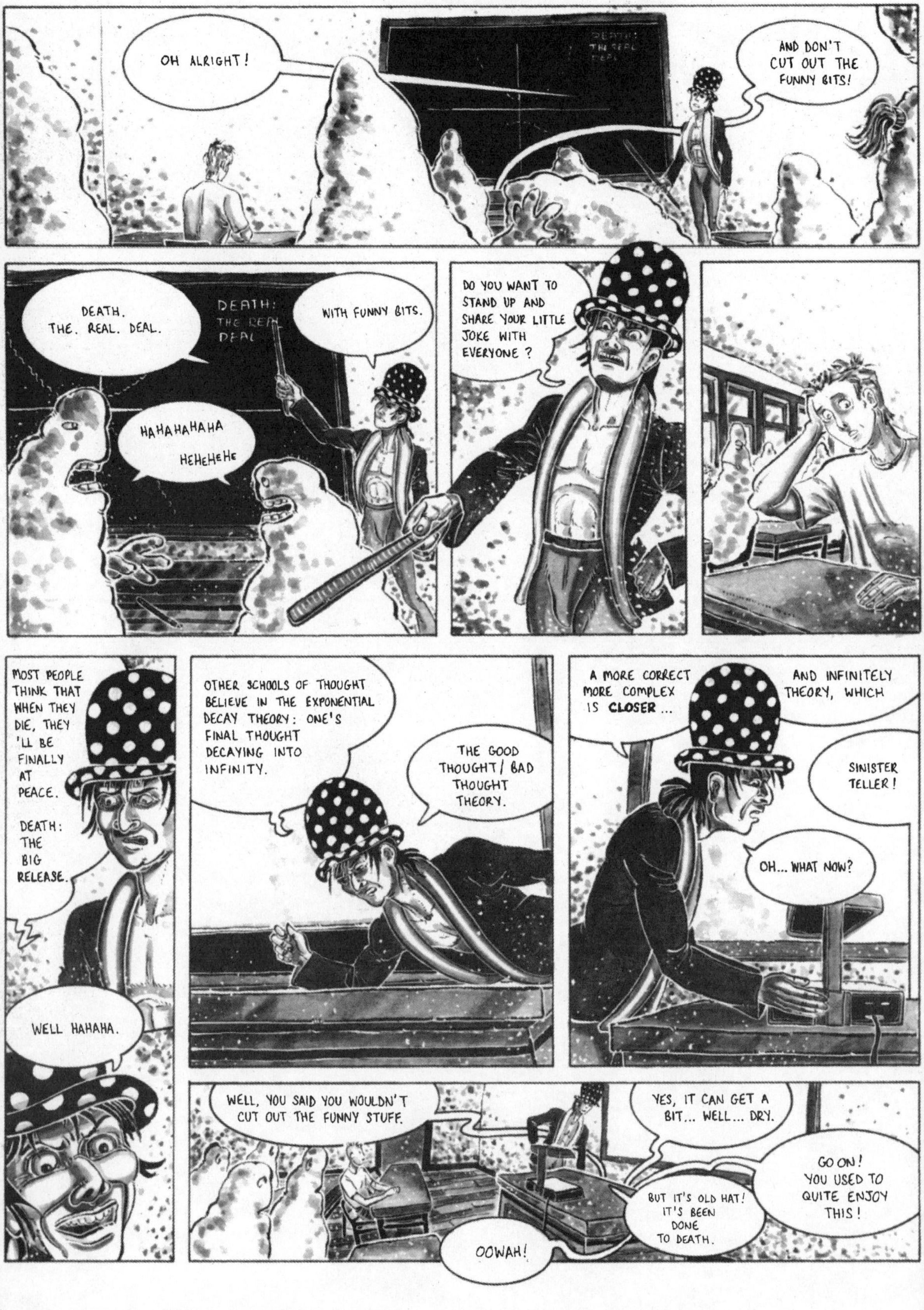
OH ALRIGHT!
DEATH: THE REAL DEAL
AND DON'T CUT OUT THE FUNNY BITS!
DEATH. THE. REAL. DEAL.
DEATH: THE REAL DEAL
WITH FUNNY BITS.
HAHAHAHAHA
HEHEHEHE
DO YOU WANT TO STAND UP AND SHARE YOUR LITTLE JOKE WITH EVERYONE?
MOST PEOPLE THINK THAT WHEN THEY DIE, THEY 'LL BE FINALLY AT PEACE.
DEATH: THE BIG RELEASE.
WELL HAHAHA.
OTHER SCHOOLS OF THOUGHT BELIEVE IN THE EXPONENTIAL DECAY THEORY: ONE'S FINAL THOUGHT DECAYING INTO INFINITY.
THE GOOD THOUGHT/ BAD THOUGHT THEORY.
A MORE CORRECT MORE COMPLEX IS CLOSER ...
AND INFINITELY THEORY, WHICH
SINISTER TELLER!
OH... WHAT NOW?
WELL, YOU SAID YOU WOULDN'T CUT OUT THE FUNNY STUFF.
YES, IT CAN GET A BIT... WELL... DRY.
BUT IT'S OLD HAT! IT'S BEEN DONE TO DEATH.
GO ON! YOU USED TO QUITE ENJOY THIS!
OOWAH!

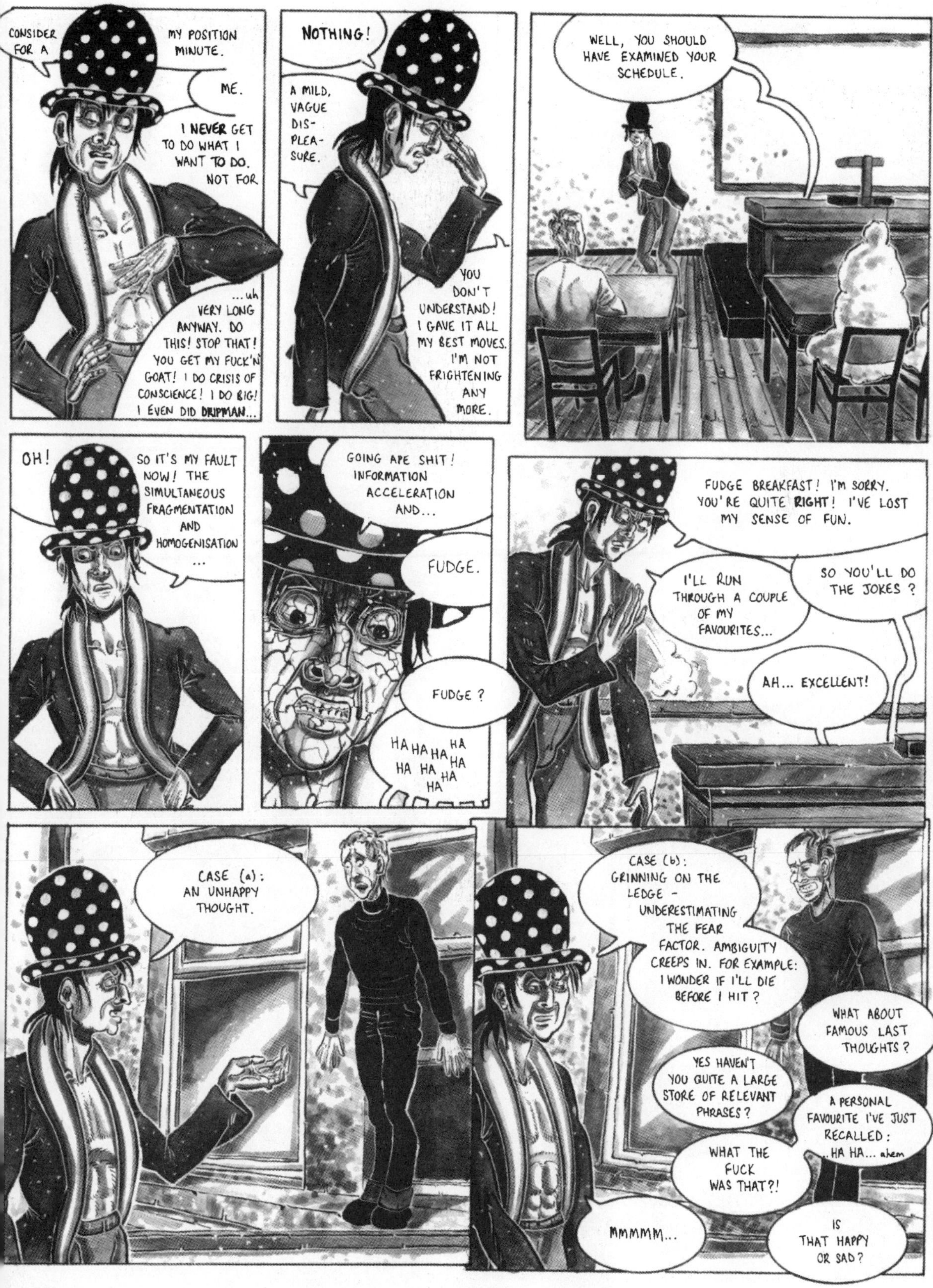
CONSIDER FOR A
MY POSITION MINUTE.
ME.
I NEVER GET TO DO WHAT I WANT TO DO. NOT FOR
...uh VERY LONG ANYWAY. DO THIS! STOP THAT! YOU GET MY FUCK'N GOAT! I DO CRISIS OF CONSCIENCE! I DO BIG! I EVEN DID DRIPMAN...
NOTHING!
A MILD, VAGUE DIS-PLEA-SURE.
YOU DON'T UNDERSTAND! I GAVE IT ALL MY BEST MOVES. I'M NOT FRIGHTENING ANY MORE.
WELL, YOU SHOULD HAVE EXAMINED YOUR SCHEDULE.
OH!
SO IT'S MY FAULT NOW! THE SIMULTANEOUS FRAGMENTATION AND HOMOGENISATION ...
GOING APE SHIT! INFORMATION ACCELERATION AND...
FUDGE.
FUDGE ?
HA HA HA HA HA HA HA HA HA
FUDGE BREAKFAST! I'M SORRY. YOU'RE QUITE RIGHT! I'VE LOST MY SENSE OF FUN.
I'LL RUN THROUGH A COUPLE OF MY FAVOURITES...
SO YOU'LL DO THE JOKES ?
AH... EXCELLENT!
CASE (a): AN UNHAPPY THOUGHT.
CASE (b): GRINNING ON THE LEDGE - UNDERESTIMATING THE FEAR FACTOR. AMBIGUITY CREEPS IN. FOR EXAMPLE: I WONDER IF I'LL DIE BEFORE I HIT ?
WHAT ABOUT FAMOUS LAST THOUGHTS ?
YES HAVEN'T YOU QUITE A LARGE STORE OF RELEVANT PHRASES ?
A PERSONAL FAVOURITE I'VE JUST RECALLED : ..HA HA... ahem
WHAT THE FUCK WAS THAT?!
MMMMM...
IS THAT HAPPY OR SAD ?

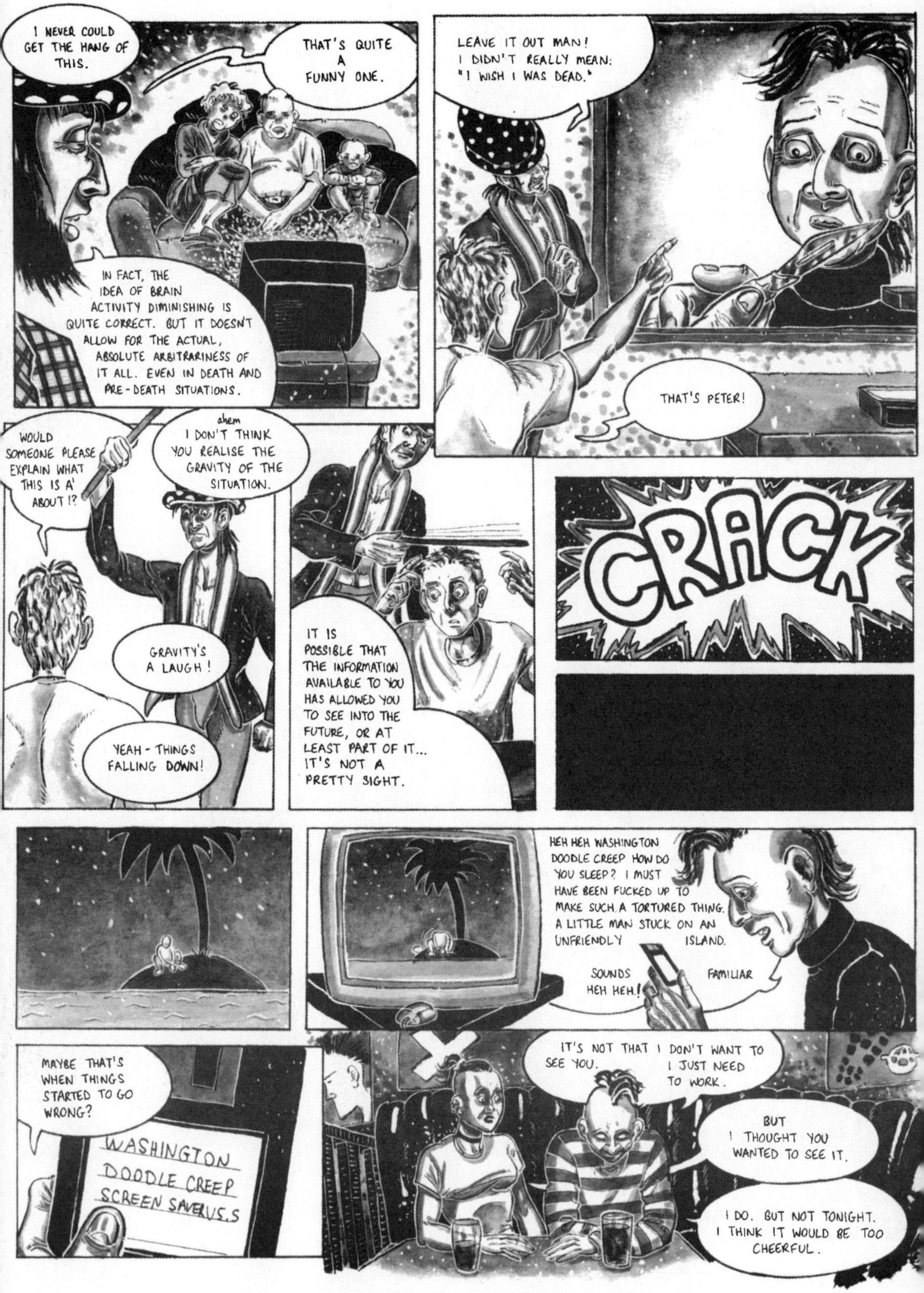
I NEVER COULD GET THE HANG OF THIS.
THAT'S QUITE A FUNNY ONE.
IN FACT, THE IDEA OF BRAIN ACTIVITY DIMINISHING IS QUITE CORRECT. BUT IT DOESN'T ALLOW FOR THE ACTUAL, ABSOLUTE ARBITRARINESS OF IT ALL. EVEN IN DEATH AND PRE-DEATH SITUATIONS.
LEAVE IT OUT MAN! I DIDN'T REALLY MEAN: "I WISH I WAS DEAD."
THAT'S PETER!
WOULD SOMEONE PLEASE EXPLAIN WHAT THIS IS A' ABOUT!?
ahem I DON'T THINK YOU REALISE THE GRAVITY OF THE SITUATION.
GRAVITY'S A LAUGH!
YEAH - THINGS FALLING DOWN!
IT IS POSSIBLE THAT THE INFORMATION AVAILABLE TO YOU HAS ALLOWED YOU TO SEE INTO THE FUTURE, OR AT LEAST PART OF IT... IT'S NOT A PRETTY SIGHT.
CRACK
HEH HEH WASHINGTON DOODLE CREEP HOW DO YOU SLEEP? I MUST HAVE BEEN FUCKED UP TO MAKE SUCH A TORTURED THING. A LITTLE MAN STUCK ON AN UNFRIENDLY ISLAND.
SOUNDS FAMILIAR HEH HEH!
MAYBE THAT'S WHEN THINGS STARTED TO GO WRONG?
WASHINGTON DOODLE CREEP SCREEN SAVER U.S.S
IT'S NOT THAT I DON'T WANT TO SEE YOU. I JUST NEED TO WORK.
BUT I THOUGHT YOU WANTED TO SEE IT.
I DO. BUT NOT TONIGHT. I THINK IT WOULD BE TOO CHEERFUL.

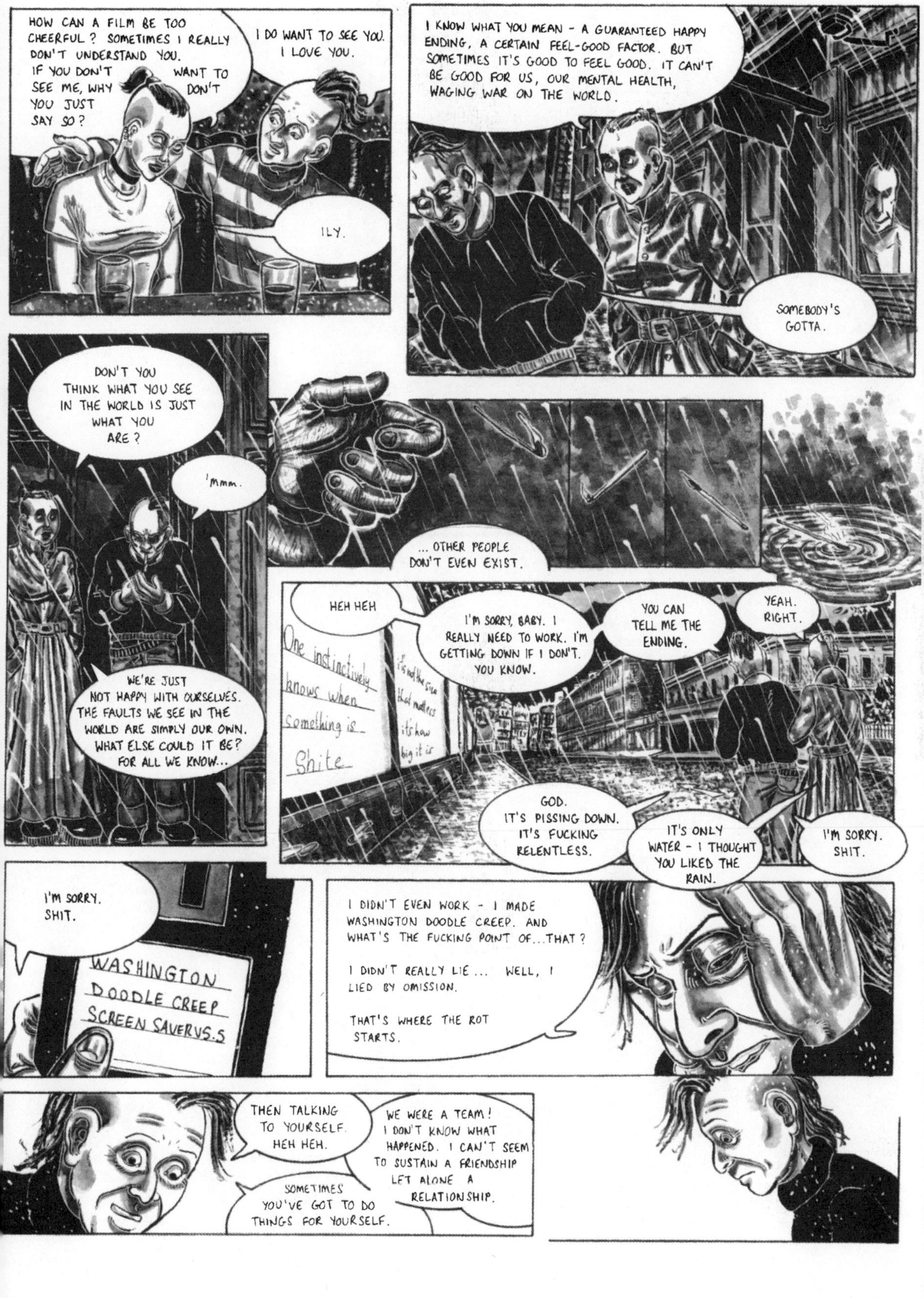
HOW CAN A FILM BE TOO CHEERFUL? SOMETIMES I REALLY DON'T UNDERSTAND YOU. IF YOU DON'T WANT TO SEE ME, WHY DON'T YOU JUST SAY SO?
I DO WANT TO SEE YOU. I LOVE YOU.
ILY.
I KNOW WHAT YOU MEAN - A GUARANTEED HAPPY ENDING, A CERTAIN FEEL-GOOD FACTOR. BUT SOMETIMES IT'S GOOD TO FEEL GOOD. IT CAN'T BE GOOD FOR US, OUR MENTAL HEALTH, WAGING WAR ON THE WORLD.
SOMEBODY'S GOTTA.
DON'T YOU THINK WHAT YOU SEE IN THE WORLD IS JUST WHAT YOU ARE?
'mmm.
WE'RE JUST NOT HAPPY WITH OURSELVES. THE FAULTS WE SEE IN THE WORLD ARE SIMPLY OUR OWN. WHAT ELSE COULD IT BE? FOR ALL WE KNOW...
... OTHER PEOPLE DON'T EVEN EXIST.
HEH HEH
One instinctively knows when something is Shite
it's not the size that matters it's how big it is
I'M SORRY, BABY. I REALLY NEED TO WORK. I'M GETTING DOWN IF I DON'T. YOU KNOW.
YOU CAN TELL ME THE ENDING.
YEAH. RIGHT.
GOD. IT'S PISSING DOWN. IT'S FUCKING RELENTLESS.
IT'S ONLY WATER - I THOUGHT YOU LIKED THE RAIN.
I'M SORRY. SHIT.
I'M SORRY. SHIT.
WASHINGTON DOODLE CREEP SCREEN SAVER V.S.S
I DIDN'T EVEN WORK - I MADE WASHINGTON DOODLE CREEP. AND WHAT'S THE FUCKING POINT OF... THAT?
I DIDN'T REALLY LIE... WELL, I LIED BY OMISSION.
THAT'S WHERE THE ROT STARTS.
THEN TALKING TO YOURSELF. HEH HEH.
SOMETIMES YOU'VE GOT TO DO THINGS FOR YOURSELF.
WE WERE A TEAM! I DON'T KNOW WHAT HAPPENED. I CAN'T SEEM TO SUSTAIN A FRIENDSHIP LET ALONE A RELATIONSHIP.

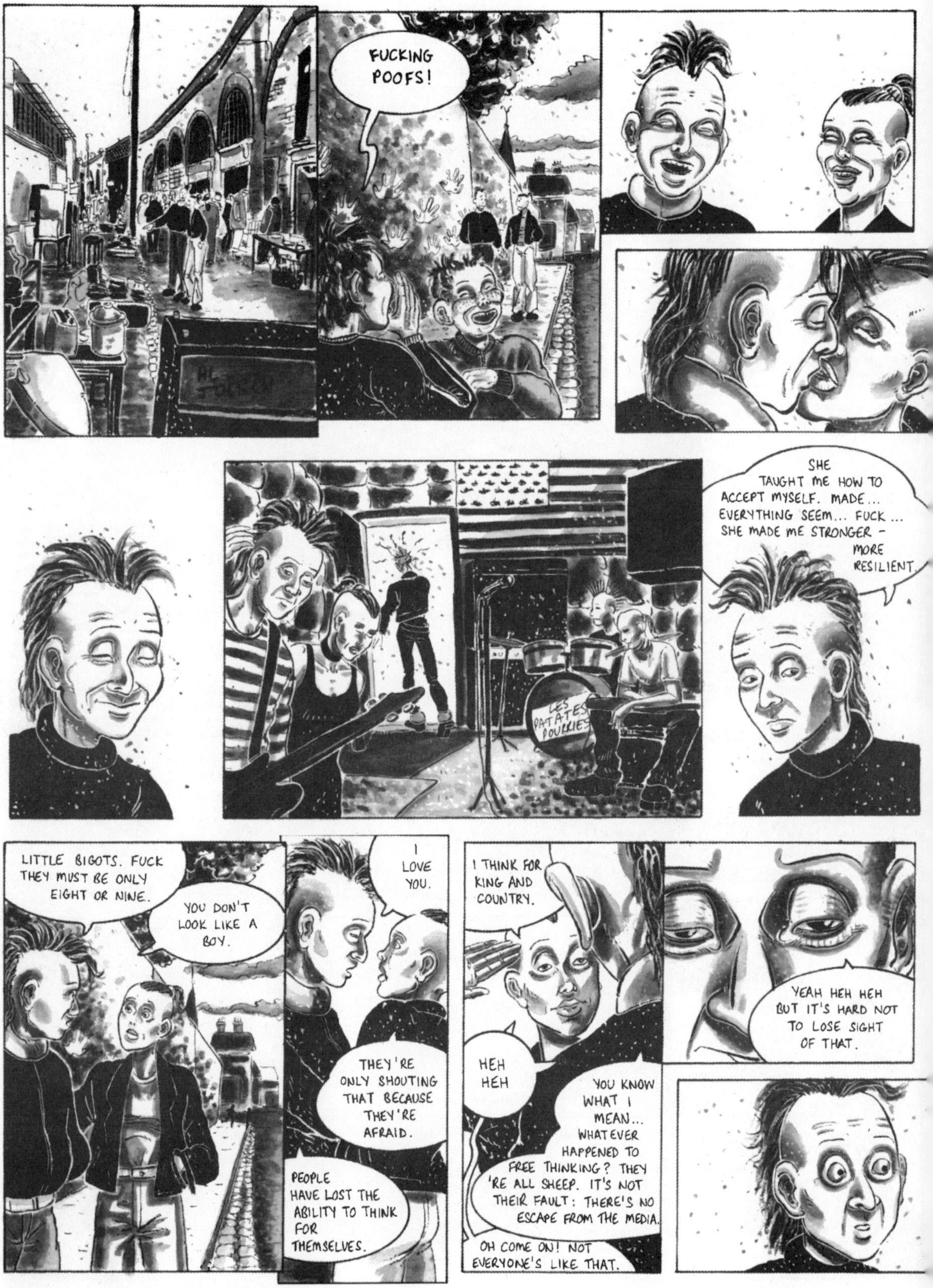
FUCKING POOFS!
SHE TAUGHT ME HOW TO ACCEPT MYSELF. MADE... EVERYTHING SEEM... FUCK... SHE MADE ME STRONGER - MORE RESILIENT
LES PATATES POURRIES
LITTLE BIGOTS. FUCK THEY MUST BE ONLY EIGHT OR NINE.
YOU DON'T LOOK LIKE A BOY.
I LOVE YOU.
THEY'RE ONLY SHOUTING THAT BECAUSE THEY'RE AFRAID.
PEOPLE HAVE LOST THE ABILITY TO THINK FOR THEMSELVES.
I THINK FOR KING AND COUNTRY.
HEH HEH
YOU KNOW WHAT I MEAN... WHATEVER HAPPENED TO FREE THINKING? THEY'RE ALL SHEEP. IT'S NOT THEIR FAULT: THERE'S NO ESCAPE FROM THE MEDIA.
OH COME ON! NOT EVERYONE'S LIKE THAT.
YEAH HEH HEH BUT IT'S HARD NOT TO LOSE SIGHT OF THAT.

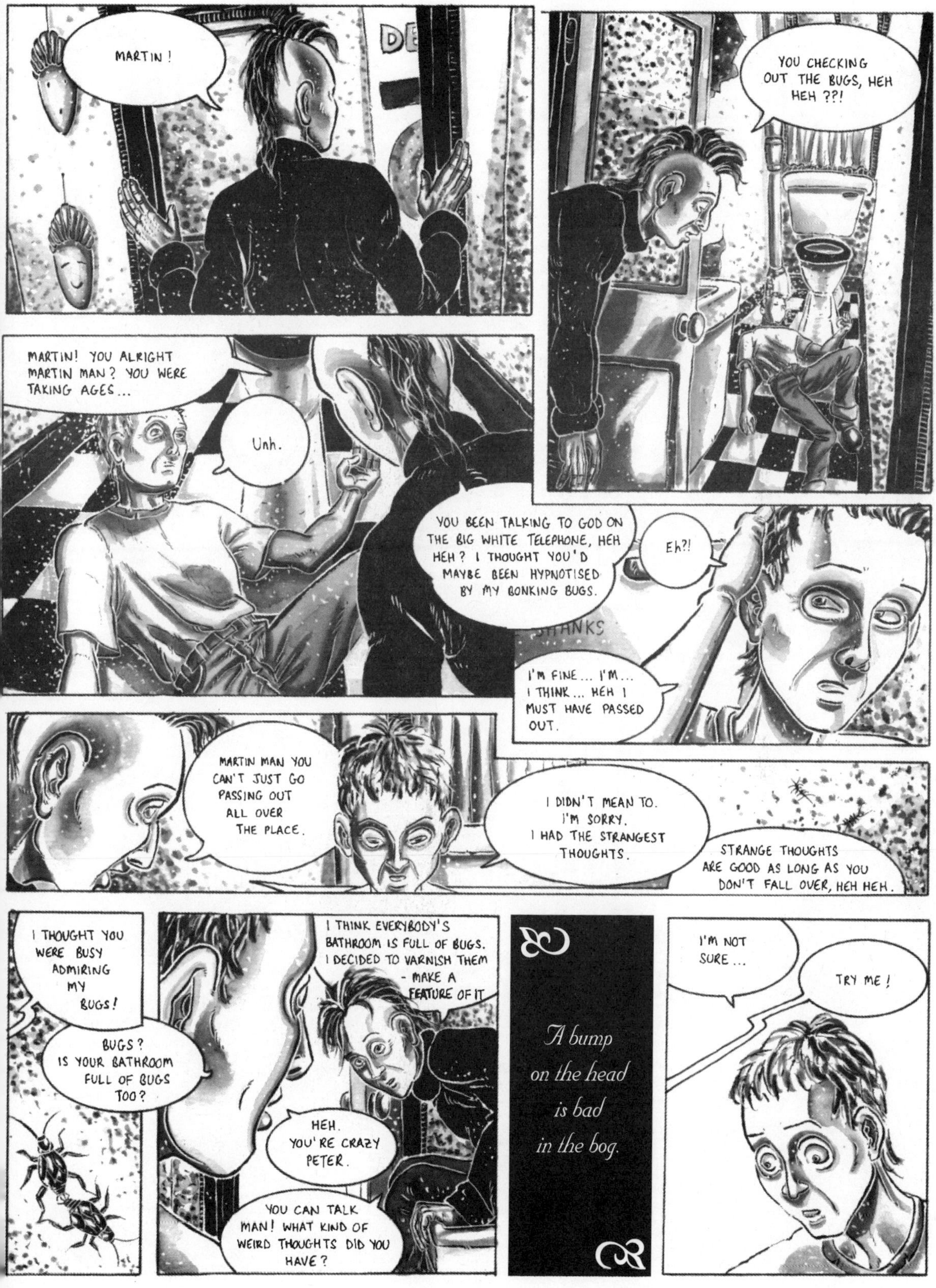
MARTIN !
DE
YOU CHECKING OUT THE BUGS, HEH HEH ??!
MARTIN! YOU ALRIGHT MARTIN MAN? YOU WERE TAKING AGES...
Unh.
YOU BEEN TALKING TO GOD ON THE BIG WHITE TELEPHONE, HEH HEH? I THOUGHT YOU'D MAYBE BEEN HYPNOTISED BY MY BONKING BUGS.
Eh?!
I'M FINE... I'M... I THINK... HEH I MUST HAVE PASSED OUT.
MARTIN MAN YOU CAN'T JUST GO PASSING OUT ALL OVER THE PLACE.
I DIDN'T MEAN TO. I'M SORRY. I HAD THE STRANGEST THOUGHTS.
STRANGE THOUGHTS ARE GOOD AS LONG AS YOU DON'T FALL OVER, HEH HEH.
I THOUGHT YOU WERE BUSY ADMIRING MY BUGS!
BUGS? IS YOUR BATHROOM FULL OF BUGS TOO?
I THINK EVERYBODY'S BATHROOM IS FULL OF BUGS. I DECIDED TO VARNISH THEM - MAKE A FEATURE OF IT
HEH. YOU'RE CRAZY PETER.
YOU CAN TALK MAN! WHAT KIND OF WEIRD THOUGHTS DID YOU HAVE?
A bump on the head is bad in the bog.
I'M NOT SURE...
TRY ME!

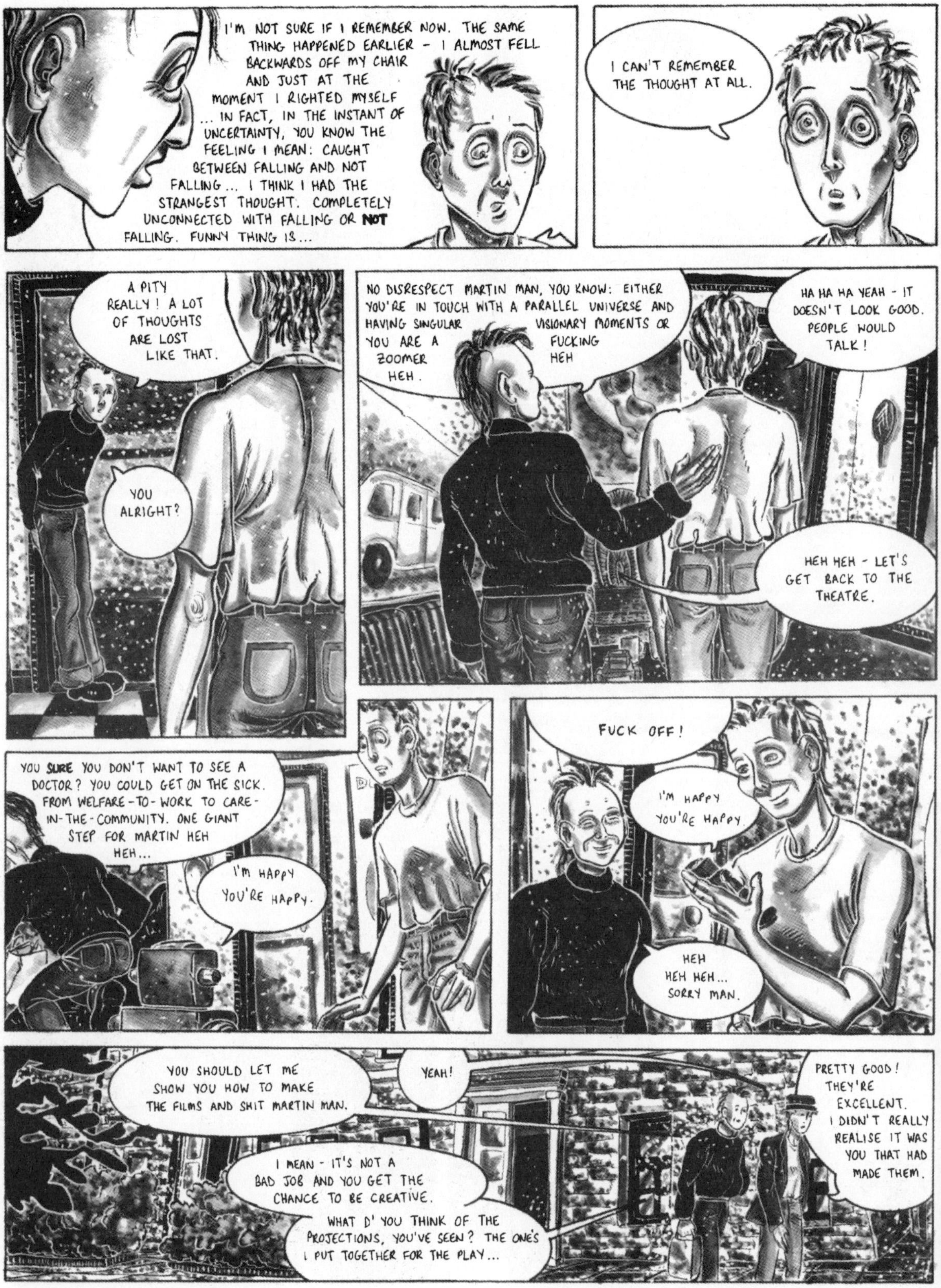

I'M NOT SURE IF I REMEMBER NOW. THE SAME THING HAPPENED EARLIER - I ALMOST FELL BACKWARDS OFF MY CHAIR AND JUST AT THE MOMENT I RIGHTED MYSELF ... IN FACT, IN THE INSTANT OF UNCERTAINTY, YOU KNOW THE FEELING I MEAN: CAUGHT BETWEEN FALLING AND NOT FALLING ... I THINK I HAD THE STRANGEST THOUGHT. COMPLETELY UNCONNECTED WITH FALLING OR **NOT** FALLING. FUNNY THING IS...
I CAN'T REMEMBER THE THOUGHT AT ALL.
A PITY REALLY! A LOT OF THOUGHTS ARE LOST LIKE THAT.
YOU ALRIGHT?
NO DISRESPECT MARTIN MAN, YOU KNOW: EITHER YOU'RE IN TOUCH WITH A PARALLEL UNIVERSE AND HAVING SINGULAR VISIONARY MOMENTS OR YOU ARE A FUCKING ZOOMER HEH HEH.
HA HA HA YEAH - IT DOESN'T LOOK GOOD. PEOPLE WOULD TALK!
HEH HEH - LET'S GET BACK TO THE THEATRE.
YOU **SURE** YOU DON'T WANT TO SEE A DOCTOR? YOU COULD GET ON THE SICK. FROM WELFARE-TO-WORK TO CARE-IN-THE-COMMUNITY. ONE GIANT STEP FOR MARTIN HEH HEH...
I'M HAPPY YOU'RE HAPPY.
FUCK OFF!
I'M HAPPY YOU'RE HAPPY.
HEH HEH HEH... SORRY MAN.
YOU SHOULD LET ME SHOW YOU HOW TO MAKE THE FILMS AND SHIT MARTIN MAN.
YEAH!
I MEAN - IT'S NOT A BAD JOB AND YOU GET THE CHANCE TO BE CREATIVE.
WHAT D' YOU THINK OF THE PROJECTIONS, YOU'VE SEEN? THE ONE'S I PUT TOGETHER FOR THE PLAY...
PRETTY GOOD! THEY'RE EXCELLENT. I DIDN'T REALLY REALISE IT WAS YOU THAT HAD MADE THEM.

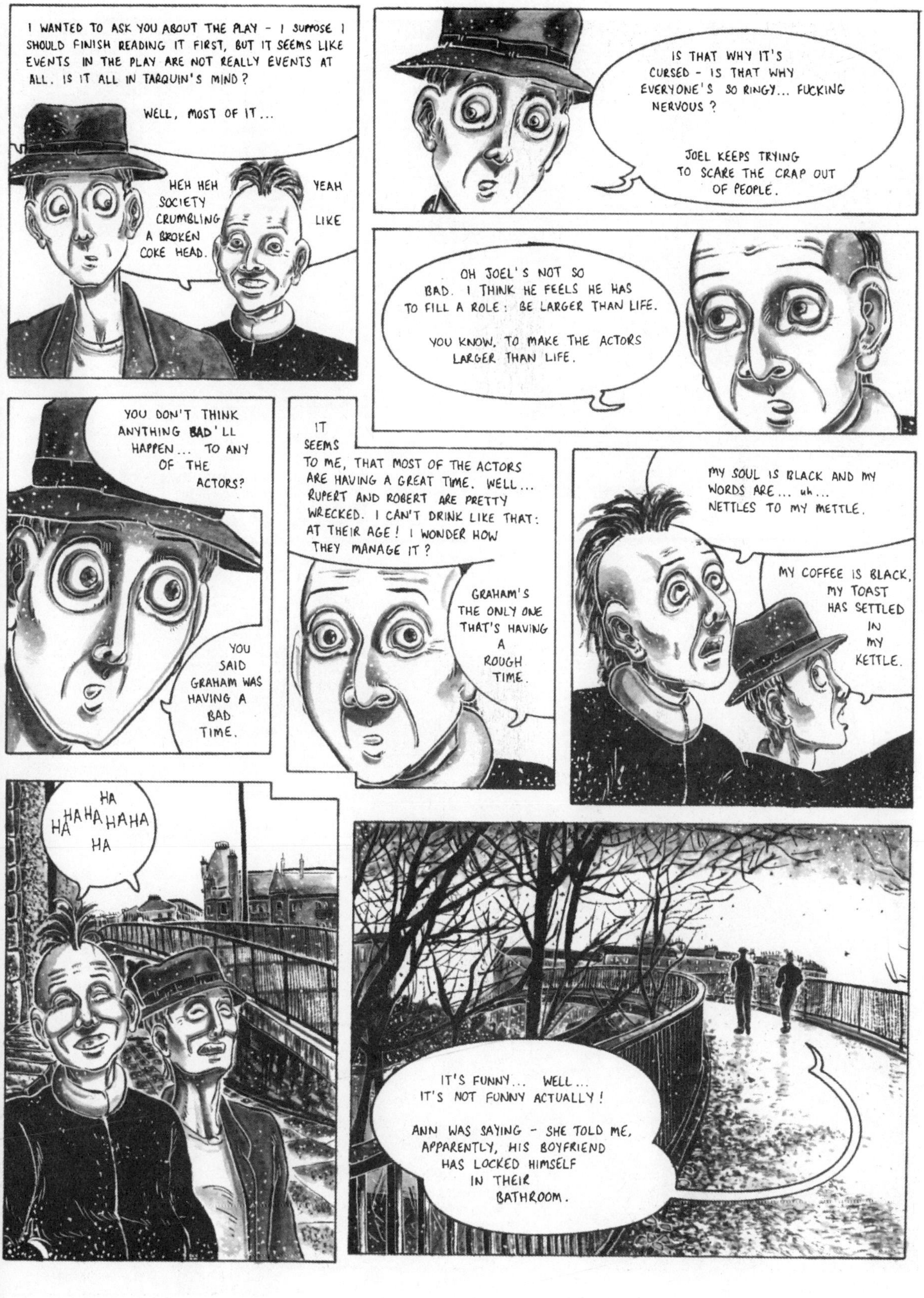
I WANTED TO ASK YOU ABOUT THE PLAY - I SUPPOSE I SHOULD FINISH READING IT FIRST, BUT IT SEEMS LIKE EVENTS IN THE PLAY ARE NOT REALLY EVENTS AT ALL. IS IT ALL IN TARQUIN'S MIND?
WELL, MOST OF IT...
HEH HEH SOCIETY CRUMBLING A BROKEN COKE HEAD.
YEAH LIKE
IS THAT WHY IT'S CURSED - IS THAT WHY EVERYONE'S SO RINGY... FUCKING NERVOUS?
JOEL KEEPS TRYING TO SCARE THE CRAP OUT OF PEOPLE.
OH JOEL'S NOT SO BAD. I THINK HE FEELS HE HAS TO FILL A ROLE: BE LARGER THAN LIFE.
YOU KNOW, TO MAKE THE ACTORS LARGER THAN LIFE.
YOU DON'T THINK ANYTHING BAD'LL HAPPEN... TO ANY OF THE ACTORS?
YOU SAID GRAHAM WAS HAVING A BAD TIME.
IT SEEMS TO ME, THAT MOST OF THE ACTORS ARE HAVING A GREAT TIME. WELL... RUPERT AND ROBERT ARE PRETTY WRECKED. I CAN'T DRINK LIKE THAT: AT THEIR AGE! I WONDER HOW THEY MANAGE IT?
GRAHAM'S THE ONLY ONE THAT'S HAVING A ROUGH TIME.
MY SOUL IS BLACK AND MY WORDS ARE... uh... NETTLES TO MY METTLE.
MY COFFEE IS BLACK, MY TOAST HAS SETTLED IN MY KETTLE.
HA HAHA HAHA HA HA
IT'S FUNNY... WELL... IT'S NOT FUNNY ACTUALLY!
ANN WAS SAYING - SHE TOLD ME, APPARENTLY, HIS BOYFRIEND HAS LOCKED HIMSELF IN THEIR BATHROOM.

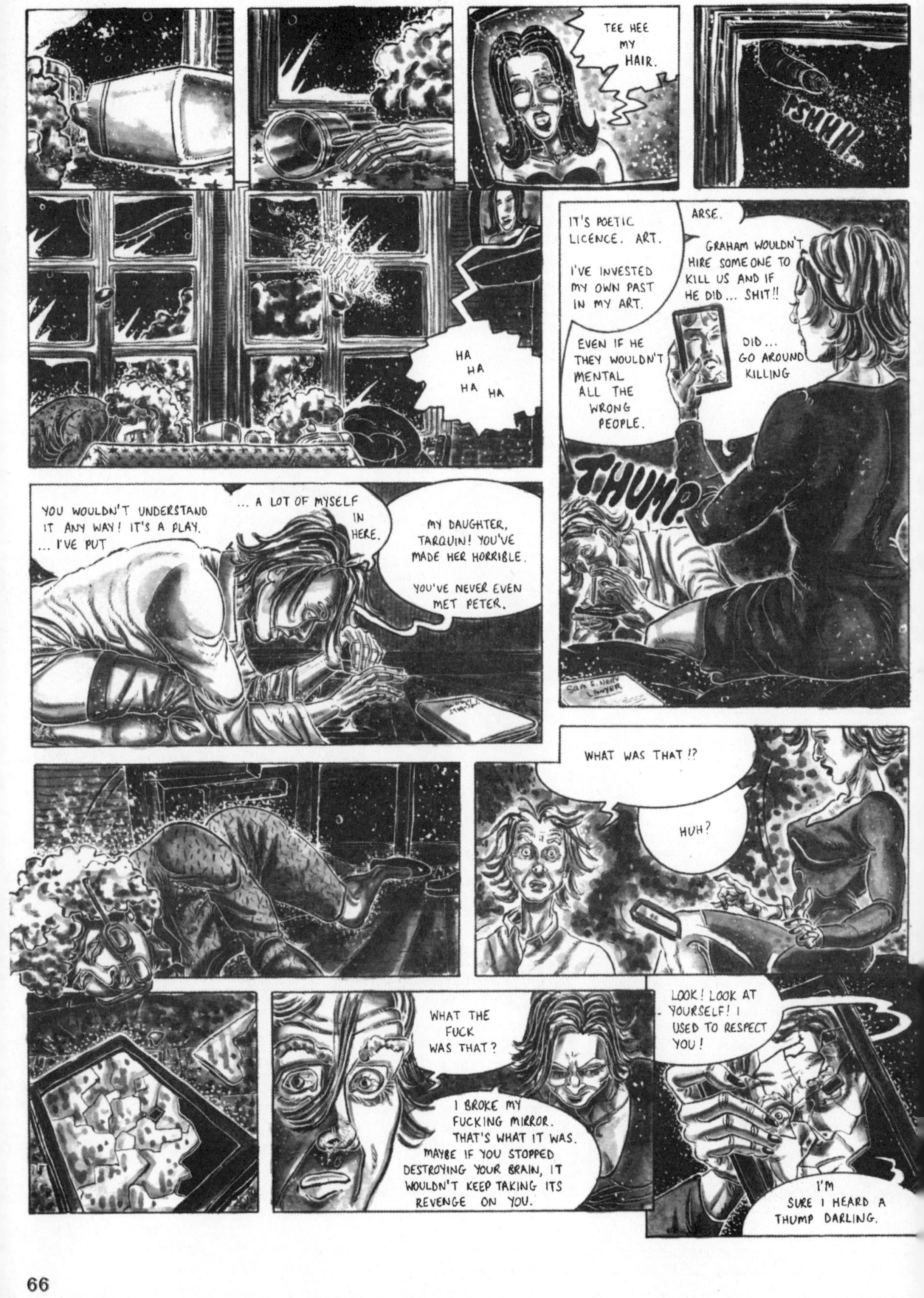
TEE HEE MY HAIR.
PSHHH...
PSHHH...
HA HA HA HA
IT'S POETIC LICENCE. ART.
I'VE INVESTED MY OWN PAST IN MY ART.
ARSE.
GRAHAM WOULDN'T HIRE SOMEONE TO KILL US AND IF HE DID... SHIT!!
EVEN IF HE THEY WOULDN'T MENTAL ALL THE WRONG PEOPLE.
DID... GO AROUND KILLING
THUMP
YOU WOULDN'T UNDERSTAND IT ANY WAY! IT'S A PLAY. ... I'VE PUT
... A LOT OF MYSELF IN HERE.
MY DAUGHTER, TARQUIN! YOU'VE MADE HER HORRIBLE.
YOU'VE NEVER EVEN MET PETER.
WHAT WAS THAT !?
HUH?
WHAT THE FUCK WAS THAT?
I BROKE MY FUCKING MIRROR. THAT'S WHAT IT WAS.
MAYBE IF YOU STOPPED DESTROYING YOUR BRAIN, IT WOULDN'T KEEP TAKING ITS REVENGE ON YOU.
LOOK! LOOK AT YOURSELF! I USED TO RESPECT YOU!
I'M SURE I HEARD A THUMP DARLING.

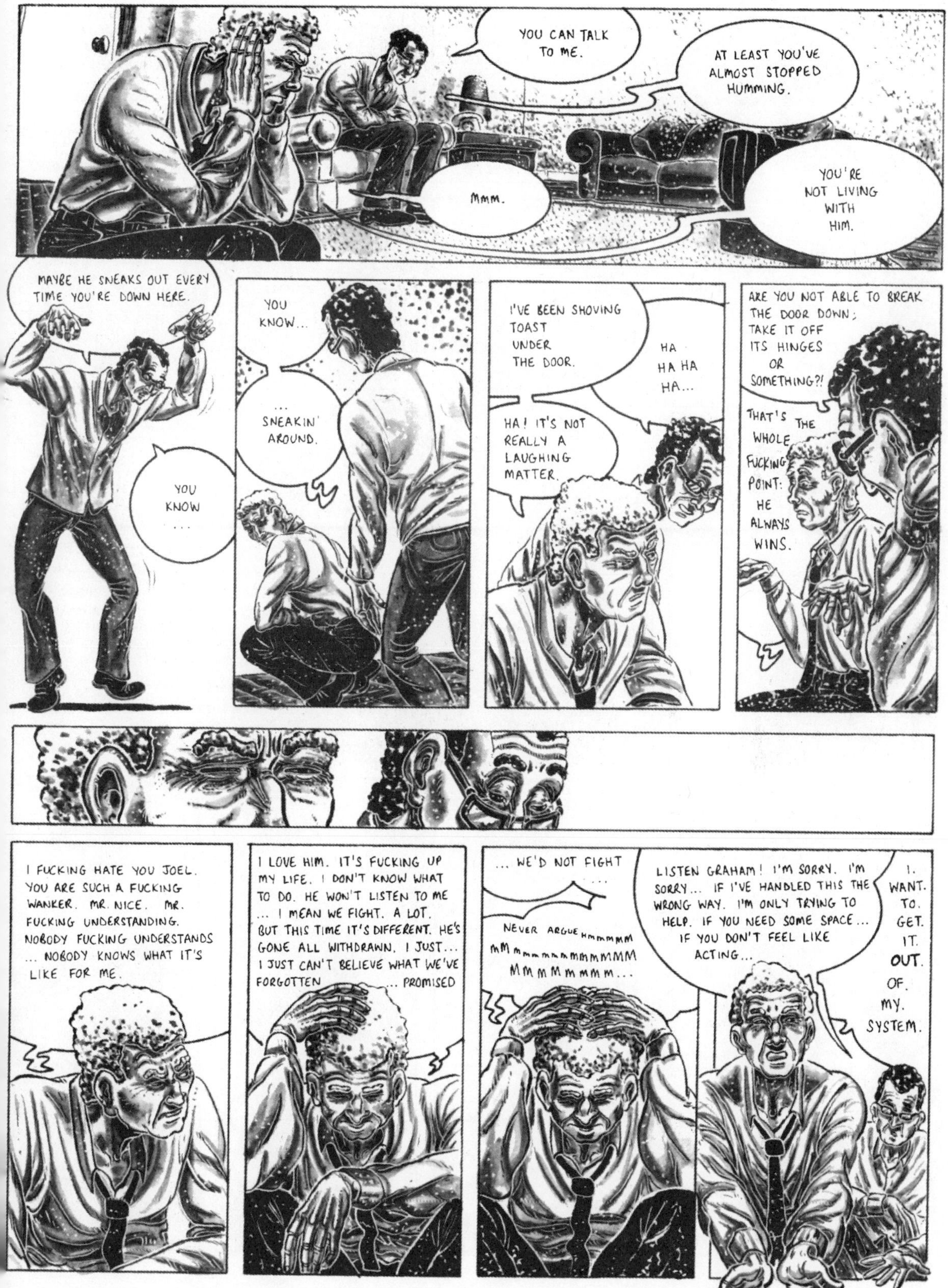
YOU CAN TALK TO ME.
AT LEAST YOU'VE ALMOST STOPPED HUMMING.
MMM.
YOU'RE NOT LIVING WITH HIM.
MAYBE HE SNEAKS OUT EVERY TIME YOU'RE DOWN HERE.
YOU KNOW . . .
YOU KNOW...
... SNEAKIN' AROUND.
I'VE BEEN SHOVING TOAST UNDER THE DOOR.
HA HA HA HA...
HA! IT'S NOT REALLY A LAUGHING MATTER.
ARE YOU NOT ABLE TO BREAK THE DOOR DOWN; TAKE IT OFF ITS HINGES OR SOMETHING?!
THAT'S THE WHOLE FUCKING POINT: HE ALWAYS WINS.
I FUCKING HATE YOU JOEL. YOU ARE SUCH A FUCKING WANKER. MR. NICE. MR. FUCKING UNDERSTANDING. NOBODY FUCKING UNDERSTANDS ... NOBODY KNOWS WHAT IT'S LIKE FOR ME.
I LOVE HIM. IT'S FUCKING UP MY LIFE. I DON'T KNOW WHAT TO DO. HE WON'T LISTEN TO ME ... I MEAN WE FIGHT. A LOT. BUT THIS TIME IT'S DIFFERENT. HE'S GONE ALL WITHDRAWN. I JUST... I JUST CAN'T BELIEVE WHAT WE'VE FORGOTTEN ... PROMISED
... WE'D NOT FIGHT ...
NEVER ARGUE HMMMMM MMMMMMMMMMMMMM MMMMMMMM...
LISTEN GRAHAM! I'M SORRY. I'M SORRY... IF I'VE HANDLED THIS THE WRONG WAY. I'M ONLY TRYING TO HELP. IF YOU NEED SOME SPACE... IF YOU DON'T FEEL LIKE ACTING...
I. WANT. TO. GET. IT. OUT. OF. MY. SYSTEM.

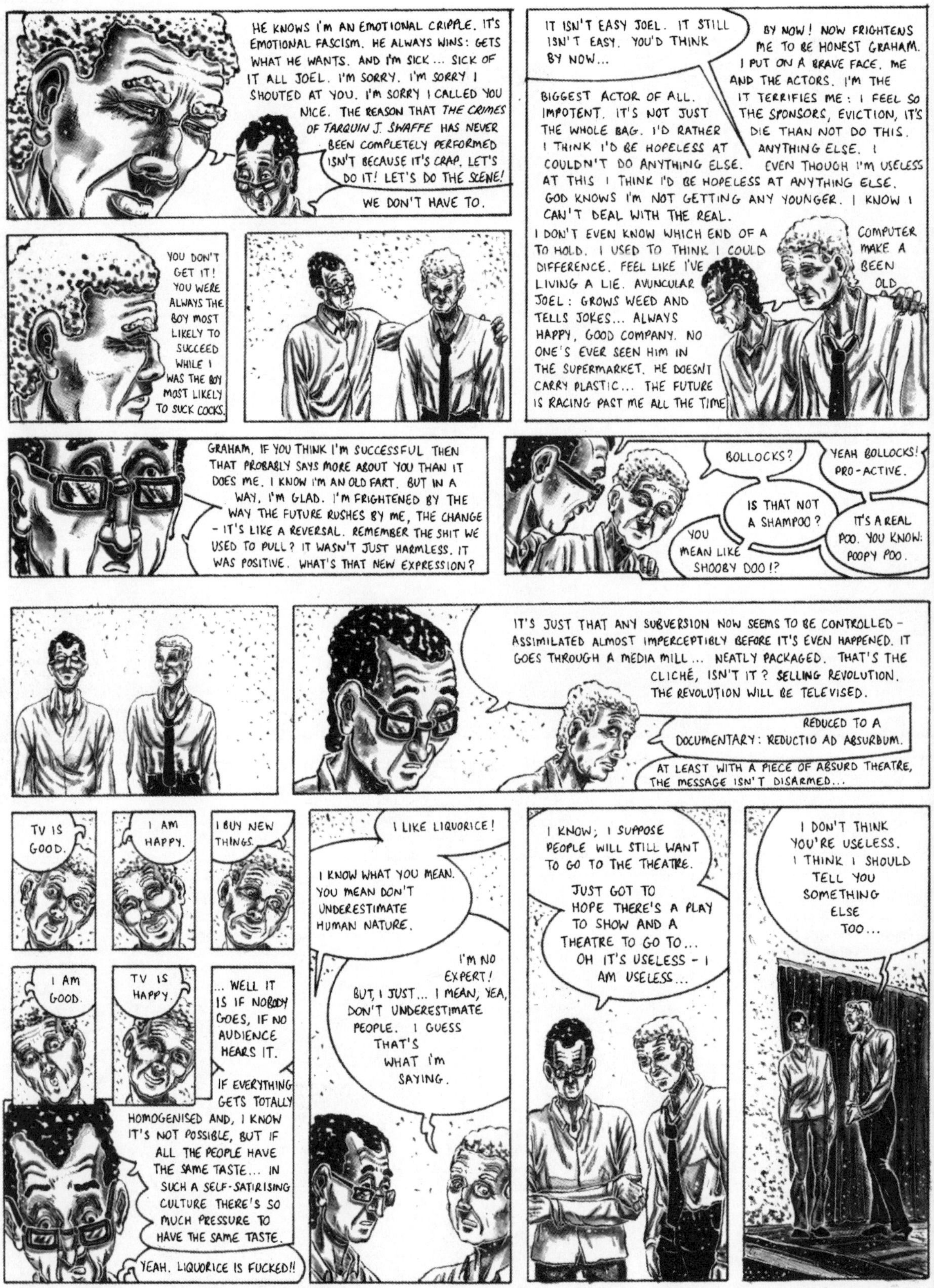
HE KNOWS I'M AN EMOTIONAL CRIPPLE. IT'S EMOTIONAL FASCISM. HE ALWAYS WINS: GETS WHAT HE WANTS. AND I'M SICK... SICK OF IT ALL JOEL. I'M SORRY. I'M SORRY I SHOUTED AT YOU. I'M SORRY I CALLED YOU NICE. THE REASON THAT *THE CRIMES OF TARQUIN J. SWAFFE* HAS NEVER BEEN COMPLETELY PERFORMED ISN'T BECAUSE IT'S CRAP. LET'S DO IT! LET'S DO THE SCENE!
WE DON'T HAVE TO.
IT ISN'T EASY JOEL. IT STILL ISN'T EASY. YOU'D THINK BY NOW...
BY NOW! NOW FRIGHTENS ME TO BE HONEST GRAHAM. I PUT ON A BRAVE FACE. ME AND THE ACTORS. I'M THE
BIGGEST ACTOR OF ALL. IT TERRIFIES ME: I FEEL SO
IMPOTENT. IT'S NOT JUST THE SPONSORS, EVICTION, IT'S
THE WHOLE BAG. I'D RATHER DIE THAN NOT DO THIS.
I THINK I'D BE HOPELESS AT ANYTHING ELSE. I
COULDN'T DO ANYTHING ELSE. EVEN THOUGH I'M USELESS AT THIS I THINK I'D BE HOPELESS AT ANYTHING ELSE. GOD KNOWS I'M NOT GETTING ANY YOUNGER. I KNOW I CAN'T DEAL WITH THE REAL.
I DON'T EVEN KNOW WHICH END OF A COMPUTER
TO HOLD. I USED TO THINK I COULD MAKE A
DIFFERENCE. FEEL LIKE I'VE BEEN
LIVING A LIE. AVUNCULAR OLD
JOEL: GROWS WEED AND TELLS JOKES... ALWAYS HAPPY, GOOD COMPANY. NO ONE'S EVER SEEN HIM IN THE SUPERMARKET. HE DOESN'T CARRY PLASTIC... THE FUTURE IS RACING PAST ME ALL THE TIME
YOU DON'T GET IT! YOU WERE ALWAYS THE BOY MOST LIKELY TO SUCCEED WHILE I WAS THE BOY MOST LIKELY TO SUCK COCKS.
GRAHAM, IF YOU THINK I'M SUCCESSFUL THEN THAT PROBABLY SAYS MORE ABOUT YOU THAN IT DOES ME. I KNOW I'M AN OLD FART. BUT IN A WAY, I'M GLAD. I'M FRIGHTENED BY THE WAY THE FUTURE RUSHES BY ME, THE CHANGE - IT'S LIKE A REVERSAL. REMEMBER THE SHIT WE USED TO PULL? IT WASN'T JUST HARMLESS. IT WAS POSITIVE. WHAT'S THAT NEW EXPRESSION?
BOLLOCKS?
YEAH BOLLOCKS! PRO-ACTIVE.
IS THAT NOT A SHAMPOO?
IT'S A REAL POO. YOU KNOW: POOPY POO.
YOU MEAN LIKE SHOOBY DOO!?
IT'S JUST THAT ANY SUBVERSION NOW SEEMS TO BE CONTROLLED - ASSIMILATED ALMOST IMPERCEPTIBLY BEFORE IT'S EVEN HAPPENED. IT GOES THROUGH A MEDIA MILL... NEATLY PACKAGED. THAT'S THE CLICHÉ, ISN'T IT? SELLING REVOLUTION. THE REVOLUTION WILL BE TELEVISED.
REDUCED TO A DOCUMENTARY: REDUCTIO AD ABSURBUM.
AT LEAST WITH A PIECE OF ABSURD THEATRE, THE MESSAGE ISN'T DISARMED...
TV IS GOOD.
I AM HAPPY.
I BUY NEW THINGS.
I AM GOOD.
TV IS HAPPY.
... WELL IT IS IF NOBODY GOES, IF NO AUDIENCE HEARS IT.
IF EVERYTHING GETS TOTALLY HOMOGENISED AND, I KNOW IT'S NOT POSSIBLE, BUT IF ALL THE PEOPLE HAVE THE SAME TASTE... IN SUCH A SELF-SATIRISING CULTURE THERE'S SO MUCH PRESSURE TO HAVE THE SAME TASTE.
YEAH. LIQUORICE IS FUCKED!!
I LIKE LIQUORICE!
I KNOW WHAT YOU MEAN. YOU MEAN DON'T UNDERESTIMATE HUMAN NATURE.
I'M NO EXPERT! BUT, I JUST... I MEAN, YEA, DON'T UNDERESTIMATE PEOPLE. I GUESS THAT'S WHAT I'M SAYING.
I KNOW; I SUPPOSE PEOPLE WILL STILL WANT TO GO TO THE THEATRE.
JUST GOT TO HOPE THERE'S A PLAY TO SHOW AND A THEATRE TO GO TO... OH IT'S USELESS - I AM USELESS...
I DON'T THINK YOU'RE USELESS. I THINK I SHOULD TELL YOU SOMETHING ELSE TOO...

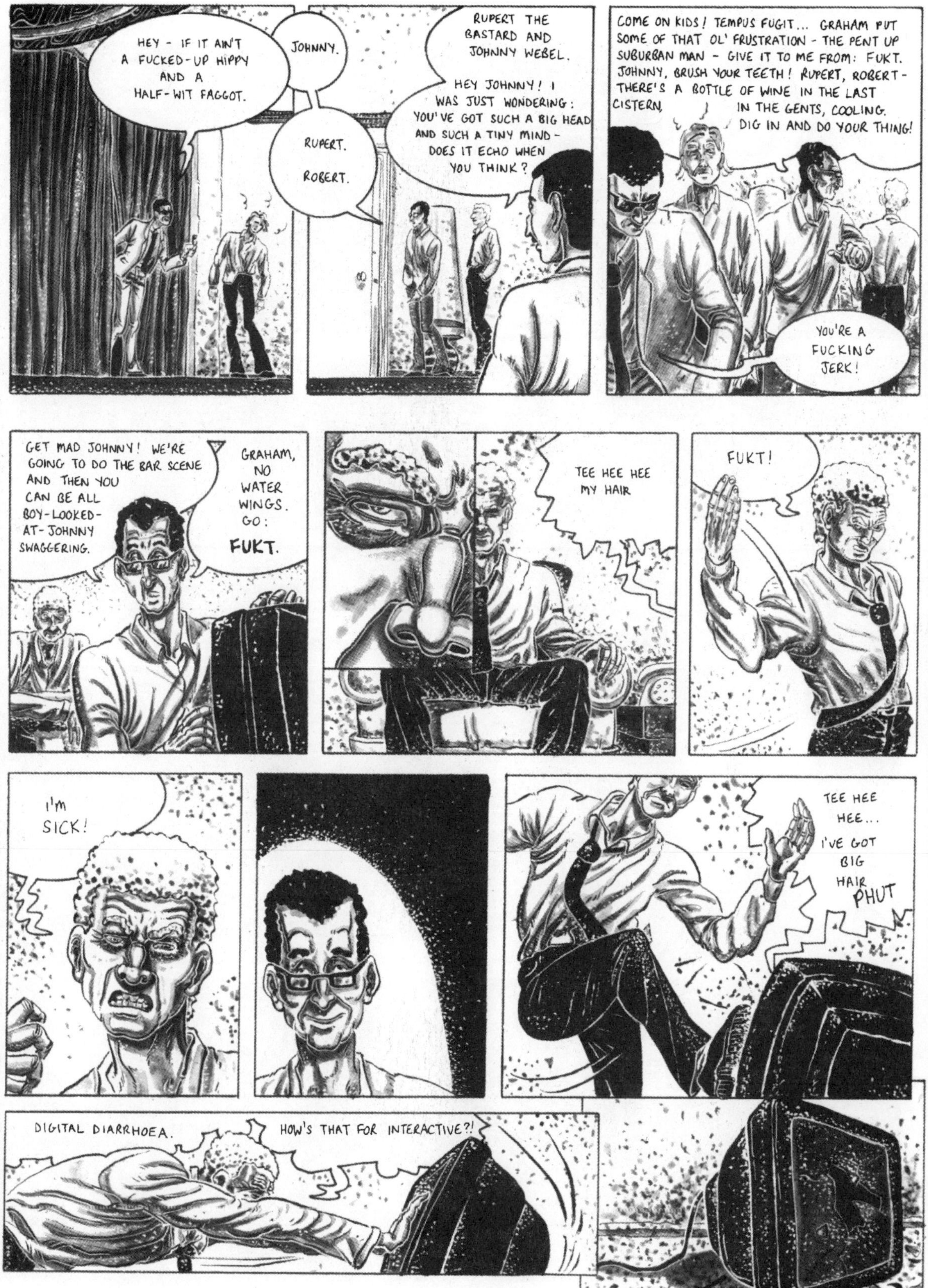
HEY - IF IT AIN'T A FUCKED-UP HIPPY AND A HALF-WIT FAGGOT.
JOHNNY.
RUPERT.
ROBERT.
RUPERT THE BASTARD AND JOHNNY WEBEL.
HEY JOHNNY! I WAS JUST WONDERING: YOU'VE GOT SUCH A BIG HEAD AND SUCH A TINY MIND - DOES IT ECHO WHEN YOU THINK?
COME ON KIDS! TEMPUS FUGIT... GRAHAM PUT SOME OF THAT OL' FRUSTRATION - THE PENT UP SUBURBAN MAN - GIVE IT TO ME FROM: FUKT. JOHNNY, BRUSH YOUR TEETH! RUPERT, ROBERT - THERE'S A BOTTLE OF WINE IN THE LAST CISTERN IN THE GENTS, COOLING. DIG IN AND DO YOUR THING!
YOU'RE A FUCKING JERK!
GET MAD JOHNNY! WE'RE GOING TO DO THE BAR SCENE AND THEN YOU CAN BE ALL BOY-LOOKED-AT-JOHNNY SWAGGERING.
GRAHAM, NO WATER WINGS. GO: FUKT.
TEE HEE HEE MY HAIR
FUKT!
I'M SICK!
TEE HEE HEE... I'VE GOT BIG HAIR
PHUT
DIGITAL DIARRHOEA.
HOW'S THAT FOR INTERACTIVE?!

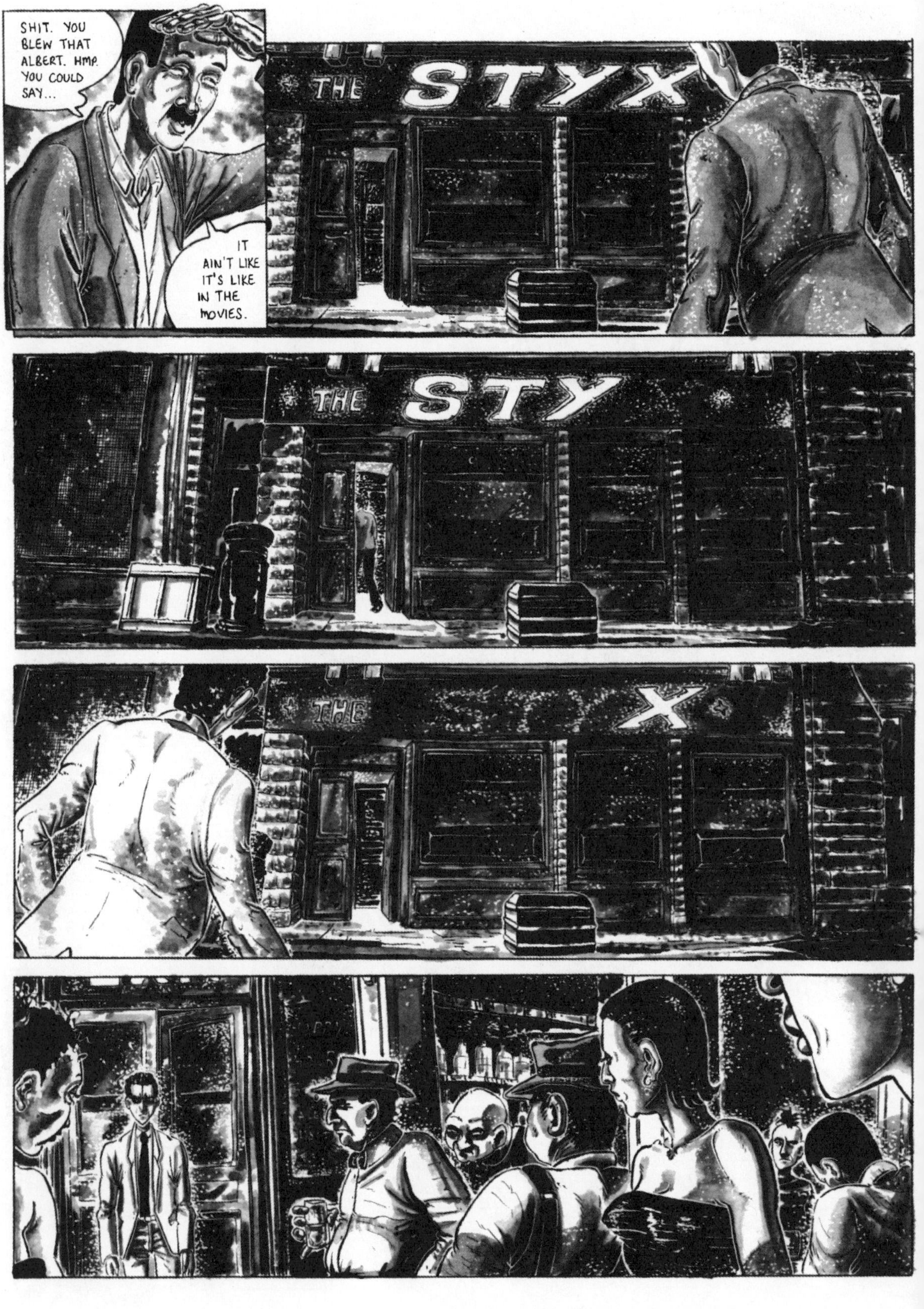
SHIT. YOU BLEW THAT ALBERT. HMP. YOU COULD SAY...
IT AIN'T LIKE IT'S LIKE IN THE MOVIES.
THE STYX
THE STY
THE X

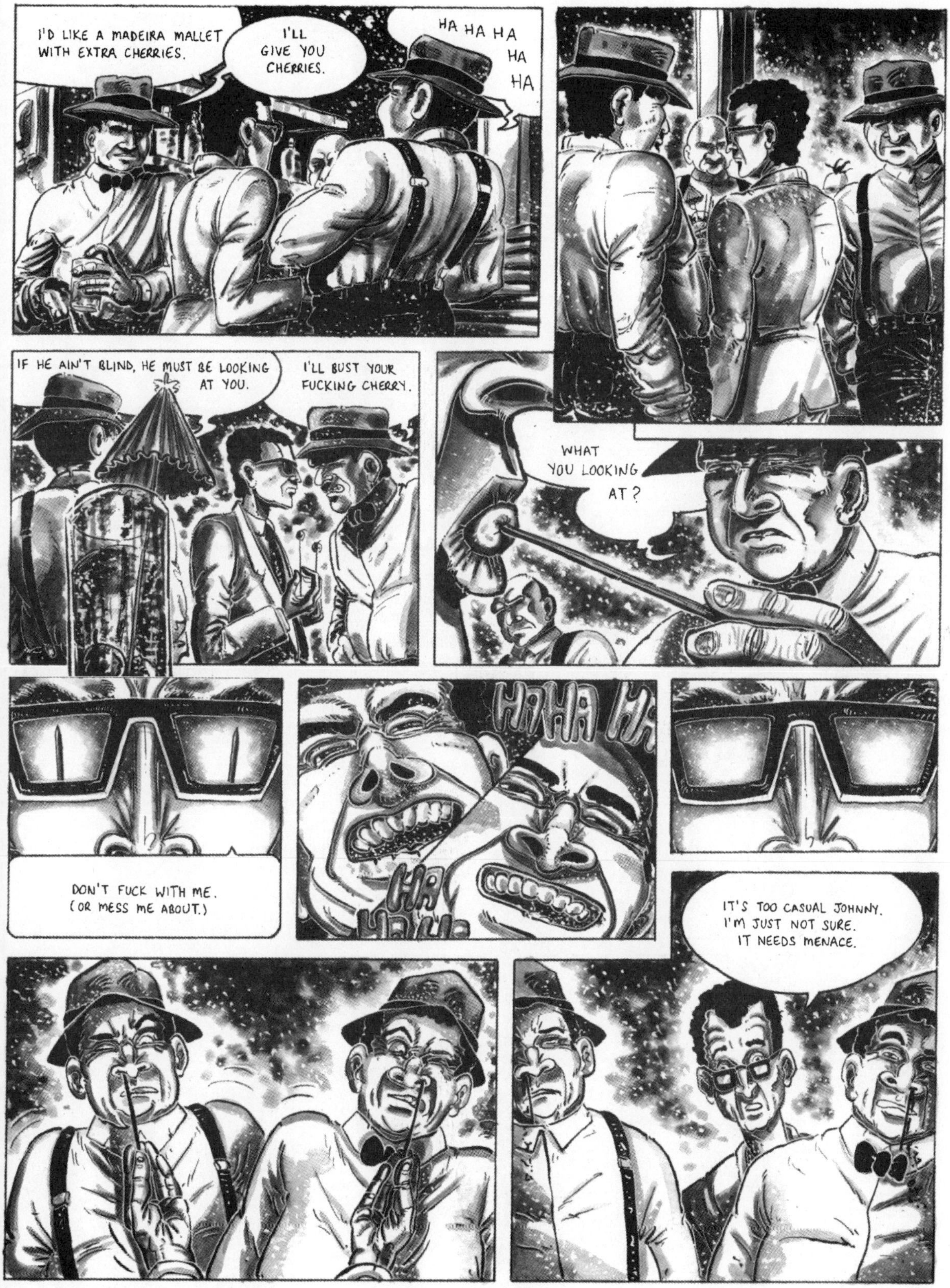
I'D LIKE A MADEIRA MALLET WITH EXTRA CHERRIES.
I'LL GIVE YOU CHERRIES.
HA HA HA HA HA
IF HE AIN'T BLIND, HE MUST BE LOOKING AT YOU.
I'LL BUST YOUR FUCKING CHERRY.
WHAT YOU LOOKING AT?
DON'T FUCK WITH ME. (OR MESS ME ABOUT.)
HAHA HA
IT'S TOO CASUAL JOHNNY. I'M JUST NOT SURE. IT NEEDS MENACE.

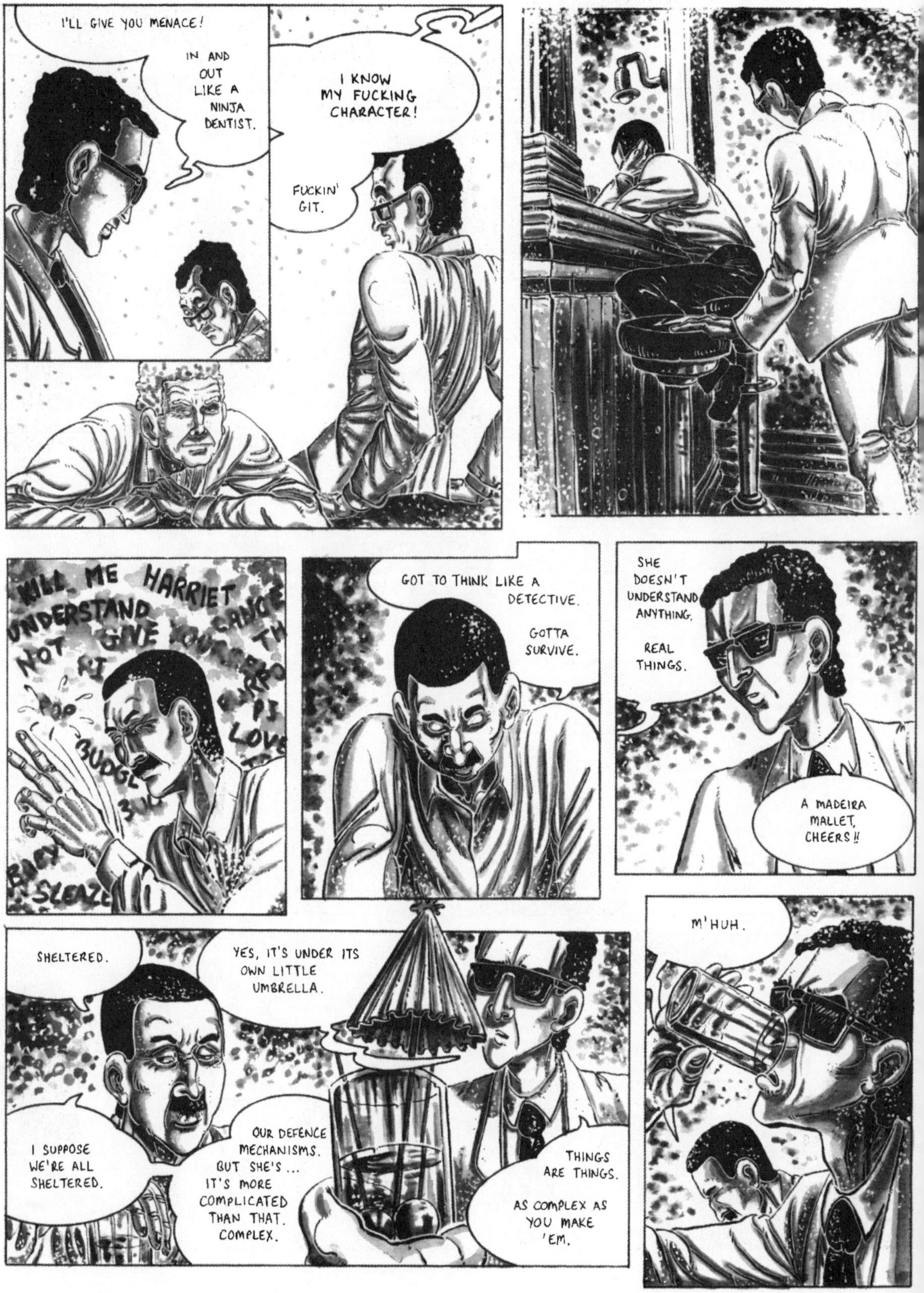
I'LL GIVE YOU MENACE!
IN AND OUT LIKE A NINJA DENTIST.
I KNOW MY FUCKING CHARACTER!
FUCKIN' GIT.
ME HARRIET
UNDERSTAND
NOT GIVE
SLEAZE
GOT TO THINK LIKE A DETECTIVE.
GOTTA SURVIVE.
SHE DOESN'T UNDERSTAND ANYTHING.
REAL THINGS.
A MADEIRA MALLET, CHEERS !!
SHELTERED.
YES, IT'S UNDER ITS OWN LITTLE UMBRELLA.
I SUPPOSE WE'RE ALL SHELTERED.
OUR DEFENCE MECHANISMS. BUT SHE'S ... IT'S MORE COMPLICATED THAN THAT. COMPLEX.
THINGS ARE THINGS.
AS COMPLEX AS YOU MAKE 'EM.
M'HUH.

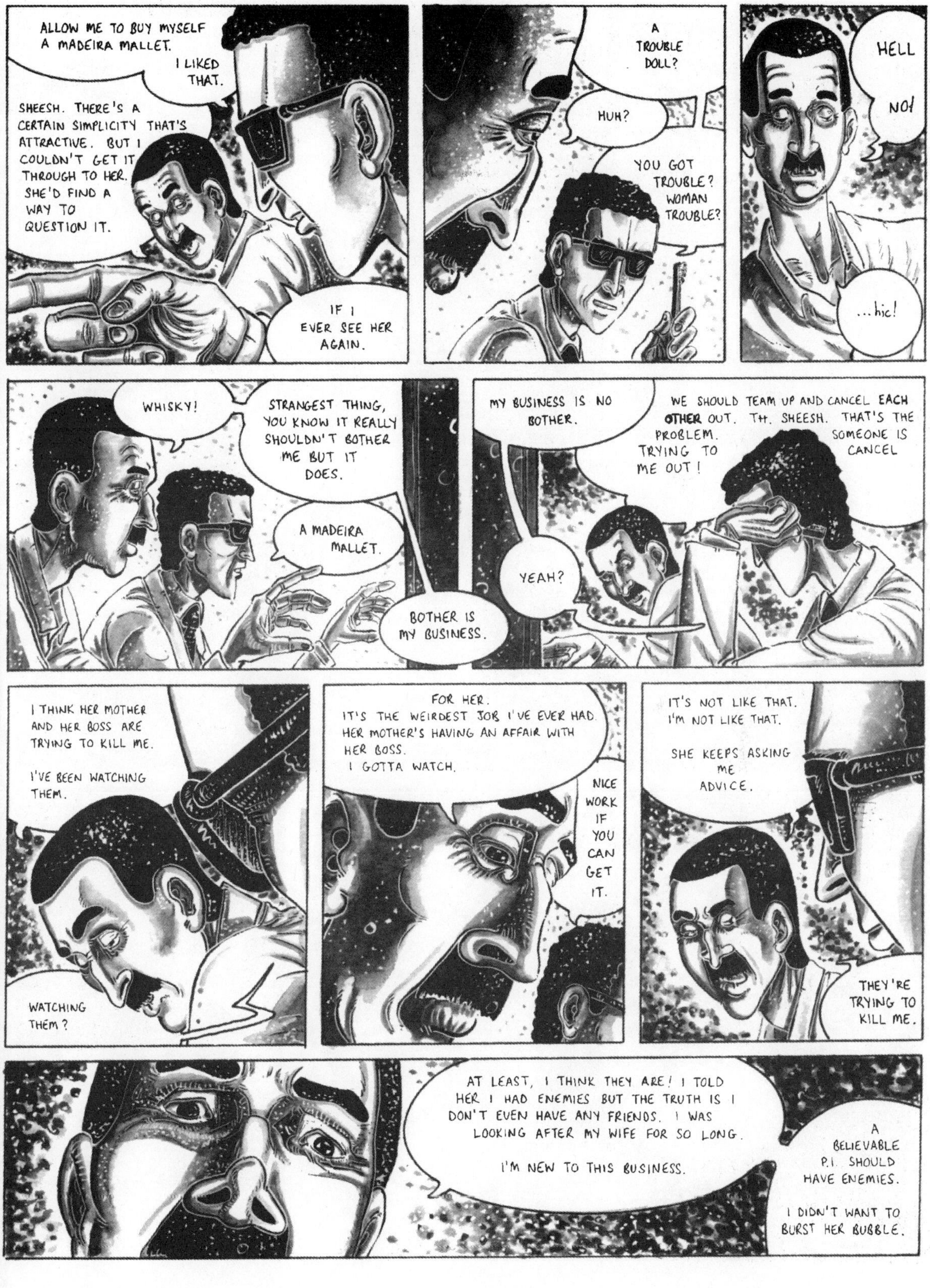
ALLOW ME TO BUY MYSELF A MADEIRA MALLET.
I LIKED THAT.
SHEESH. THERE'S A CERTAIN SIMPLICITY THAT'S ATTRACTIVE. BUT I COULDN'T GET IT THROUGH TO HER. SHE'D FIND A WAY TO QUESTION IT.
IF I EVER SEE HER AGAIN.
A TROUBLE DOLL?
HUH?
YOU GOT TROUBLE? WOMAN TROUBLE?
HELL
NO!
...hic!
WHISKY!
STRANGEST THING, YOU KNOW IT REALLY SHOULDN'T BOTHER ME BUT IT DOES.
A MADEIRA MALLET.
BOTHER IS MY BUSINESS.
MY BUSINESS IS NO BOTHER.
WE SHOULD TEAM UP AND CANCEL EACH OTHER OUT. TH. SHEESH. THAT'S THE PROBLEM. SOMEONE IS TRYING TO CANCEL ME OUT!
YEAH?
I THINK HER MOTHER AND HER BOSS ARE TRYING TO KILL ME.
I'VE BEEN WATCHING THEM.
WATCHING THEM?
FOR HER. IT'S THE WEIRDEST JOB I'VE EVER HAD. HER MOTHER'S HAVING AN AFFAIR WITH HER BOSS. I GOTTA WATCH.
NICE WORK IF YOU CAN GET IT.
IT'S NOT LIKE THAT. I'M NOT LIKE THAT.
SHE KEEPS ASKING ME ADVICE.
THEY'RE TRYING TO KILL ME.
AT LEAST, I THINK THEY ARE! I TOLD HER I HAD ENEMIES BUT THE TRUTH IS I DON'T EVEN HAVE ANY FRIENDS. I WAS LOOKING AFTER MY WIFE FOR SO LONG.
I'M NEW TO THIS BUSINESS.
A BELIEVABLE P.I. SHOULD HAVE ENEMIES.
I DIDN'T WANT TO BURST HER BUBBLE.

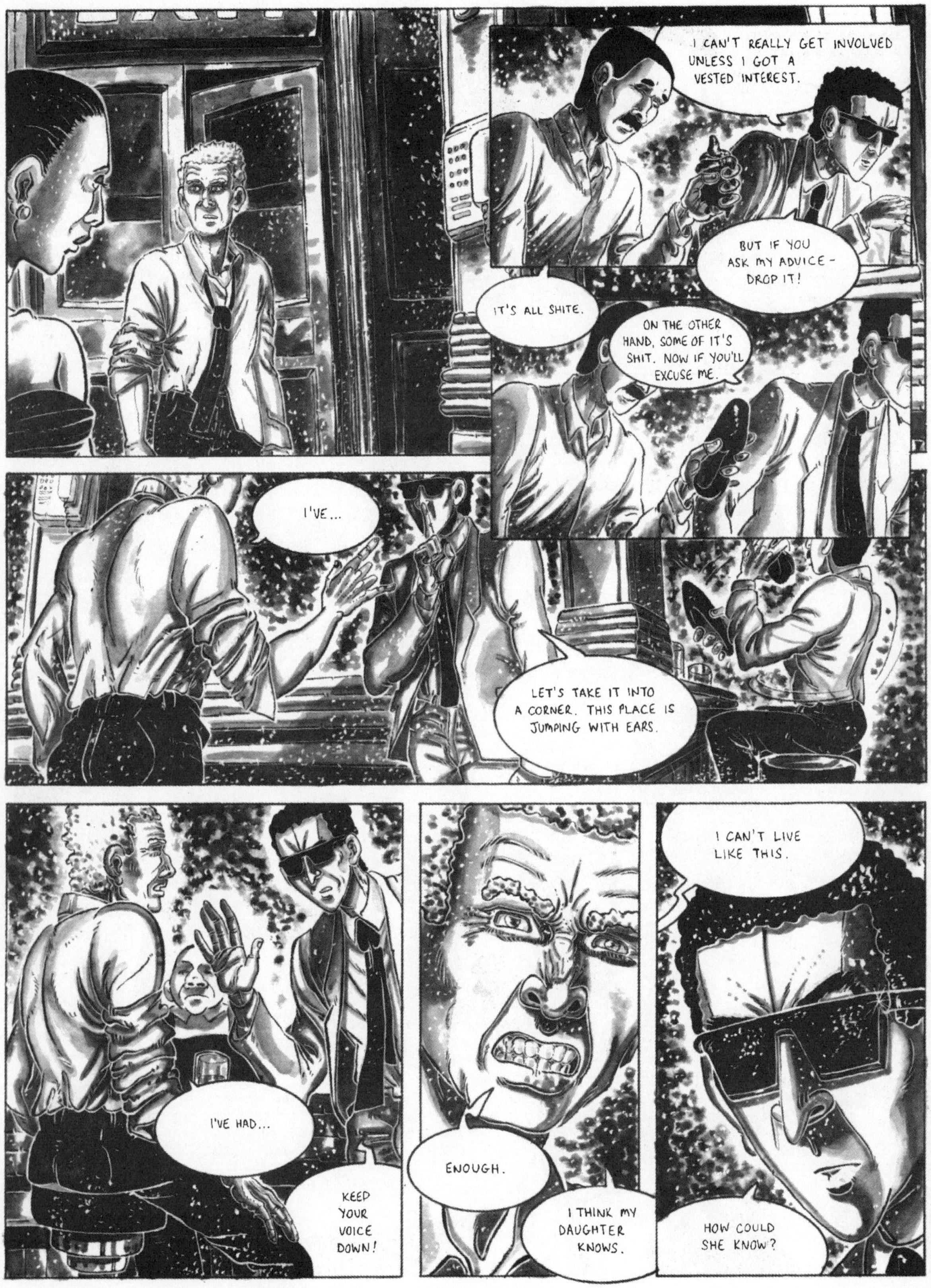

I CAN'T REALLY GET INVOLVED UNLESS I GOT A VESTED INTEREST.
BUT IF YOU ASK MY ADVICE - DROP IT!
IT'S ALL SHITE.
ON THE OTHER HAND, SOME OF IT'S SHIT. NOW IF YOU'LL EXCUSE ME.
I'VE...
LET'S TAKE IT INTO A CORNER. THIS PLACE IS JUMPING WITH EARS.
I'VE HAD...
KEEP YOUR VOICE DOWN!
ENOUGH.
I THINK MY DAUGHTER KNOWS.
I CAN'T LIVE LIKE THIS.
HOW COULD SHE KNOW?

The place where all ideas meet.

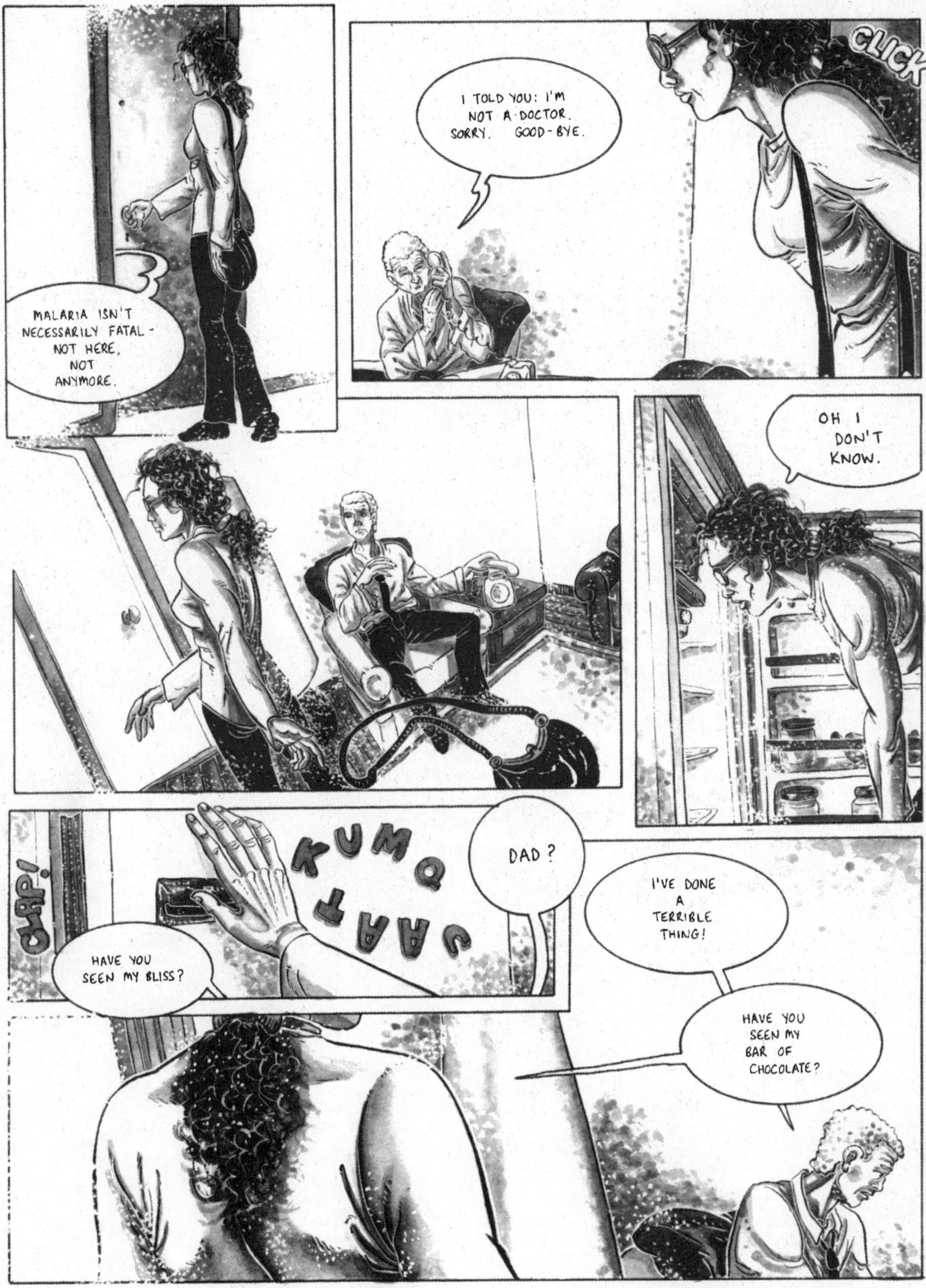
MALARIA ISN'T NECESSARILY FATAL - NOT HERE, NOT ANYMORE.
I TOLD YOU: I'M NOT A DOCTOR. SORRY. GOOD-BYE.
CLICK
OH I DON'T KNOW.
CLAP!
KUMQUAT
DAD?
HAVE YOU SEEN MY BLISS?
I'VE DONE A TERRIBLE THING!
HAVE YOU SEEN MY BAR OF CHOCOLATE?

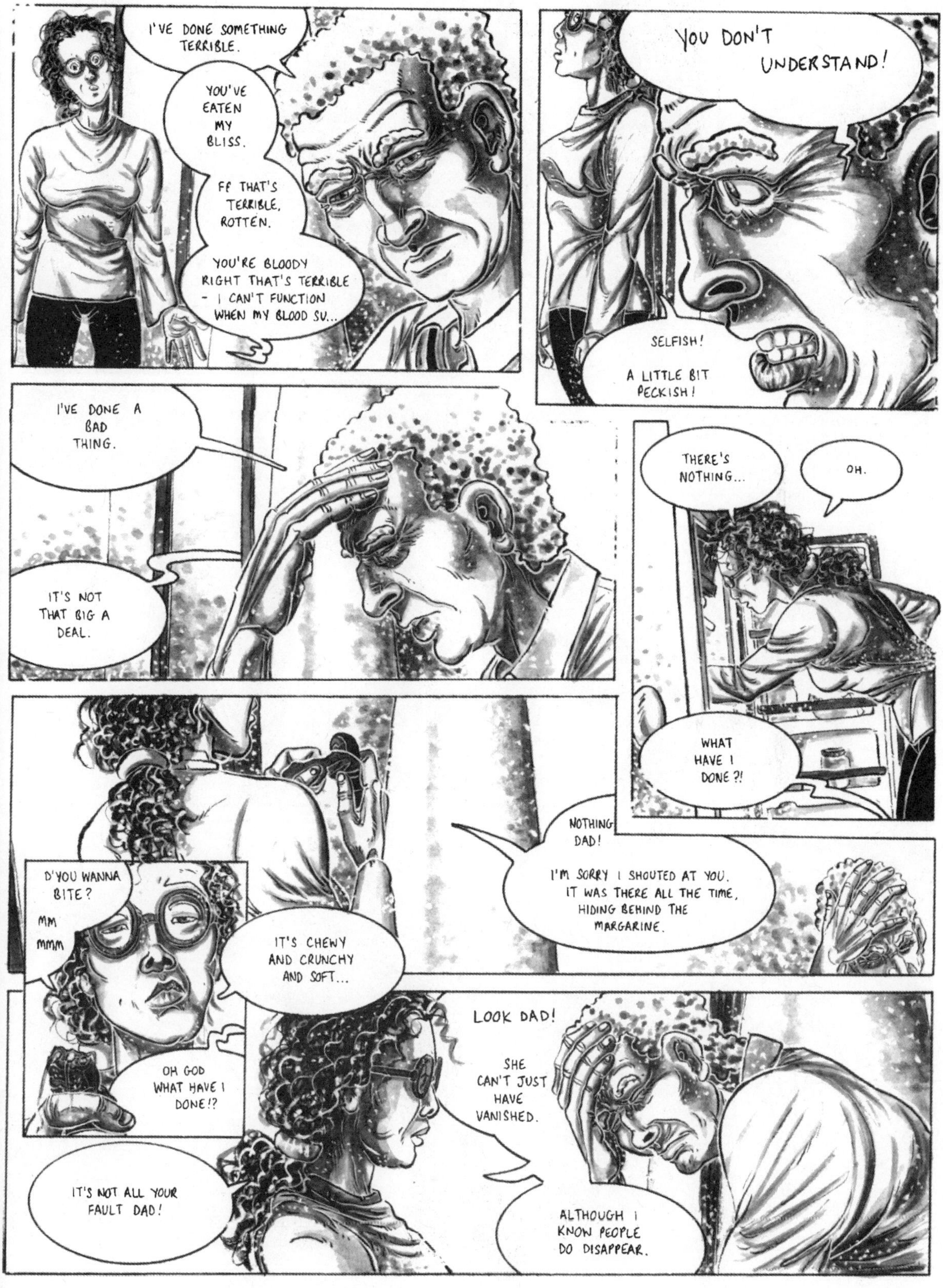
I'VE DONE SOMETHING TERRIBLE.
YOU'VE EATEN MY BLISS.
FF THAT'S TERRIBLE, ROTTEN.
YOU'RE BLOODY RIGHT THAT'S TERRIBLE - I CAN'T FUNCTION WHEN MY BLOOD SU...
YOU DON'T UNDERSTAND!
SELFISH!
A LITTLE BIT PECKISH!
I'VE DONE A BAD THING.
IT'S NOT THAT BIG A DEAL.
THERE'S NOTHING...
OH.
WHAT HAVE I DONE?!
NOTHING DAD!
I'M SORRY I SHOUTED AT YOU. IT WAS THERE ALL THE TIME, HIDING BEHIND THE MARGARINE.
D'YOU WANNA BITE?
MM
MMM
IT'S CHEWY AND CRUNCHY AND SOFT...
OH GOD WHAT HAVE I DONE!?
IT'S NOT ALL YOUR FAULT DAD!
LOOK DAD!
SHE CAN'T JUST HAVE VANISHED.
ALTHOUGH I KNOW PEOPLE DO DISAPPEAR.

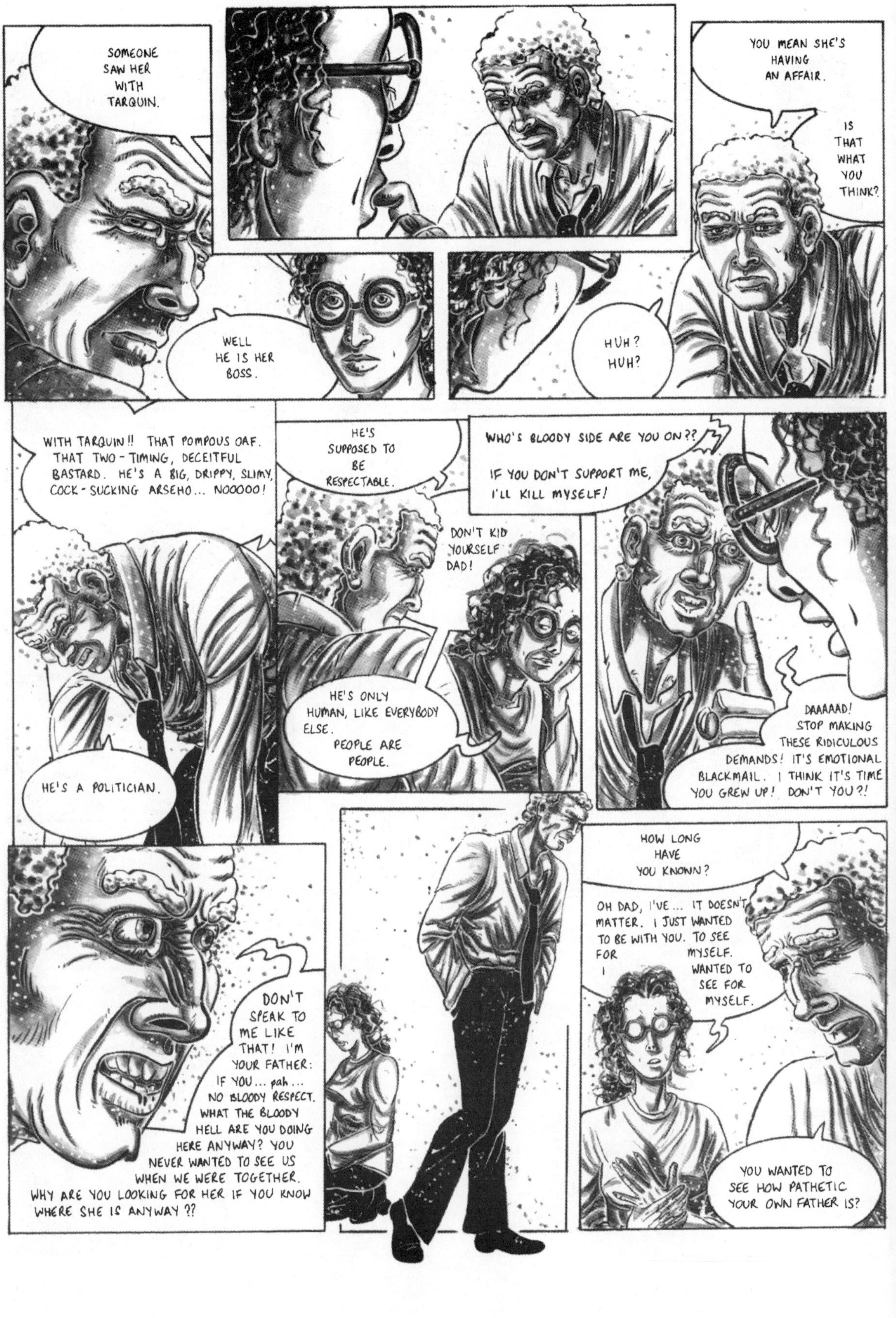
SOMEONE SAW HER WITH TARQUIN.
YOU MEAN SHE'S HAVING AN AFFAIR.
IS THAT WHAT YOU THINK?
WELL HE IS HER BOSS.
HUH? HUH?
WITH TARQUIN!! THAT POMPOUS OAF. THAT TWO-TIMING, DECEITFUL BASTARD. HE'S A BIG, DRIPPY, SLIMY, COCK-SUCKING ARSEHO... NOOOOO!
HE'S A POLITICIAN.
HE'S SUPPOSED TO BE RESPECTABLE.
DON'T KID YOURSELF DAD!
HE'S ONLY HUMAN, LIKE EVERYBODY ELSE. PEOPLE ARE PEOPLE.
WHO'S BLOODY SIDE ARE YOU ON??
IF YOU DON'T SUPPORT ME, I'LL KILL MYSELF!
DAAAAAD! STOP MAKING THESE RIDICULOUS DEMANDS! IT'S EMOTIONAL BLACKMAIL. I THINK IT'S TIME YOU GREW UP! DON'T YOU?!
DON'T SPEAK TO ME LIKE THAT! I'M YOUR FATHER: IF YOU... pah... NO BLOODY RESPECT. WHAT THE BLOODY HELL ARE YOU DOING HERE ANYWAY? YOU NEVER WANTED TO SEE US WHEN WE WERE TOGETHER. WHY ARE YOU LOOKING FOR HER IF YOU KNOW WHERE SHE IS ANYWAY??
HOW LONG HAVE YOU KNOWN?
OH DAD, I'VE... IT DOESN'T MATTER. I JUST WANTED TO BE WITH YOU. TO SEE FOR MYSELF. I WANTED TO SEE FOR MYSELF.
YOU WANTED TO SEE HOW PATHETIC YOUR OWN FATHER IS?

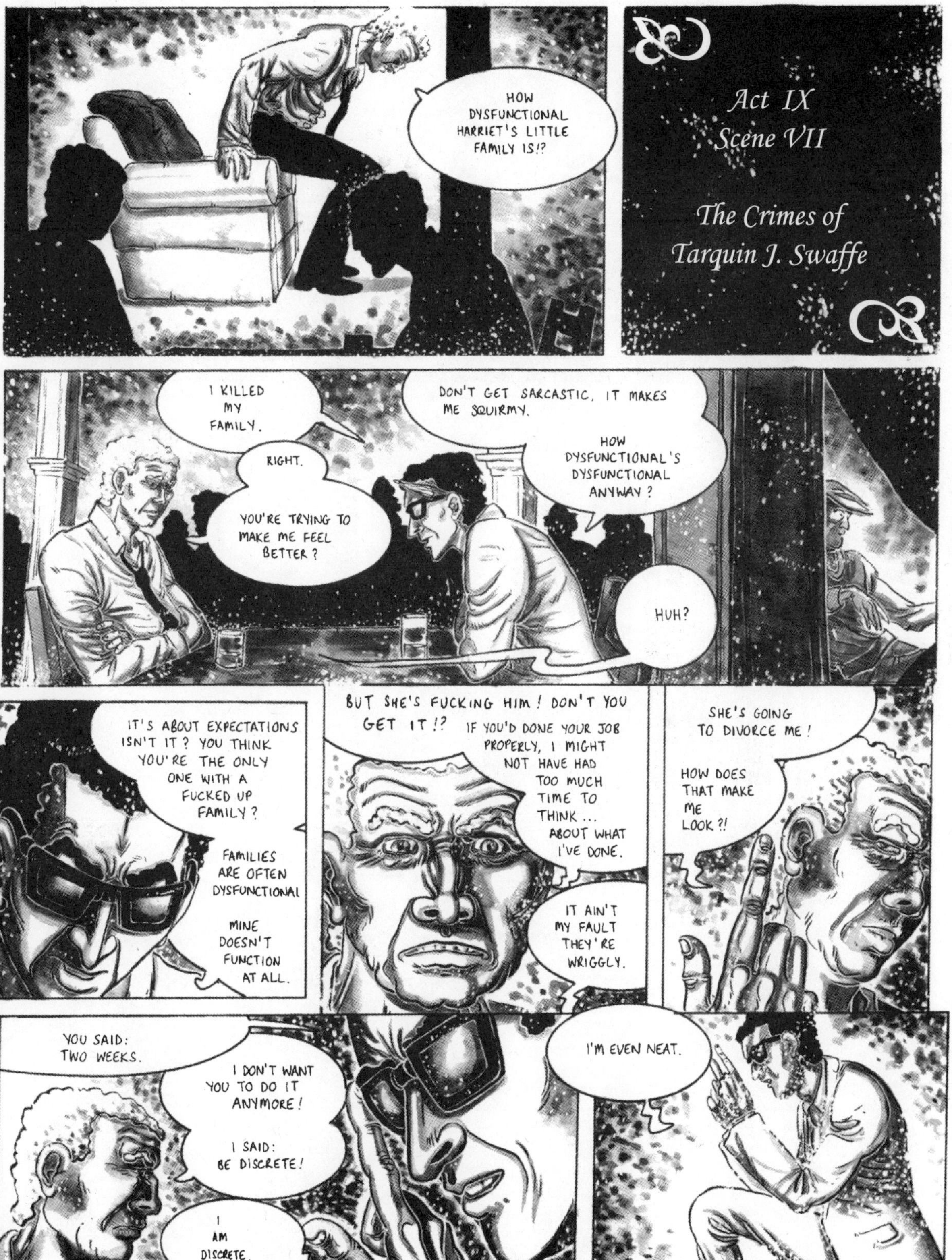
HOW DYSFUNCTIONAL HARRIET'S LITTLE FAMILY IS!?
Act IX
Scene VII
The Crimes of Tarquin J. Swaffe
I KILLED MY FAMILY.
DON'T GET SARCASTIC, IT MAKES ME SQUIRMY.
RIGHT.
YOU'RE TRYING TO MAKE ME FEEL BETTER?
HOW DYSFUNCTIONAL'S DYSFUNCTIONAL ANYWAY?
HUH?
IT'S ABOUT EXPECTATIONS ISN'T IT? YOU THINK YOU'RE THE ONLY ONE WITH A FUCKED UP FAMILY?
FAMILIES ARE OFTEN DYSFUNCTIONAL
MINE DOESN'T FUNCTION AT ALL.
BUT SHE'S FUCKING HIM! DON'T YOU GET IT!?
IF YOU'D DONE YOUR JOB PROPERLY, I MIGHT NOT HAVE HAD TOO MUCH TIME TO THINK ... ABOUT WHAT I'VE DONE.
IT AIN'T MY FAULT THEY'RE WRIGGLY.
SHE'S GOING TO DIVORCE ME!
HOW DOES THAT MAKE ME LOOK?!
YOU SAID: TWO WEEKS.
I DON'T WANT YOU TO DO IT ANYMORE!
I SAID: BE DISCRETE!
I AM DISCRETE.
I'M EVEN NEAT.

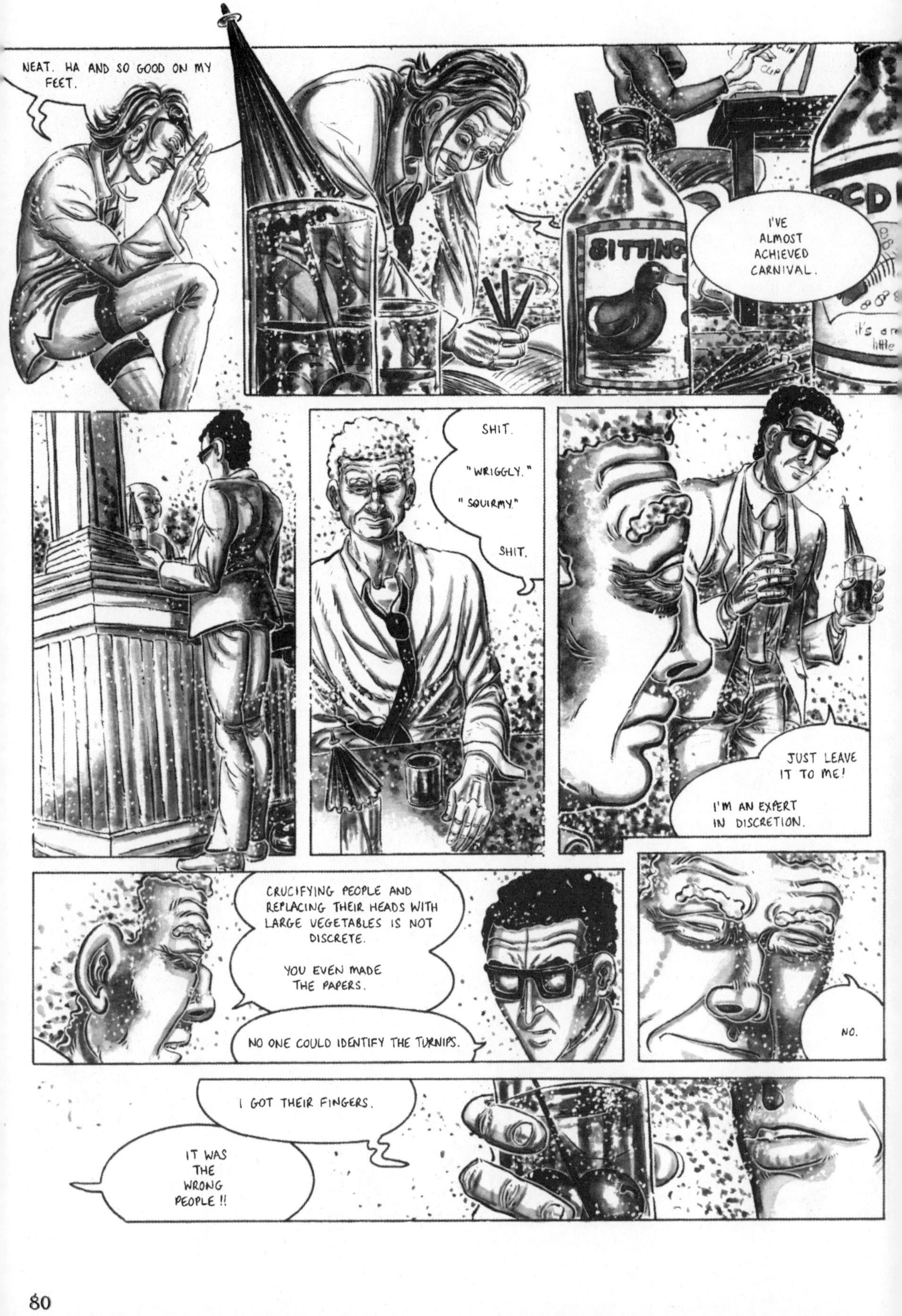
NEAT. HA AND SO GOOD ON MY FEET.
I'VE ALMOST ACHIEVED CARNIVAL.
SHIT.
"WRIGGLY."
"SQUIRMY."
SHIT.
JUST LEAVE IT TO ME!
I'M AN EXPERT IN DISCRETION.
CRUCIFYING PEOPLE AND REPLACING THEIR HEADS WITH LARGE VEGETABLES IS NOT DISCRETE.
YOU EVEN MADE THE PAPERS.
NO ONE COULD IDENTIFY THE TURNIPS.
NO.
I GOT THEIR FINGERS.
IT WAS THE WRONG PEOPLE !!

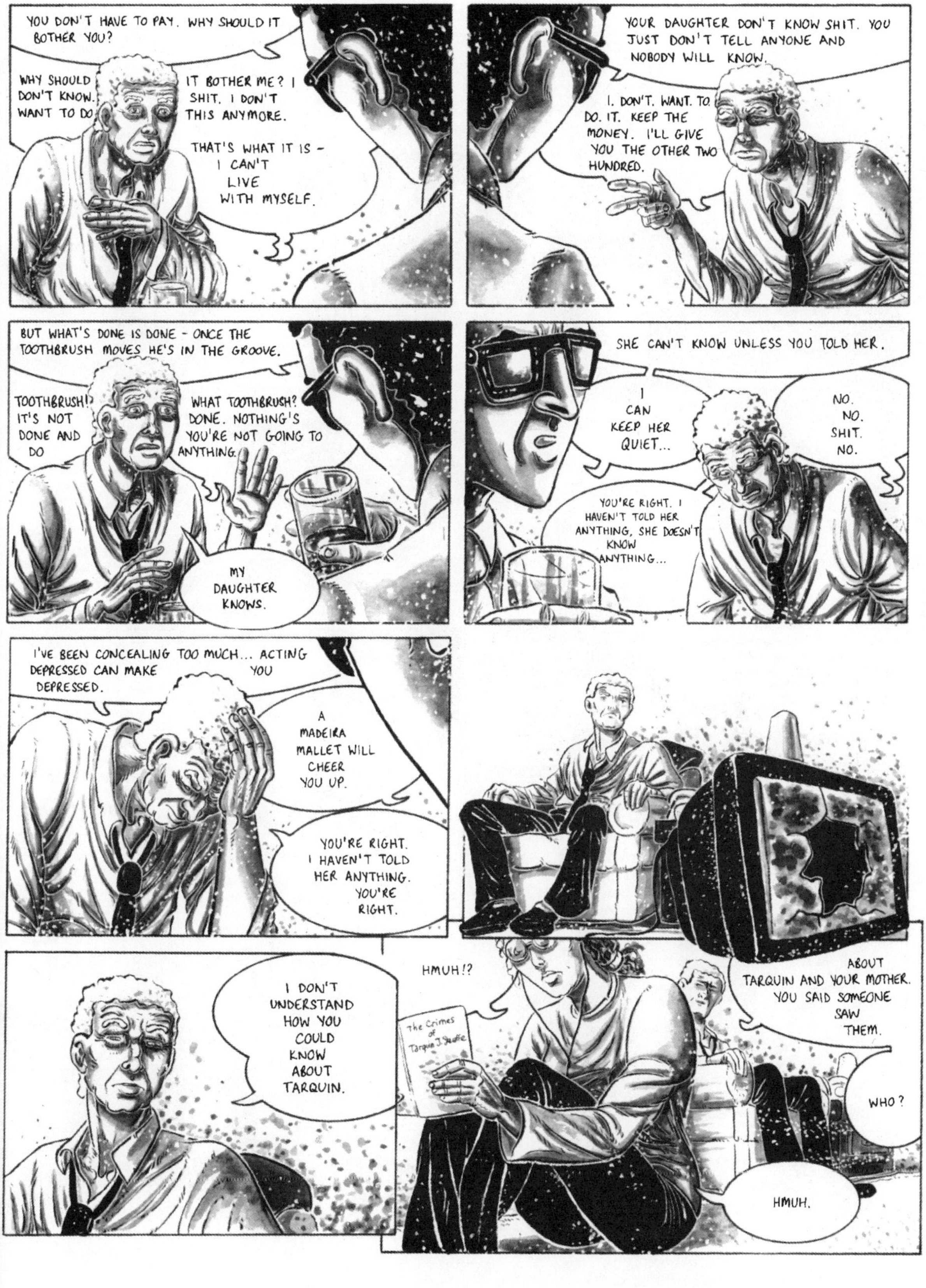
YOU DON'T HAVE TO PAY. WHY SHOULD IT BOTHER YOU?
WHY SHOULD IT BOTHER ME? I DON'T KNOW. SHIT. I DON'T WANT TO DO THIS ANYMORE.
THAT'S WHAT IT IS - I CAN'T LIVE WITH MYSELF.
YOUR DAUGHTER DON'T KNOW SHIT. YOU JUST DON'T TELL ANYONE AND NOBODY WILL KNOW.
I. DON'T. WANT. TO. DO. IT. KEEP THE MONEY. I'LL GIVE YOU THE OTHER TWO HUNDRED.
BUT WHAT'S DONE IS DONE - ONCE THE TOOTHBRUSH MOVES HE'S IN THE GROOVE.
TOOTHBRUSH! WHAT TOOTHBRUSH? IT'S NOT DONE. NOTHING'S DONE AND YOU'RE NOT GOING TO DO ANYTHING.
MY DAUGHTER KNOWS.
SHE CAN'T KNOW UNLESS YOU TOLD HER.
I CAN KEEP HER QUIET...
NO. NO. SHIT. NO.
YOU'RE RIGHT. I HAVEN'T TOLD HER ANYTHING, SHE DOESN'T KNOW ANYTHING...
I'VE BEEN CONCEALING TOO MUCH... ACTING DEPRESSED CAN MAKE YOU DEPRESSED.
A MADEIRA MALLET WILL CHEER YOU UP.
YOU'RE RIGHT. I HAVEN'T TOLD HER ANYTHING. YOU'RE RIGHT.
I DON'T UNDERSTAND HOW YOU COULD KNOW ABOUT TARQUIN.
HMUH!?
ABOUT TARQUIN AND YOUR MOTHER. YOU SAID SOMEONE SAW THEM.
WHO?
HMUH.

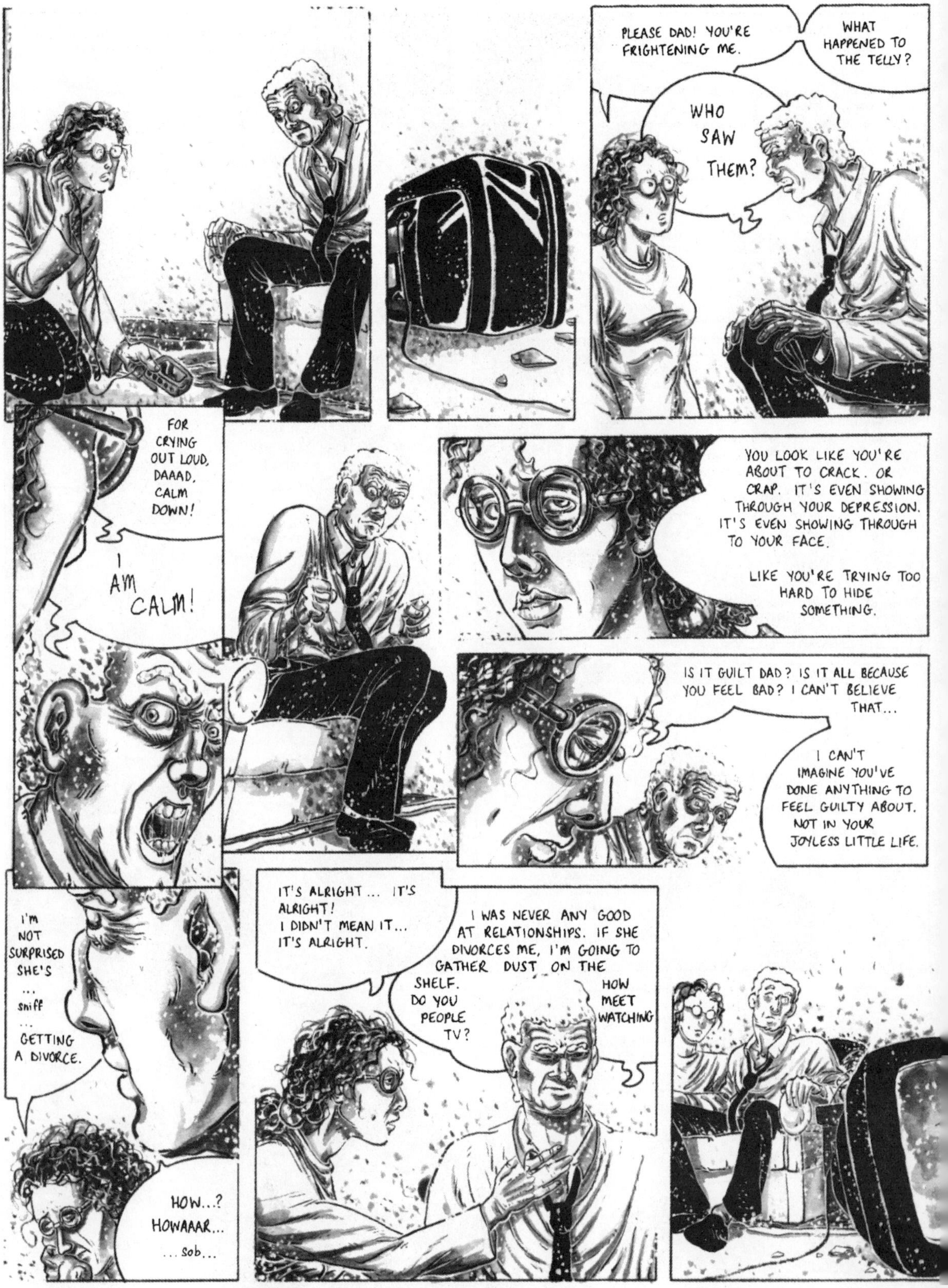
PLEASE DAD! YOU'RE FRIGHTENING ME.
WHAT HAPPENED TO THE TELLY?
WHO SAW THEM?
FOR CRYING OUT LOUD, DAAAD, CALM DOWN!
I AM CALM!
YOU LOOK LIKE YOU'RE ABOUT TO CRACK. OR CRAP. IT'S EVEN SHOWING THROUGH YOUR DEPRESSION. IT'S EVEN SHOWING THROUGH TO YOUR FACE.
LIKE YOU'RE TRYING TOO HARD TO HIDE SOMETHING.
IS IT GUILT DAD? IS IT ALL BECAUSE YOU FEEL BAD? I CAN'T BELIEVE THAT...
I CAN'T IMAGINE YOU'VE DONE ANYTHING TO FEEL GUILTY ABOUT. NOT IN YOUR JOYLESS LITTLE LIFE.
I'M NOT SURPRISED SHE'S ... sniff ... GETTING A DIVORCE.
HOW...? HOWAAAR... ...sob...
IT'S ALRIGHT... IT'S ALRIGHT! I DIDN'T MEAN IT... IT'S ALRIGHT.
I WAS NEVER ANY GOOD AT RELATIONSHIPS. IF SHE DIVORCES ME, I'M GOING TO GATHER DUST ON THE SHELF.
DO YOU PEOPLE TV?
HOW MEET WATCHING

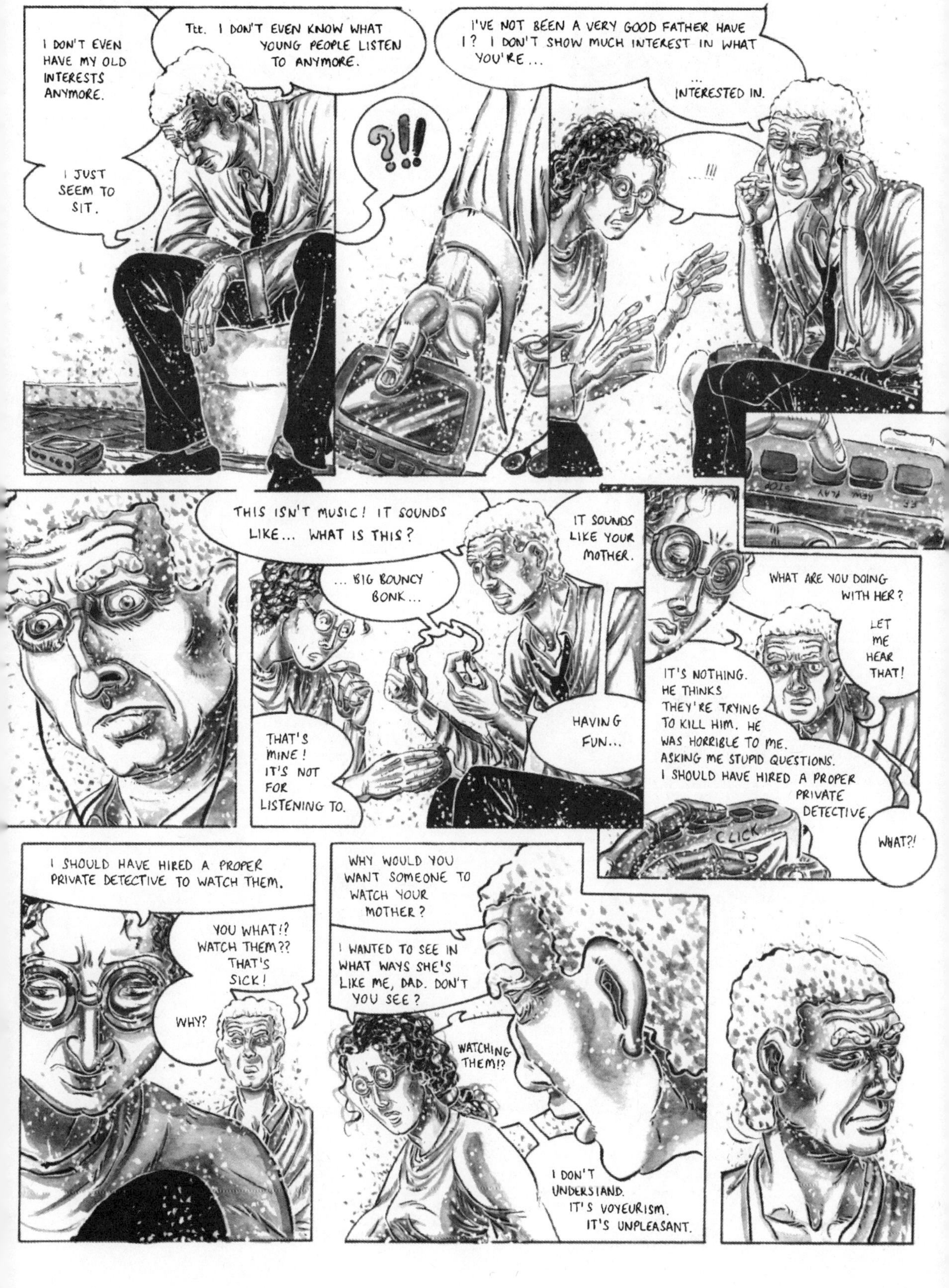
Tt. I DON'T EVEN KNOW WHAT YOUNG PEOPLE LISTEN TO ANYMORE.
I DON'T EVEN HAVE MY OLD INTERESTS ANYMORE.
I JUST SEEM TO SIT.
?!!
I'VE NOT BEEN A VERY GOOD FATHER HAVE I? I DON'T SHOW MUCH INTEREST IN WHAT YOU'RE...
... INTERESTED IN.
...!!!
STOP
PLAY
REW
FF
THIS ISN'T MUSIC! IT SOUNDS LIKE... WHAT IS THIS?
IT SOUNDS LIKE YOUR MOTHER.
... BIG BOUNCY BONK...
HAVING FUN...
THAT'S MINE! IT'S NOT FOR LISTENING TO.
WHAT ARE YOU DOING WITH HER?
LET ME HEAR THAT!
IT'S NOTHING. HE THINKS THEY'RE TRYING TO KILL HIM. HE WAS HORRIBLE TO ME. ASKING ME STUPID QUESTIONS. I SHOULD HAVE HIRED A PROPER PRIVATE DETECTIVE.
CLICK
WHAT?!
I SHOULD HAVE HIRED A PROPER PRIVATE DETECTIVE TO WATCH THEM.
YOU WHAT!? WATCH THEM?? THAT'S SICK!
WHY?
WHY WOULD YOU WANT SOMEONE TO WATCH YOUR MOTHER?
I WANTED TO SEE IN WHAT WAYS SHE'S LIKE ME, DAD. DON'T YOU SEE?
WATCHING THEM!?
I DON'T UNDERSTAND. IT'S VOYEURISM. IT'S UNPLEASANT.

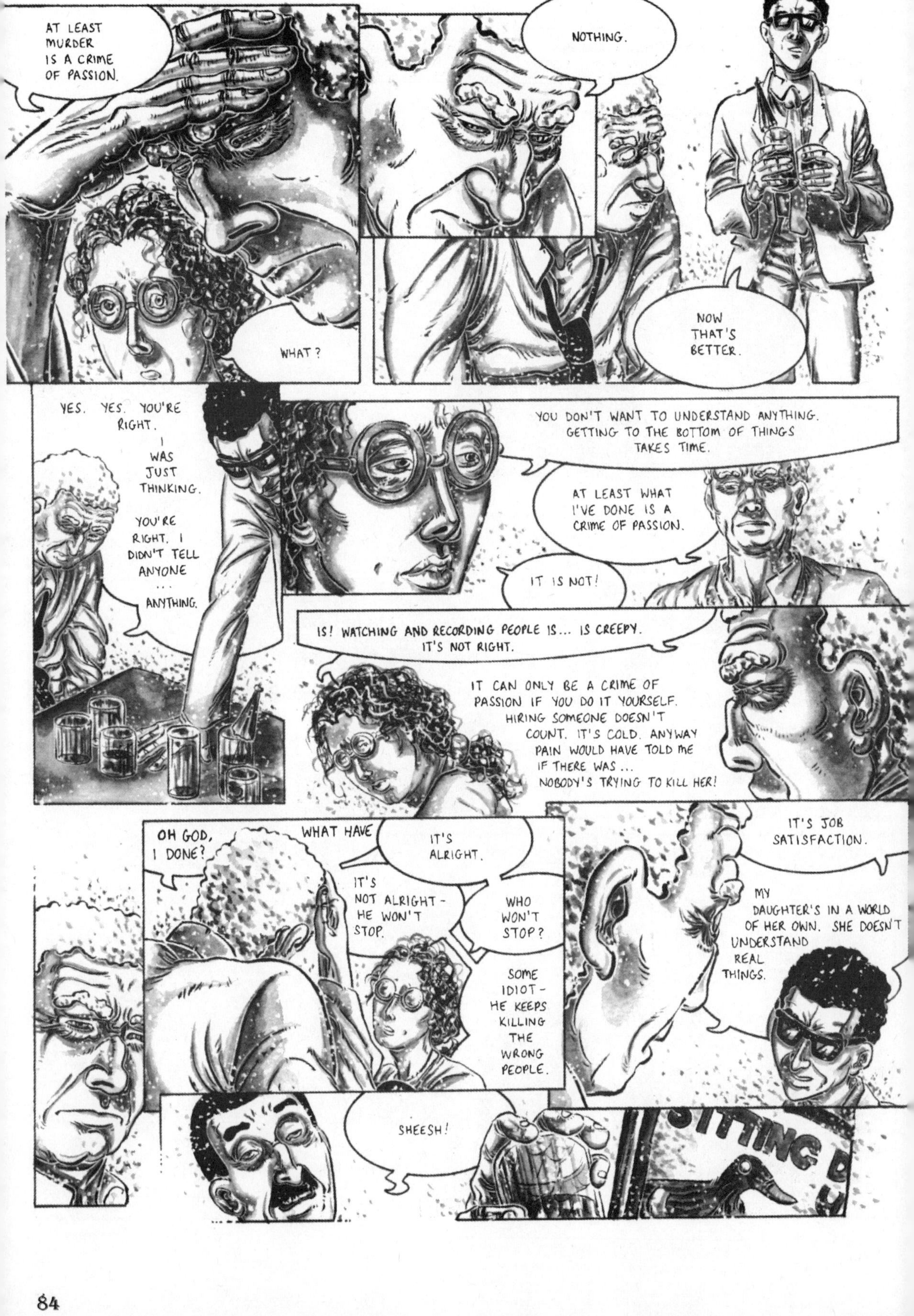
AT LEAST MURDER IS A CRIME OF PASSION.
WHAT?
NOTHING.
NOW THAT'S BETTER.
YES. YES. YOU'RE RIGHT.
I WAS JUST THINKING.
YOU'RE RIGHT. I DIDN'T TELL ANYONE . . . ANYTHING.
YOU DON'T WANT TO UNDERSTAND ANYTHING. GETTING TO THE BOTTOM OF THINGS TAKES TIME.
AT LEAST WHAT I'VE DONE IS A CRIME OF PASSION.
IT IS NOT!
IS! WATCHING AND RECORDING PEOPLE IS... IS CREEPY. IT'S NOT RIGHT.
IT CAN ONLY BE A CRIME OF PASSION IF YOU DO IT YOURSELF. HIRING SOMEONE DOESN'T COUNT. IT'S COLD. ANYWAY PAIN WOULD HAVE TOLD ME IF THERE WAS... NOBODY'S TRYING TO KILL HER!
OH GOD, I DONE?
WHAT HAVE
IT'S ALRIGHT.
IT'S NOT ALRIGHT - HE WON'T STOP.
WHO WON'T STOP?
SOME IDIOT - HE KEEPS KILLING THE WRONG PEOPLE.
IT'S JOB SATISFACTION.
MY DAUGHTER'S IN A WORLD OF HER OWN. SHE DOESN'T UNDERSTAND REAL THINGS.
SHEESH!

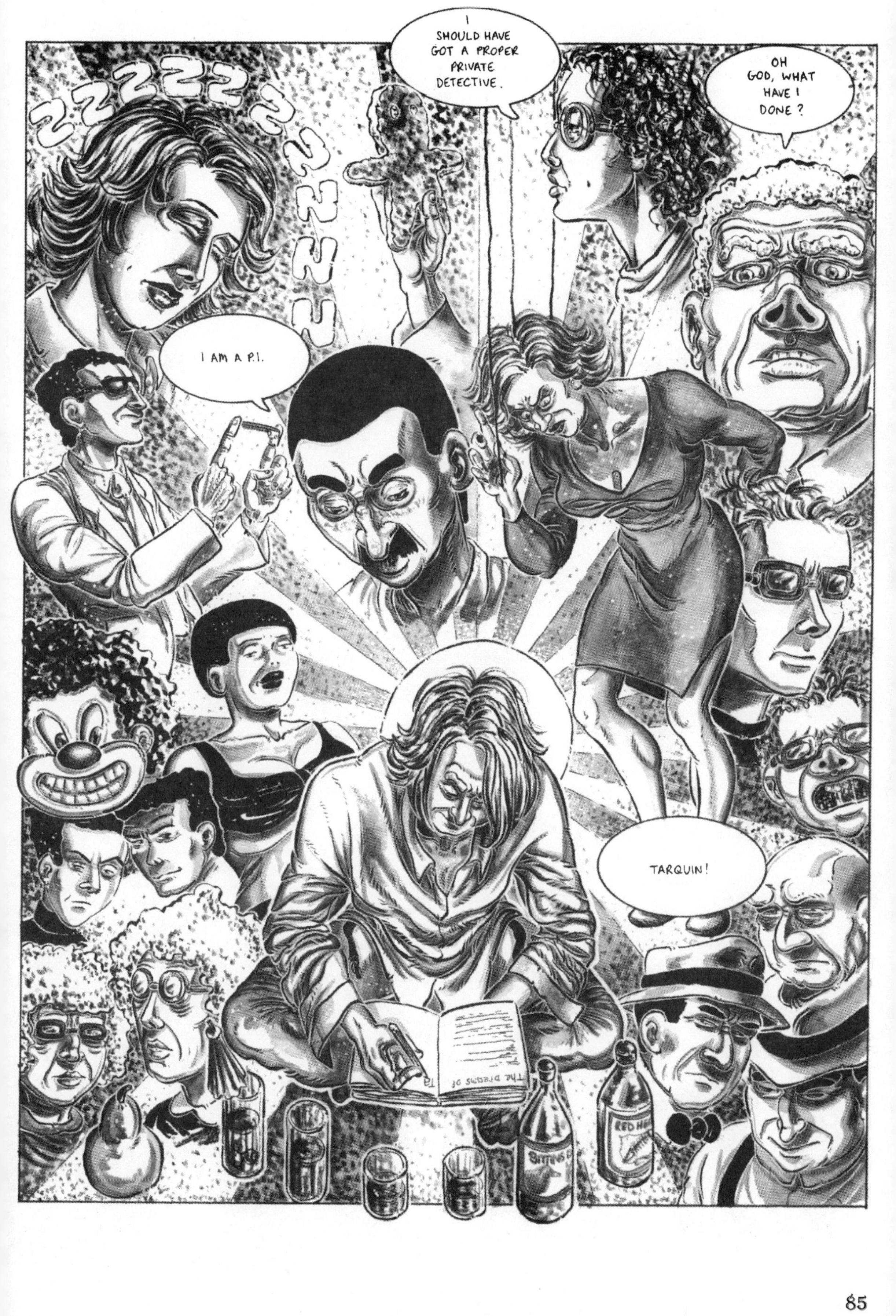
I SHOULD HAVE GOT A PROPER PRIVATE DETECTIVE.
OH GOD, WHAT HAVE I DONE?
I AM A P.I.
TARQUIN!

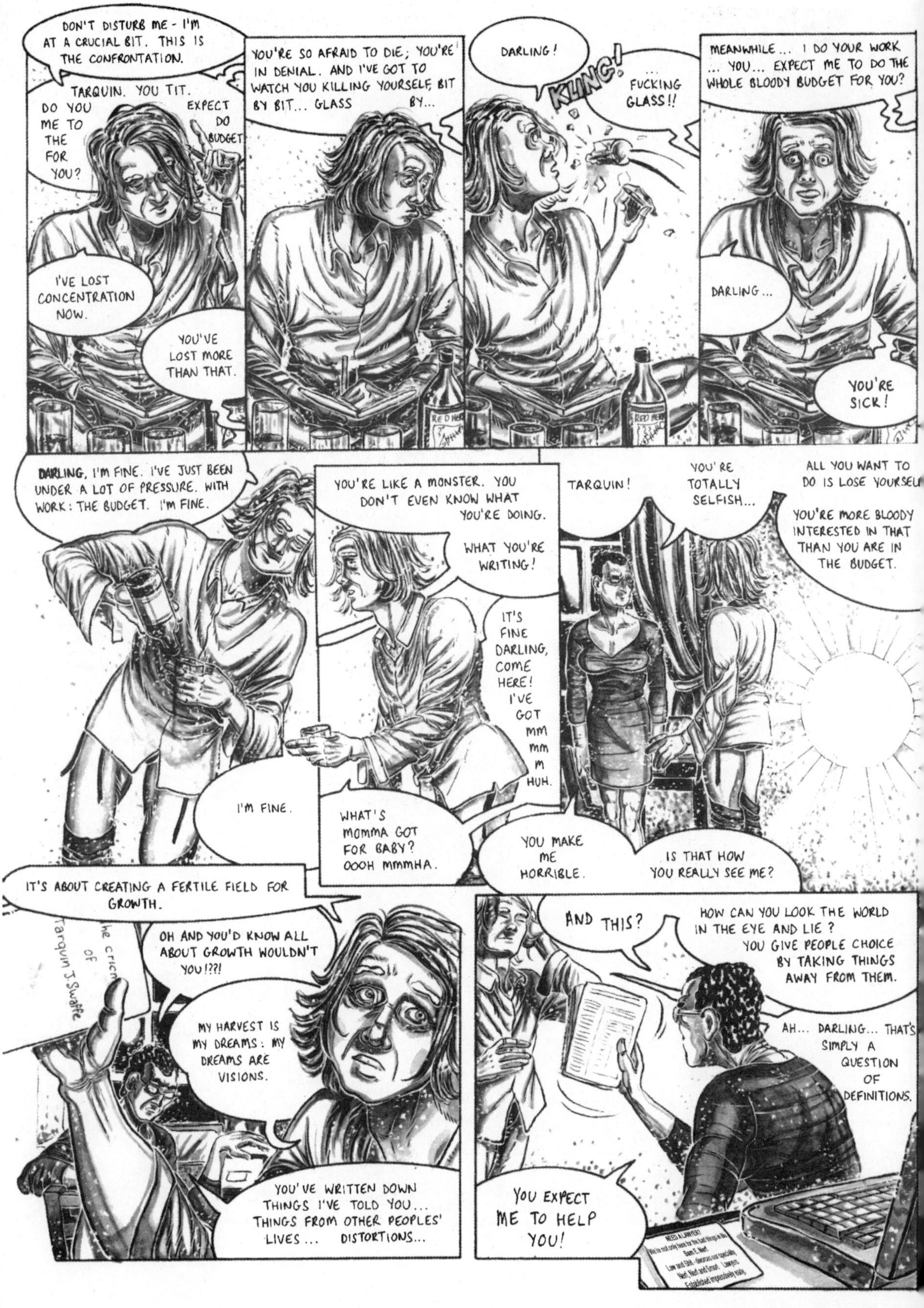
DON'T DISTURB ME - I'M AT A CRUCIAL BIT. THIS IS THE CONFRONTATION.
TARQUIN. YOU TIT.
DO YOU EXPECT ME TO DO THE BUDGET FOR YOU?
I'VE LOST CONCENTRATION NOW.
YOU'VE LOST MORE THAN THAT.
YOU'RE SO AFRAID TO DIE; YOU'RE IN DENIAL. AND I'VE GOT TO WATCH YOU KILLING YOURSELF, BIT BY BIT... GLASS BY...
DARLING!
KLING!
... FUCKING GLASS!!
MEANWHILE... I DO YOUR WORK ... YOU... EXPECT ME TO DO THE WHOLE BLOODY BUDGET FOR YOU?
DARLING...
YOU'RE SICK!
DARLING, I'M FINE. I'VE JUST BEEN UNDER A LOT OF PRESSURE. WITH WORK: THE BUDGET. I'M FINE.
I'M FINE.
YOU'RE LIKE A MONSTER. YOU DON'T EVEN KNOW WHAT YOU'RE DOING.
WHAT YOU'RE WRITING!
IT'S FINE DARLING, COME HERE! I'VE GOT MM MM M HUH.
WHAT'S MOMMA GOT FOR BABY? OOOH MMMHA.
TARQUIN!
YOU'RE TOTALLY SELFISH...
ALL YOU WANT TO DO IS LOSE YOURSELF
YOU'RE MORE BLOODY INTERESTED IN THAT THAN YOU ARE IN THE BUDGET.
YOU MAKE ME HORRIBLE.
IS THAT HOW YOU REALLY SEE ME?
IT'S ABOUT CREATING A FERTILE FIELD FOR GROWTH.
OH AND YOU'D KNOW ALL ABOUT GROWTH WOULDN'T YOU!??!
MY HARVEST IS MY DREAMS: MY DREAMS ARE VISIONS.
YOU'VE WRITTEN DOWN THINGS I'VE TOLD YOU... THINGS FROM OTHER PEOPLES' LIVES... DISTORTIONS...
AND THIS?
HOW CAN YOU LOOK THE WORLD IN THE EYE AND LIE? YOU GIVE PEOPLE CHOICE BY TAKING THINGS AWAY FROM THEM.
AH... DARLING... THAT'S SIMPLY A QUESTION OF DEFINITIONS.
YOU EXPECT ME TO HELP YOU!

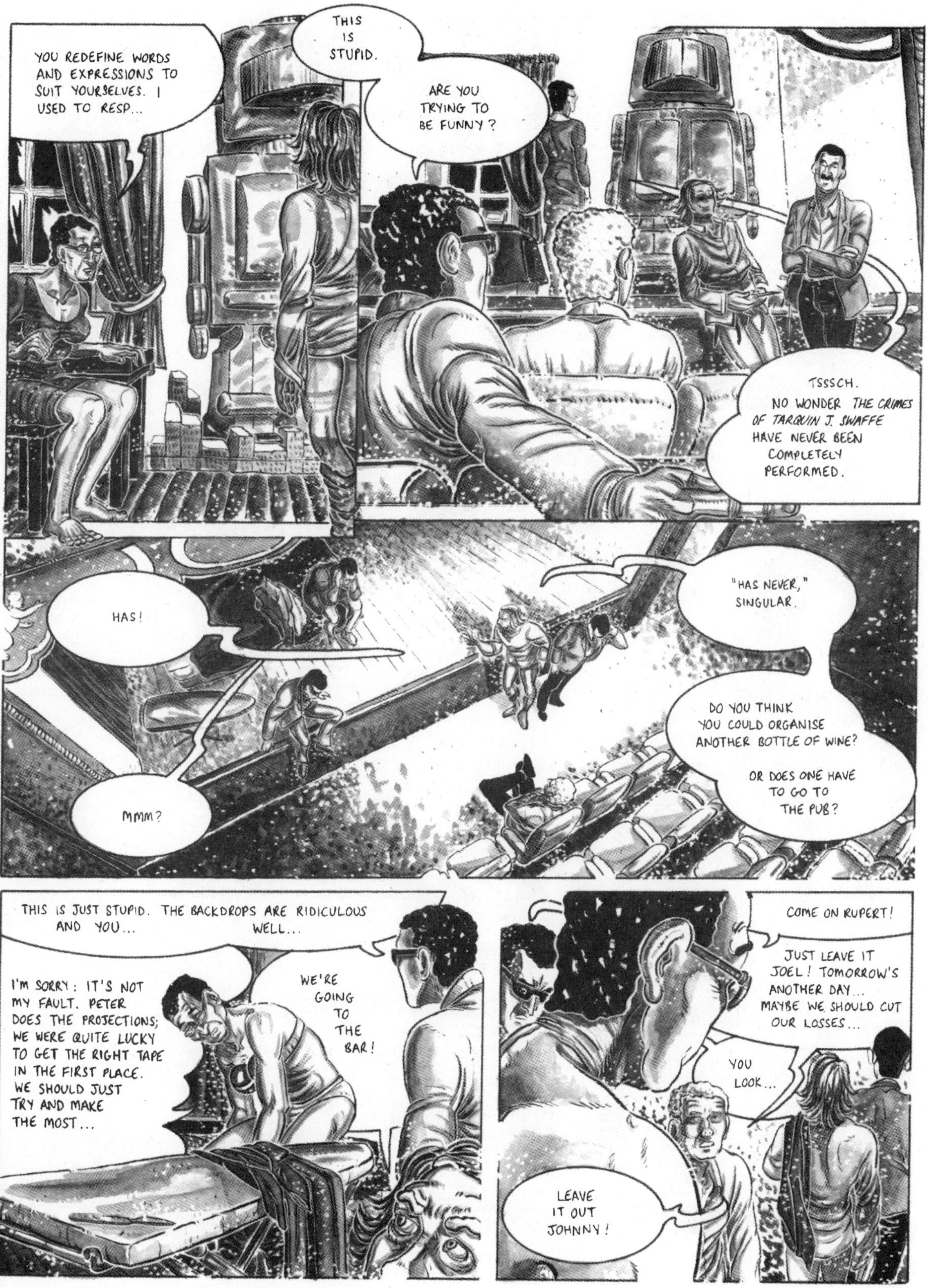

YOU REDEFINE WORDS AND EXPRESSIONS TO SUIT YOURSELVES. I USED TO RESP...
THIS IS STUPID.
ARE YOU TRYING TO BE FUNNY?
TSSSCH. NO WONDER *THE CRIMES OF TARQUIN J. SWAFFE* HAVE NEVER BEEN COMPLETELY PERFORMED.
HAS!
"HAS NEVER," SINGULAR.
MMM?
DO YOU THINK YOU COULD ORGANISE ANOTHER BOTTLE OF WINE?
OR DOES ONE HAVE TO GO TO THE PUB?
THIS IS JUST STUPID. THE BACKDROPS ARE RIDICULOUS AND YOU... WELL...
I'M SORRY: IT'S NOT MY FAULT. PETER DOES THE PROJECTIONS; WE WERE QUITE LUCKY TO GET THE RIGHT TAPE IN THE FIRST PLACE. WE SHOULD JUST TRY AND MAKE THE MOST...
WE'RE GOING TO THE BAR!
COME ON RUPERT!
JUST LEAVE IT JOEL! TOMORROW'S ANOTHER DAY... MAYBE WE SHOULD CUT OUR LOSSES...
YOU LOOK...
LEAVE IT OUT JOHNNY!

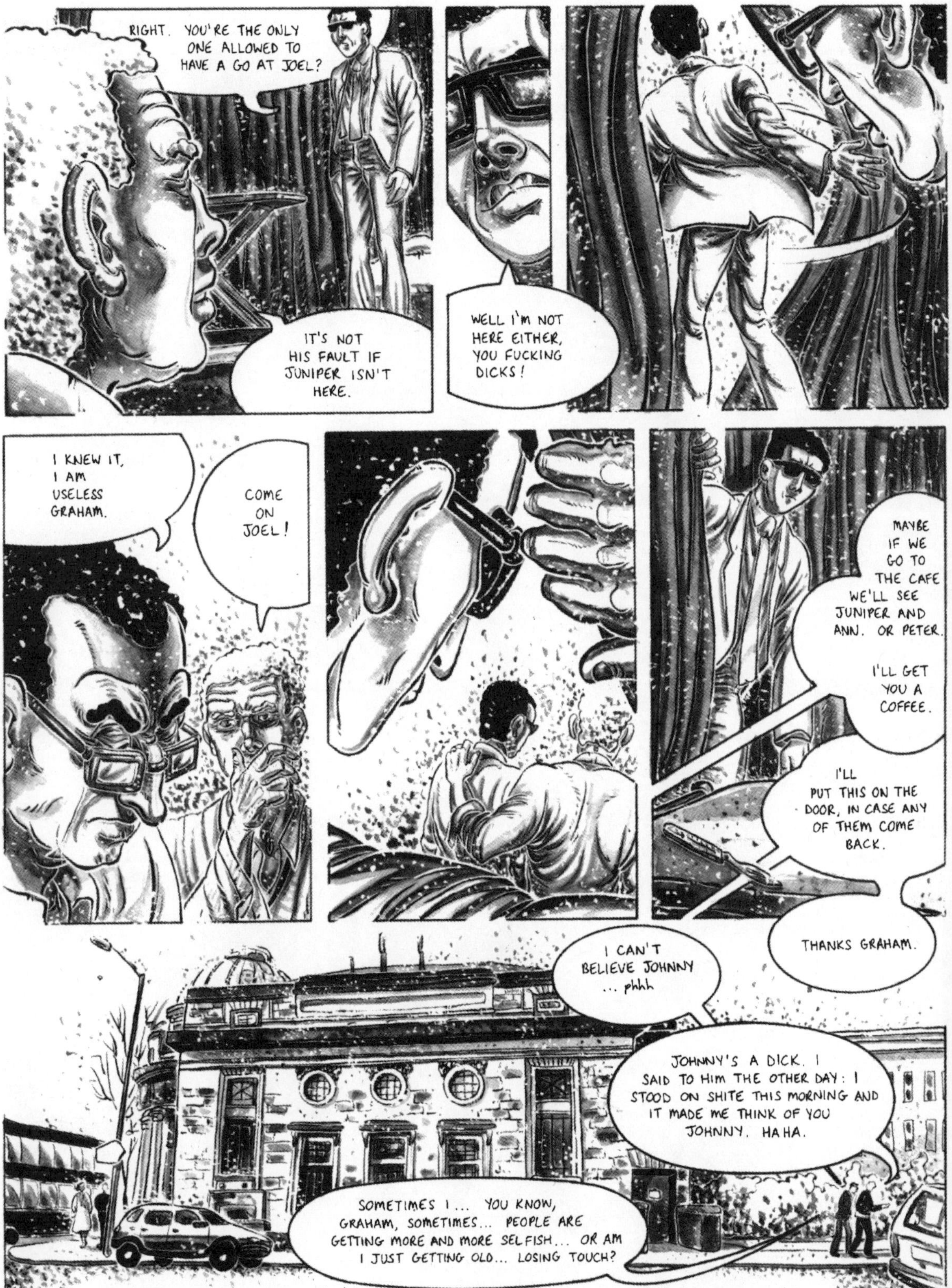
RIGHT. YOU'RE THE ONLY ONE ALLOWED TO HAVE A GO AT JOEL?
IT'S NOT HIS FAULT IF JUNIPER ISN'T HERE.
WELL I'M NOT HERE EITHER, YOU FUCKING DICKS!
I KNEW IT, I AM USELESS GRAHAM.
COME ON JOEL!
MAYBE IF WE GO TO THE CAFE WE'LL SEE JUNIPER AND ANN. OR PETER.
I'LL GET YOU A COFFEE.
I'LL PUT THIS ON THE DOOR, IN CASE ANY OF THEM COME BACK.
THANKS GRAHAM.
I CAN'T BELIEVE JOHNNY ... phhh
JOHNNY'S A DICK. I SAID TO HIM THE OTHER DAY: I STOOD ON SHITE THIS MORNING AND IT MADE ME THINK OF YOU JOHNNY. HA HA.
SOMETIMES I... YOU KNOW, GRAHAM, SOMETIMES... PEOPLE ARE GETTING MORE AND MORE SELFISH... OR AM I JUST GETTING OLD... LOSING TOUCH?

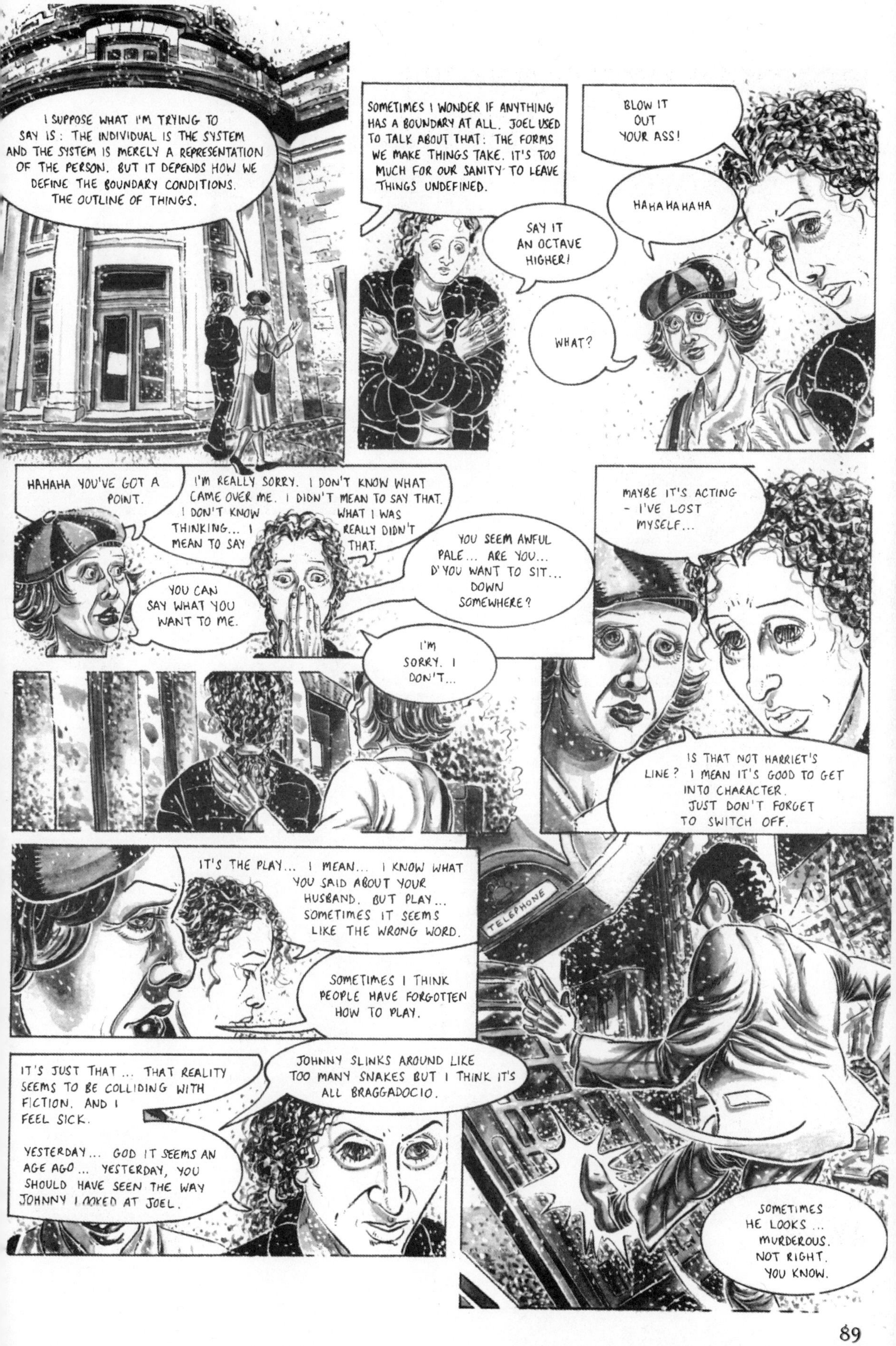
I SUPPOSE WHAT I'M TRYING TO SAY IS: THE INDIVIDUAL IS THE SYSTEM AND THE SYSTEM IS MERELY A REPRESENTATION OF THE PERSON. BUT IT DEPENDS HOW WE DEFINE THE BOUNDARY CONDITIONS. THE OUTLINE OF THINGS.
SOMETIMES I WONDER IF ANYTHING HAS A BOUNDARY AT ALL. JOEL USED TO TALK ABOUT THAT: THE FORMS WE MAKE THINGS TAKE. IT'S TOO MUCH FOR OUR SANITY TO LEAVE THINGS UNDEFINED.
SAY IT AN OCTAVE HIGHER!
BLOW IT OUT YOUR ASS!
HAHAHAHAHA
WHAT?
HAHAHA YOU'VE GOT A POINT.
I'M REALLY SORRY. I DON'T KNOW WHAT CAME OVER ME. I DIDN'T MEAN TO SAY THAT. I DON'T KNOW WHAT I WAS THINKING... I REALLY DIDN'T MEAN TO SAY THAT.
YOU CAN SAY WHAT YOU WANT TO ME.
YOU SEEM AWFUL PALE... ARE YOU... D'YOU WANT TO SIT... DOWN SOMEWHERE?
I'M SORRY. I DON'T...
MAYBE IT'S ACTING - I'VE LOST MYSELF...
IS THAT NOT HARRIET'S LINE? I MEAN IT'S GOOD TO GET INTO CHARACTER. JUST DON'T FORGET TO SWITCH OFF.
IT'S THE PLAY... I MEAN... I KNOW WHAT YOU SAID ABOUT YOUR HUSBAND. BUT PLAY... SOMETIMES IT SEEMS LIKE THE WRONG WORD.
SOMETIMES I THINK PEOPLE HAVE FORGOTTEN HOW TO PLAY.
TELEPHONE
IT'S JUST THAT ... THAT REALITY SEEMS TO BE COLLIDING WITH FICTION. AND I FEEL SICK.
YESTERDAY... GOD IT SEEMS AN AGE AGO... YESTERDAY, YOU SHOULD HAVE SEEN THE WAY JOHNNY LOOKED AT JOEL.
JOHNNY SLINKS AROUND LIKE TOO MANY SNAKES BUT I THINK IT'S ALL BRAGGADOCIO.
SOMETIMES HE LOOKS ... MURDEROUS. NOT RIGHT. YOU KNOW.

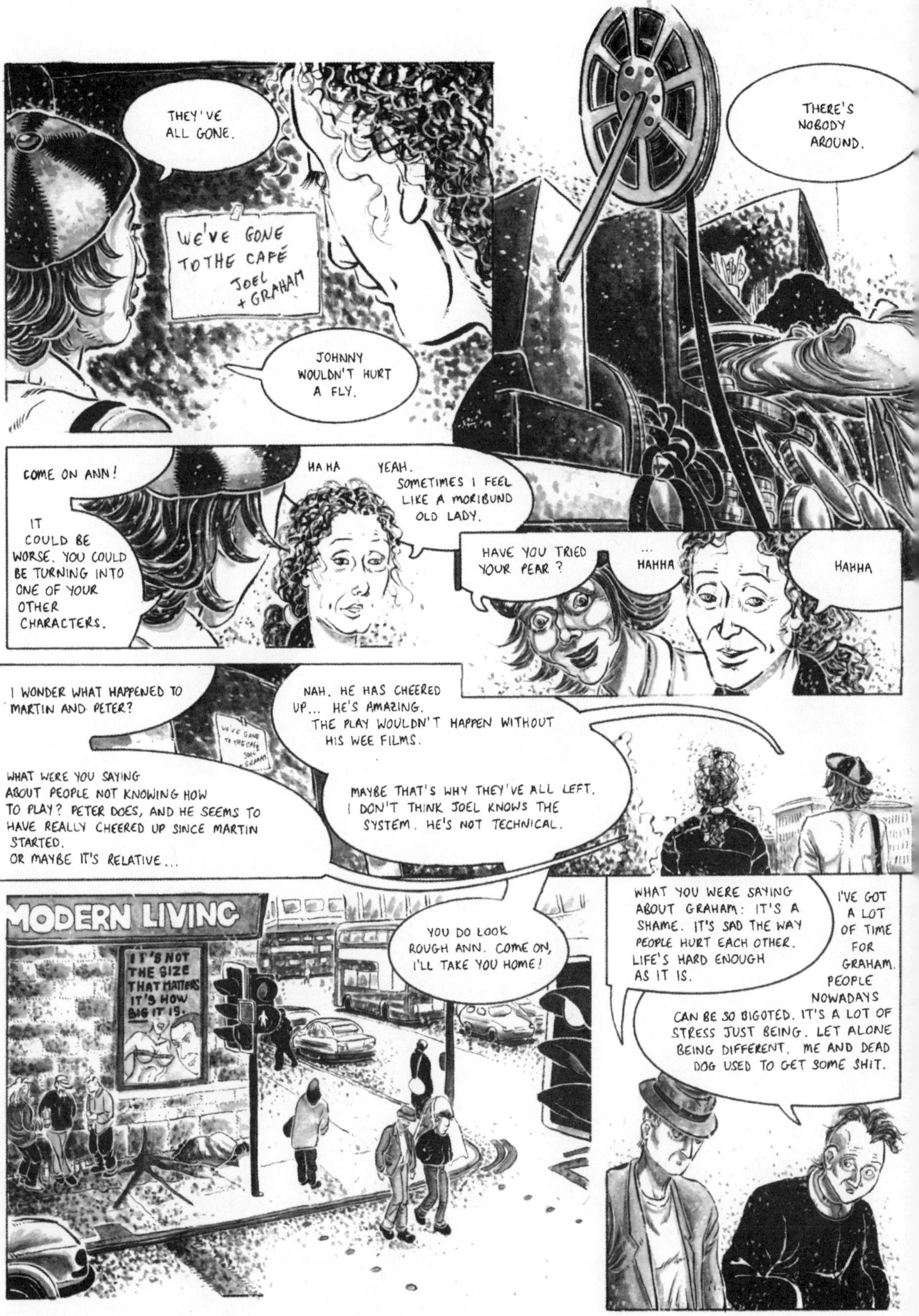

THEY'VE ALL GONE.
WE'VE GONE TO THE CAFÉ JOEL + GRAHAM
JOHNNY WOULDN'T HURT A FLY.
THERE'S NOBODY AROUND.
COME ON ANN!
IT COULD BE WORSE. YOU COULD BE TURNING INTO ONE OF YOUR OTHER CHARACTERS.
HA HA YEAH. SOMETIMES I FEEL LIKE A MORIBUND OLD LADY.
HAVE YOU TRIED YOUR PEAR?
... HAHHA
HAHHA
I WONDER WHAT HAPPENED TO MARTIN AND PETER?
NAH. HE HAS CHEERED UP... HE'S AMAZING. THE PLAY WOULDN'T HAPPEN WITHOUT HIS WEE FILMS.
WHAT WERE YOU SAYING ABOUT PEOPLE NOT KNOWING HOW TO PLAY? PETER DOES, AND HE SEEMS TO HAVE REALLY CHEERED UP SINCE MARTIN STARTED. OR MAYBE IT'S RELATIVE...
MAYBE THAT'S WHY THEY'VE ALL LEFT. I DON'T THINK JOEL KNOWS THE SYSTEM. HE'S NOT TECHNICAL.
MODERN LIVING
IT'S NOT THE SIZE THAT MATTERS IT'S HOW BIG IT IS.
YOU DO LOOK ROUGH ANN. COME ON, I'LL TAKE YOU HOME!
WHAT YOU WERE SAYING ABOUT GRAHAM: IT'S A SHAME. IT'S SAD THE WAY PEOPLE HURT EACH OTHER. LIFE'S HARD ENOUGH AS IT IS.
I'VE GOT A LOT OF TIME FOR GRAHAM. PEOPLE NOWADAYS CAN BE SO BIGOTED. IT'S A LOT OF STRESS JUST BEING. LET ALONE BEING DIFFERENT. ME AND DEAD DOG USED TO GET SOME SHIT.

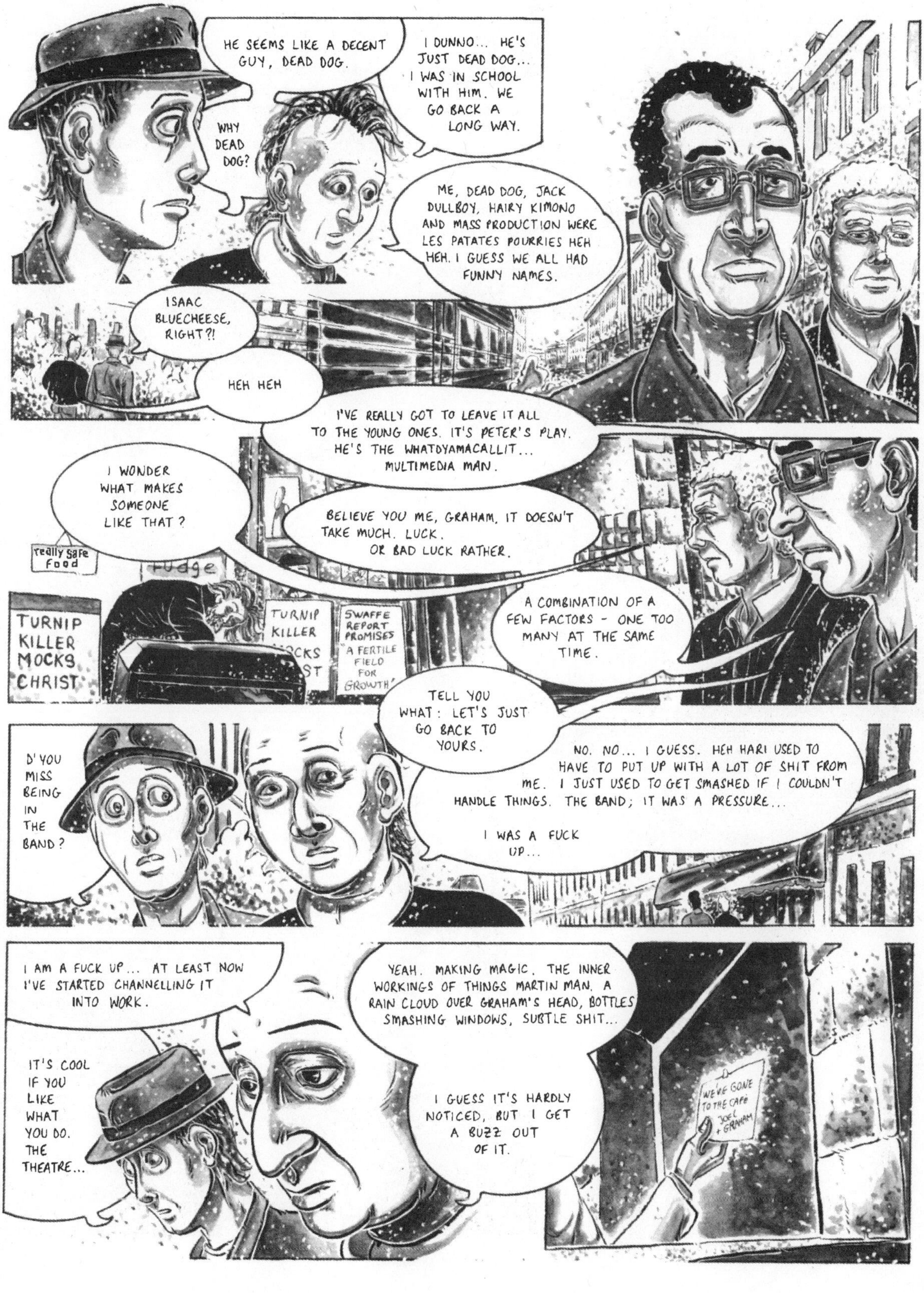
HE SEEMS LIKE A DECENT GUY, DEAD DOG.
WHY DEAD DOG?
I DUNNO... HE'S JUST DEAD DOG... I WAS IN SCHOOL WITH HIM. WE GO BACK A LONG WAY.
ME, DEAD DOG, JACK DULLBOY, HAIRY KIMONO AND MASS PRODUCTION WERE LES PATATES POURRIES HEH HEH. I GUESS WE ALL HAD FUNNY NAMES.
ISAAC BLUECHEESE, RIGHT?!
HEH HEH
I'VE REALLY GOT TO LEAVE IT ALL TO THE YOUNG ONES. IT'S PETER'S PLAY. HE'S THE WHATDYAMACALLIT... MULTIMEDIA MAN.
I WONDER WHAT MAKES SOMEONE LIKE THAT?
BELIEVE YOU ME, GRAHAM, IT DOESN'T TAKE MUCH. LUCK. OR BAD LUCK RATHER.
really safe Food
Fudge
TURNIP KILLER MOCKS CHRIST
SWAFFE REPORT PROMISES "A FERTILE FIELD FOR GROWTH"
A COMBINATION OF A FEW FACTORS - ONE TOO MANY AT THE SAME TIME.
TELL YOU WHAT: LET'S JUST GO BACK TO YOURS.
D'YOU MISS BEING IN THE BAND?
NO. NO... I GUESS. HEH HARI USED TO HAVE TO PUT UP WITH A LOT OF SHIT FROM ME. I JUST USED TO GET SMASHED IF I COULDN'T HANDLE THINGS. THE BAND; IT WAS A PRESSURE...
I WAS A FUCK UP...
I AM A FUCK UP... AT LEAST NOW I'VE STARTED CHANNELLING IT INTO WORK.
IT'S COOL IF YOU LIKE WHAT YOU DO. THE THEATRE...
YEAH. MAKING MAGIC. THE INNER WORKINGS OF THINGS MARTIN MAN. A RAIN CLOUD OVER GRAHAM'S HEAD, BOTTLES SMASHING WINDOWS, SUBTLE SHIT...
I GUESS IT'S HARDLY NOTICED, BUT I GET A BUZZ OUT OF IT.
WE'VE GONE TO THE CAFE JOEL + GRAHAM

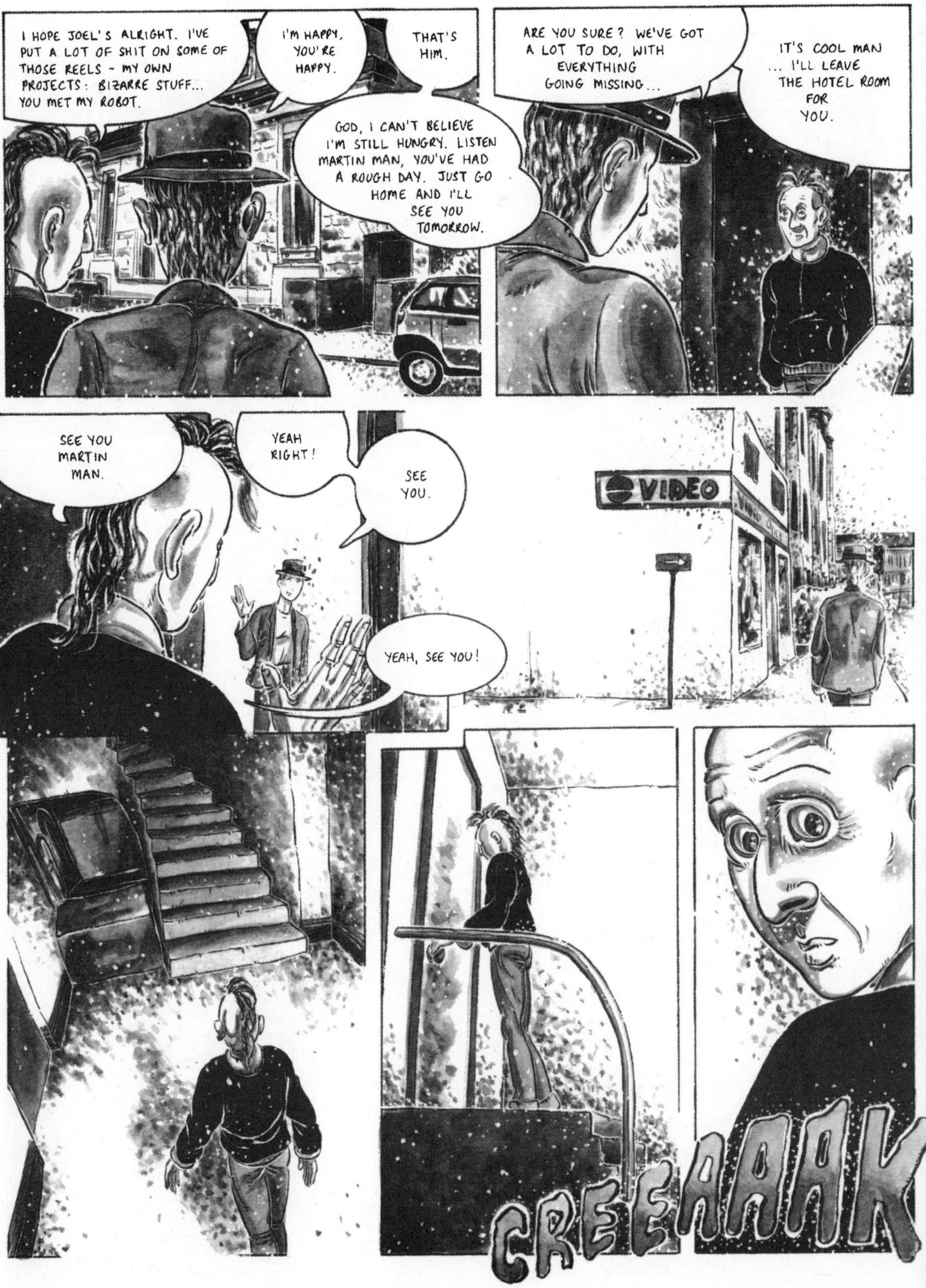
I HOPE JOEL'S ALRIGHT. I'VE PUT A LOT OF SHIT ON SOME OF THOSE REELS - MY OWN PROJECTS: BIZARRE STUFF... YOU MET MY ROBOT.
I'M HAPPY, YOU'RE HAPPY.
THAT'S HIM.
GOD, I CAN'T BELIEVE I'M STILL HUNGRY. LISTEN MARTIN MAN, YOU'VE HAD A ROUGH DAY. JUST GO HOME AND I'LL SEE YOU TOMORROW.
ARE YOU SURE? WE'VE GOT A LOT TO DO, WITH EVERYTHING GOING MISSING...
IT'S COOL MAN ... I'LL LEAVE THE HOTEL ROOM FOR YOU.
SEE YOU MARTIN MAN.
YEAH RIGHT!
SEE YOU.
YEAH, SEE YOU!
VIDEO
CREEAAAK

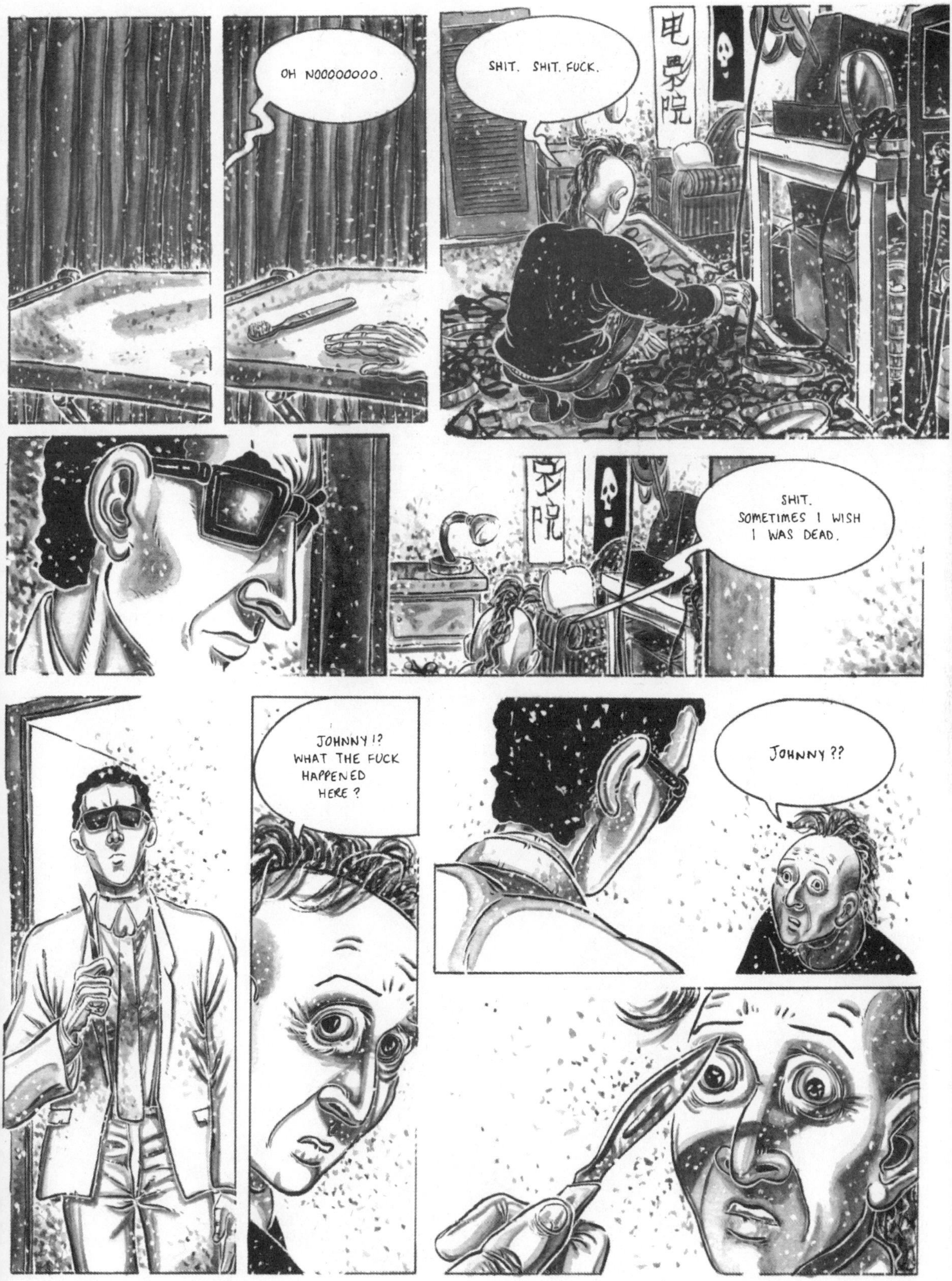
OH NOOOOOOOO.
SHIT. SHIT. FUCK.
电影院
SHIT. SOMETIMES I WISH I WAS DEAD.
JOHNNY!? WHAT THE FUCK HAPPENED HERE?
JOHNNY??

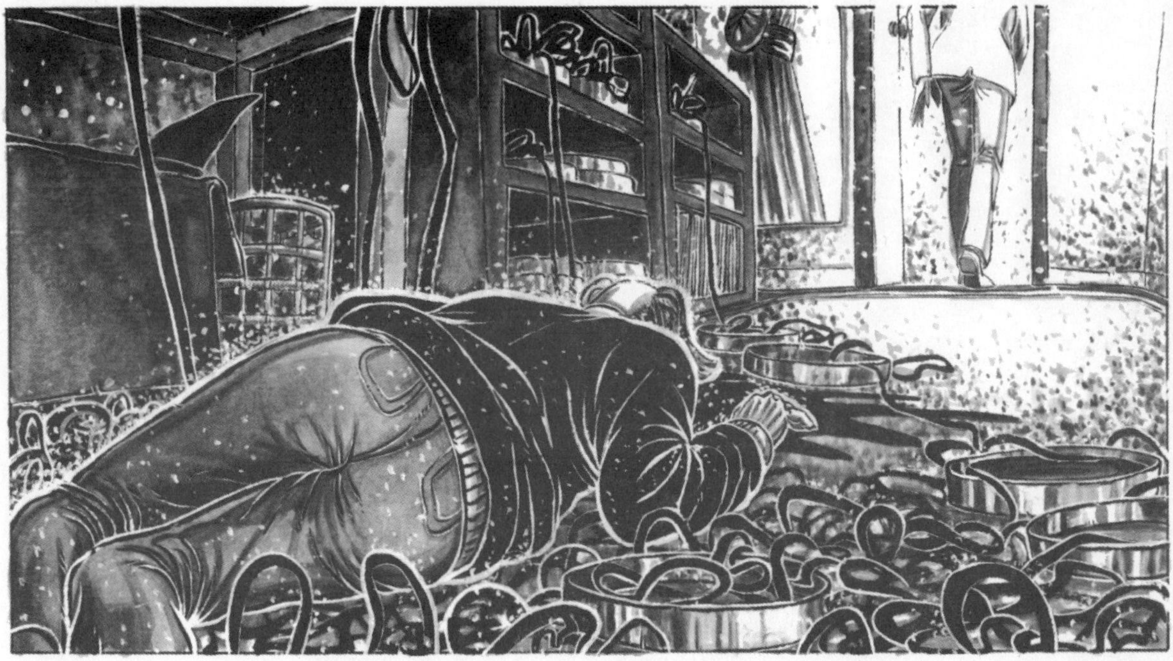

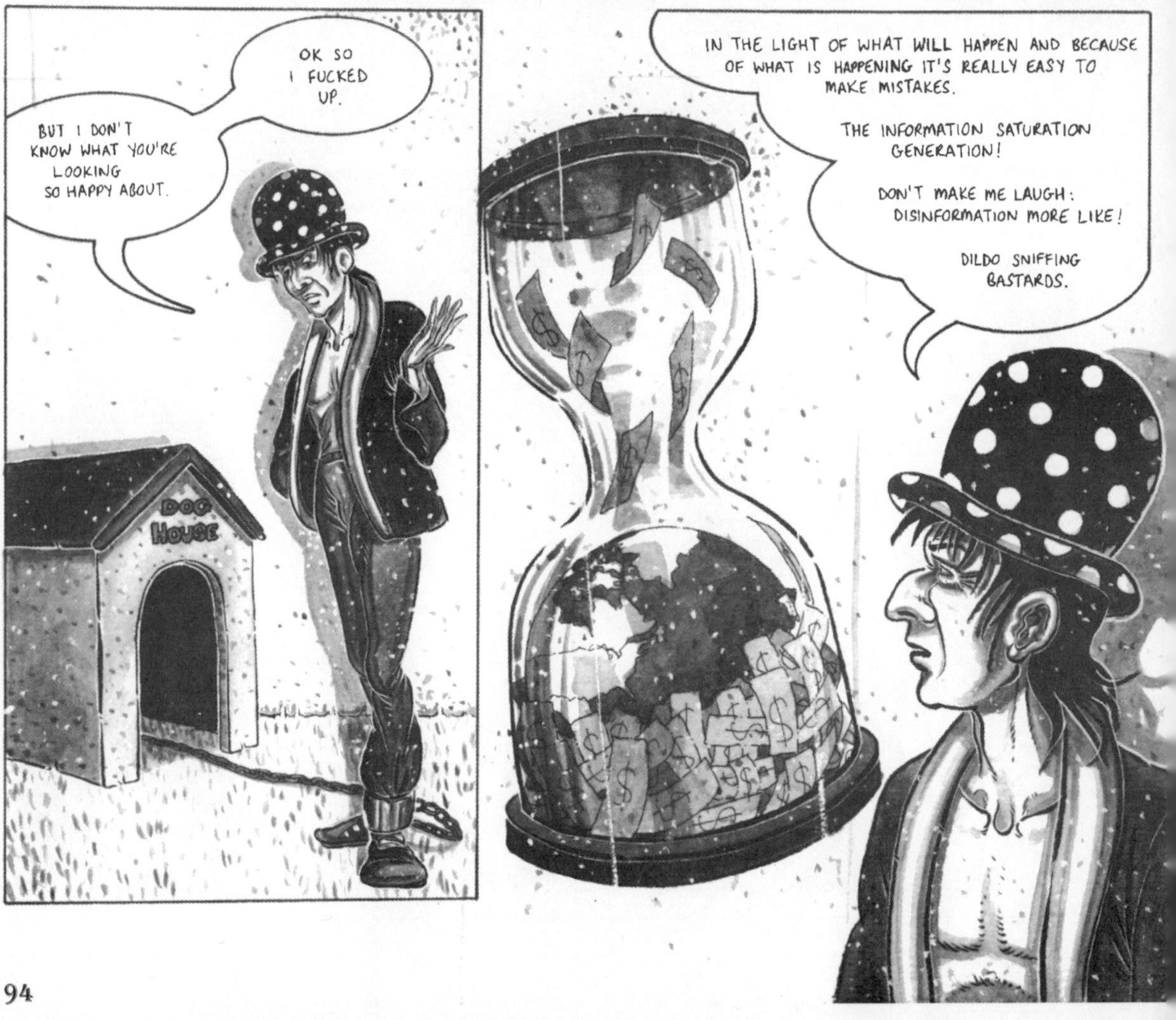
OK SO I FUCKED UP.
BUT I DON'T KNOW WHAT YOU'RE LOOKING SO HAPPY ABOUT.
DOG HOUSE
IN THE LIGHT OF WHAT WILL HAPPEN AND BECAUSE OF WHAT IS HAPPENING IT'S REALLY EASY TO MAKE MISTAKES.
THE INFORMATION SATURATION GENERATION!
DON'T MAKE ME LAUGH: DISINFORMATION MORE LIKE!
DILDO SNIFFING BASTARDS.

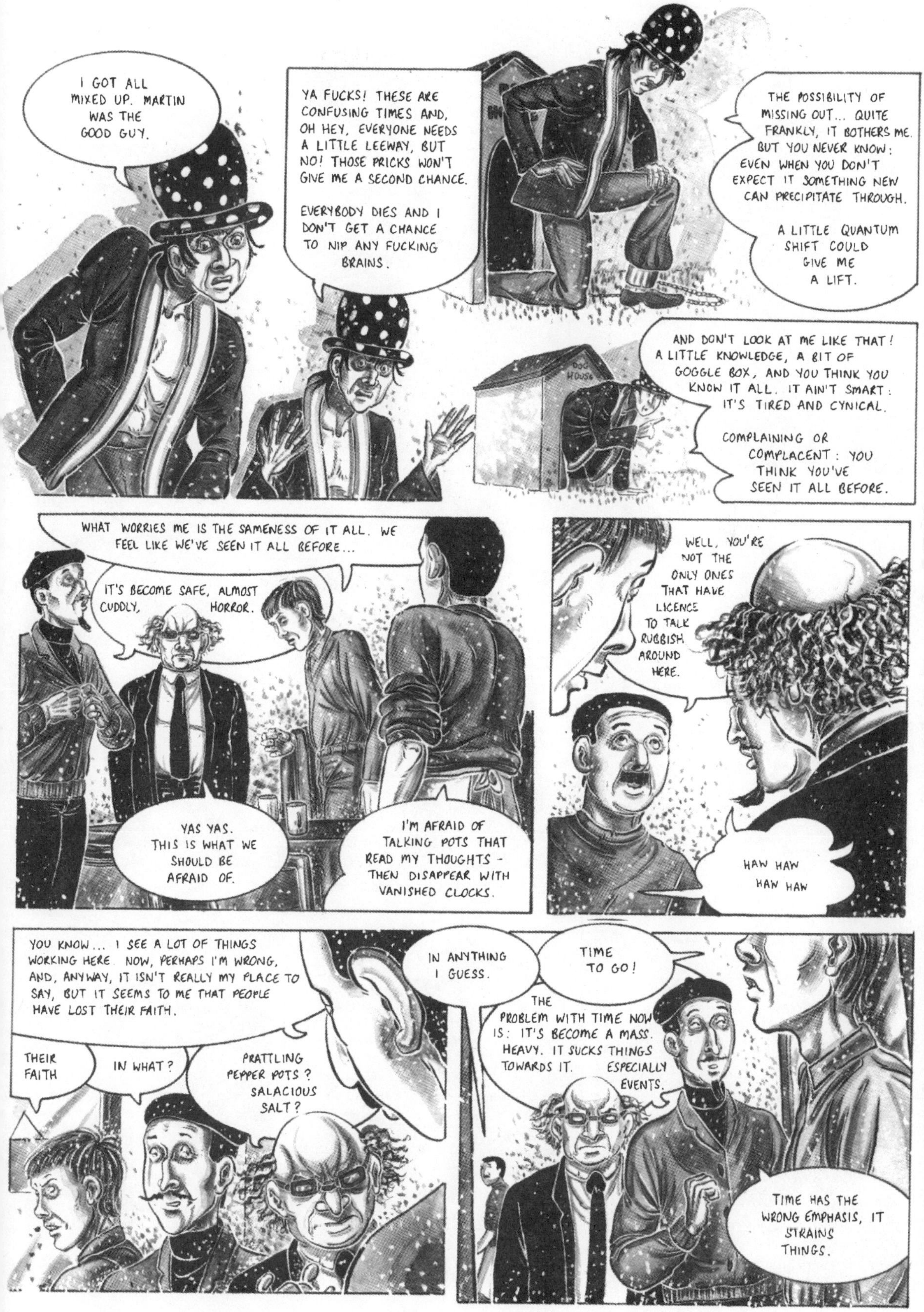
I GOT ALL MIXED UP. MARTIN WAS THE GOOD GUY.
YA FUCKS! THESE ARE CONFUSING TIMES AND, OH HEY, EVERYONE NEEDS A LITTLE LEEWAY, BUT NO! THOSE PRICKS WON'T GIVE ME A SECOND CHANCE.
EVERYBODY DIES AND I DON'T GET A CHANCE TO NIP ANY FUCKING BRAINS.
THE POSSIBILITY OF MISSING OUT... QUITE FRANKLY, IT BOTHERS ME. BUT YOU NEVER KNOW: EVEN WHEN YOU DON'T EXPECT IT SOMETHING NEW CAN PRECIPITATE THROUGH.
A LITTLE QUANTUM SHIFT COULD GIVE ME A LIFT.
DOG HOUSE
AND DON'T LOOK AT ME LIKE THAT! A LITTLE KNOWLEDGE, A BIT OF GOGGLE BOX, AND YOU THINK YOU KNOW IT ALL. IT AIN'T SMART: IT'S TIRED AND CYNICAL.
COMPLAINING OR COMPLACENT: YOU THINK YOU'VE SEEN IT ALL BEFORE.
WHAT WORRIES ME IS THE SAMENESS OF IT ALL. WE FEEL LIKE WE'VE SEEN IT ALL BEFORE...
IT'S BECOME SAFE, ALMOST CUDDLY, HORROR.
YAS YAS. THIS IS WHAT WE SHOULD BE AFRAID OF.
I'M AFRAID OF TALKING POTS THAT READ MY THOUGHTS - THEN DISAPPEAR WITH VANISHED CLOCKS.
WELL, YOU'RE NOT THE ONLY ONES THAT HAVE LICENCE TO TALK RUBBISH AROUND HERE.
HAW HAW HAW HAW
YOU KNOW... I SEE A LOT OF THINGS WORKING HERE. NOW, PERHAPS I'M WRONG, AND, ANYWAY, IT ISN'T REALLY MY PLACE TO SAY, BUT IT SEEMS TO ME THAT PEOPLE HAVE LOST THEIR FAITH.
THEIR FAITH
IN WHAT?
PRATTLING PEPPER POTS? SALACIOUS SALT?
IN ANYTHING I GUESS.
TIME TO GO!
THE PROBLEM WITH TIME NOW IS: IT'S BECOME A MASS. HEAVY. IT SUCKS THINGS TOWARDS IT. ESPECIALLY EVENTS.
TIME HAS THE WRONG EMPHASIS, IT STRAINS THINGS.

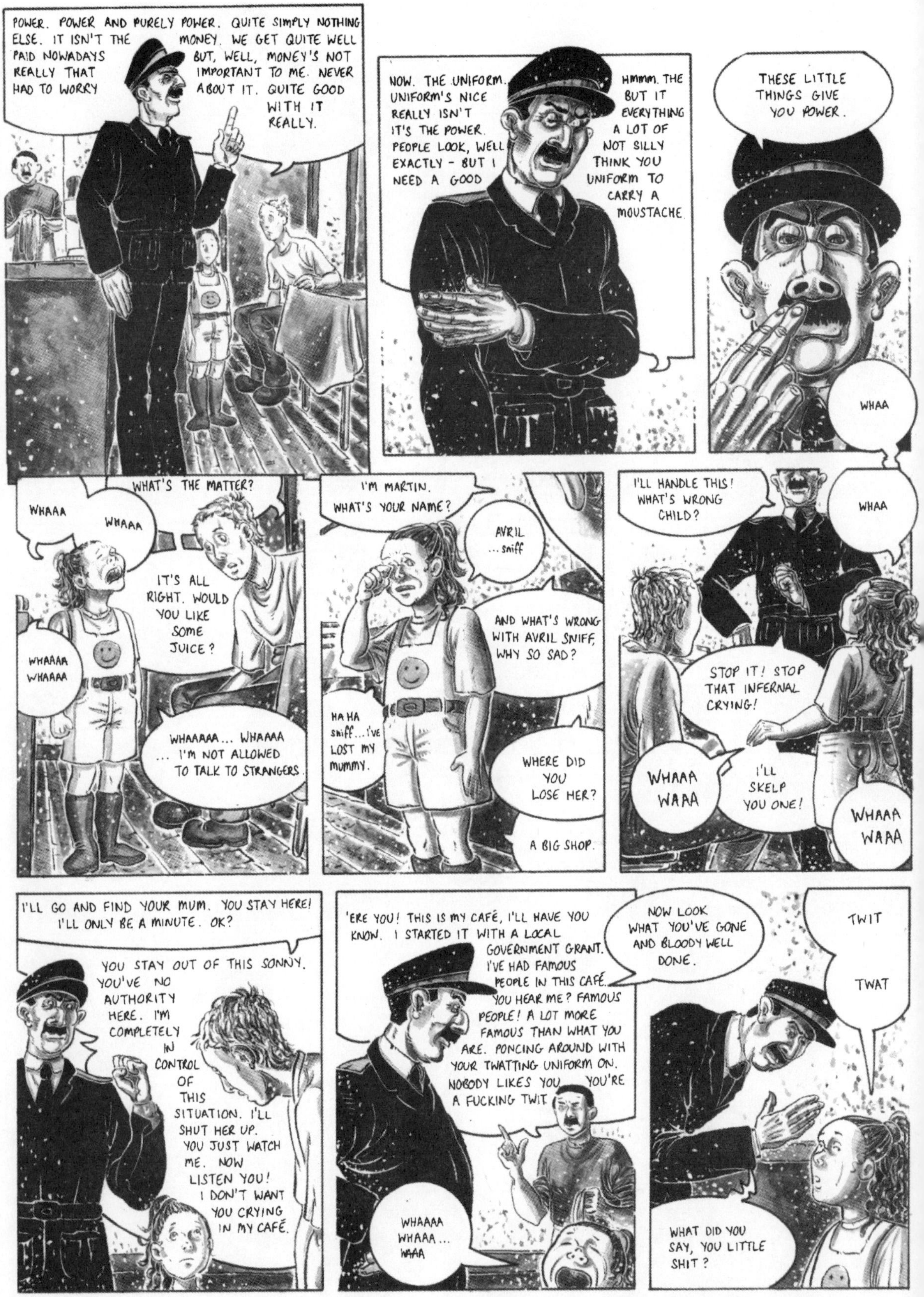
POWER. POWER AND PURELY POWER. QUITE SIMPLY NOTHING ELSE. IT ISN'T THE MONEY. WE GET QUITE WELL PAID NOWADAYS BUT, WELL, MONEY'S NOT REALLY THAT IMPORTANT TO ME. NEVER HAD TO WORRY ABOUT IT. QUITE GOOD WITH IT REALLY.
NOW. THE UNIFORM. HMMM. THE UNIFORM'S NICE BUT IT REALLY ISN'T EVERYTHING IT'S THE POWER. A LOT OF PEOPLE LOOK, WELL NOT SILLY EXACTLY - BUT I THINK YOU NEED A GOOD UNIFORM TO CARRY A MOUSTACHE.
THESE LITTLE THINGS GIVE YOU POWER.
WHAA
WHAT'S THE MATTER?
WHAAA
WHAAA
IT'S ALL RIGHT. WOULD YOU LIKE SOME JUICE?
WHAAAA WHAAAA
WHAAAAA... WHAAAA ... I'M NOT ALLOWED TO TALK TO STRANGERS.
I'M MARTIN. WHAT'S YOUR NAME?
AVRIL ...sniff
AND WHAT'S WRONG WITH AVRIL SNIFF, WHY SO SAD?
HA HA sniff... I've LOST MY MUMMY.
WHERE DID YOU LOSE HER?
A BIG SHOP.
I'LL HANDLE THIS! WHAT'S WRONG CHILD?
WHAA
STOP IT! STOP THAT INFERNAL CRYING!
WHAAA WAAA
I'LL SKELP YOU ONE!
WHAAA WAAA
I'LL GO AND FIND YOUR MUM. YOU STAY HERE! I'LL ONLY BE A MINUTE. OK?
YOU STAY OUT OF THIS SONNY. YOU'VE NO AUTHORITY HERE. I'M COMPLETELY IN CONTROL OF THIS SITUATION. I'LL SHUT HER UP. YOU JUST WATCH ME. NOW LISTEN YOU! I DON'T WANT YOU CRYING IN MY CAFÉ.
'ERE YOU! THIS IS MY CAFÉ, I'LL HAVE YOU KNOW. I STARTED IT WITH A LOCAL GOVERNMENT GRANT. I'VE HAD FAMOUS PEOPLE IN THIS CAFÉ. YOU HEAR ME? FAMOUS PEOPLE! A LOT MORE FAMOUS THAN WHAT YOU ARE. PONCING AROUND WITH YOUR TWATTING UNIFORM ON. NOBODY LIKES YOU. YOU'RE A FUCKING TWIT.
WHAAAA WHAAA... WAAA
NOW LOOK WHAT YOU'VE GONE AND BLOODY WELL DONE.
TWIT
TWAT
WHAT DID YOU SAY, YOU LITTLE SHIT?

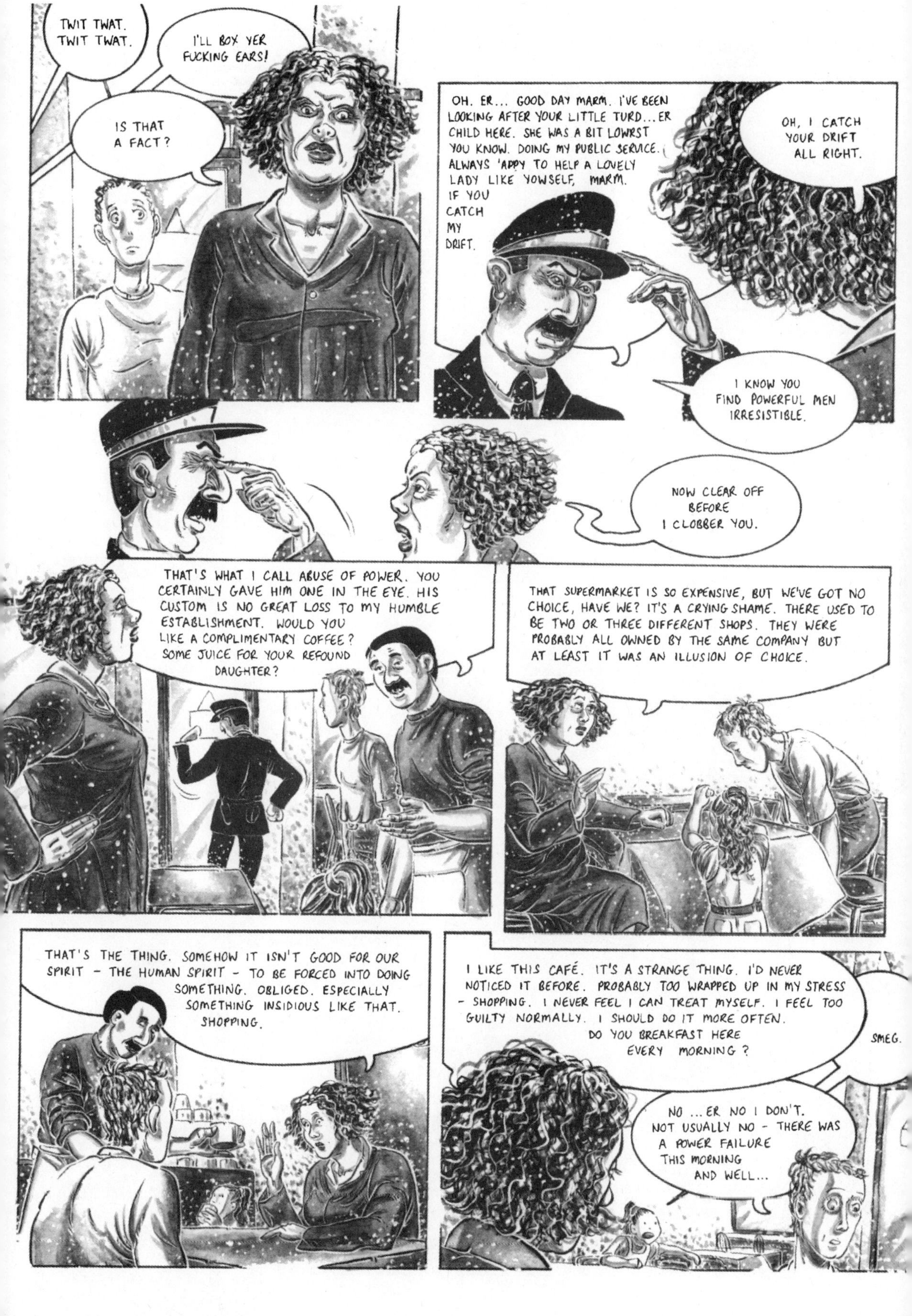
TWIT TWAT. TWIT TWAT.
I'LL BOX YER FUCKING EARS!
IS THAT A FACT?
OH. ER... GOOD DAY MARM. I'VE BEEN LOOKING AFTER YOUR LITTLE TURD... ER CHILD HERE. SHE WAS A BIT LOWRST YOU KNOW. DOING MY PUBLIC SERVICE. ALWAYS 'APPY TO HELP A LOVELY LADY LIKE YOWSELF, MARM. IF YOU CATCH MY DRIFT.
OH, I CATCH YOUR DRIFT ALL RIGHT.
I KNOW YOU FIND POWERFUL MEN IRRESISTIBLE.
NOW CLEAR OFF BEFORE I CLOBBER YOU.
THAT'S WHAT I CALL ABUSE OF POWER. YOU CERTAINLY GAVE HIM ONE IN THE EYE. HIS CUSTOM IS NO GREAT LOSS TO MY HUMBLE ESTABLISHMENT. WOULD YOU LIKE A COMPLIMENTARY COFFEE? SOME JUICE FOR YOUR REFOUND DAUGHTER?
THAT SUPERMARKET IS SO EXPENSIVE, BUT WE'VE GOT NO CHOICE, HAVE WE? IT'S A CRYING SHAME. THERE USED TO BE TWO OR THREE DIFFERENT SHOPS. THEY WERE PROBABLY ALL OWNED BY THE SAME COMPANY BUT AT LEAST IT WAS AN ILLUSION OF CHOICE.
THAT'S THE THING. SOMEHOW IT ISN'T GOOD FOR OUR SPIRIT - THE HUMAN SPIRIT - TO BE FORCED INTO DOING SOMETHING. OBLIGED. ESPECIALLY SOMETHING INSIDIOUS LIKE THAT. SHOPPING.
I LIKE THIS CAFÉ. IT'S A STRANGE THING. I'D NEVER NOTICED IT BEFORE. PROBABLY TOO WRAPPED UP IN MY STRESS - SHOPPING. I NEVER FEEL I CAN TREAT MYSELF. I FEEL TOO GUILTY NORMALLY. I SHOULD DO IT MORE OFTEN. DO YOU BREAKFAST HERE EVERY MORNING?
SMEG.
NO ... ER NO I DON'T. NOT USUALLY NO - THERE WAS A POWER FAILURE THIS MORNING AND WELL...

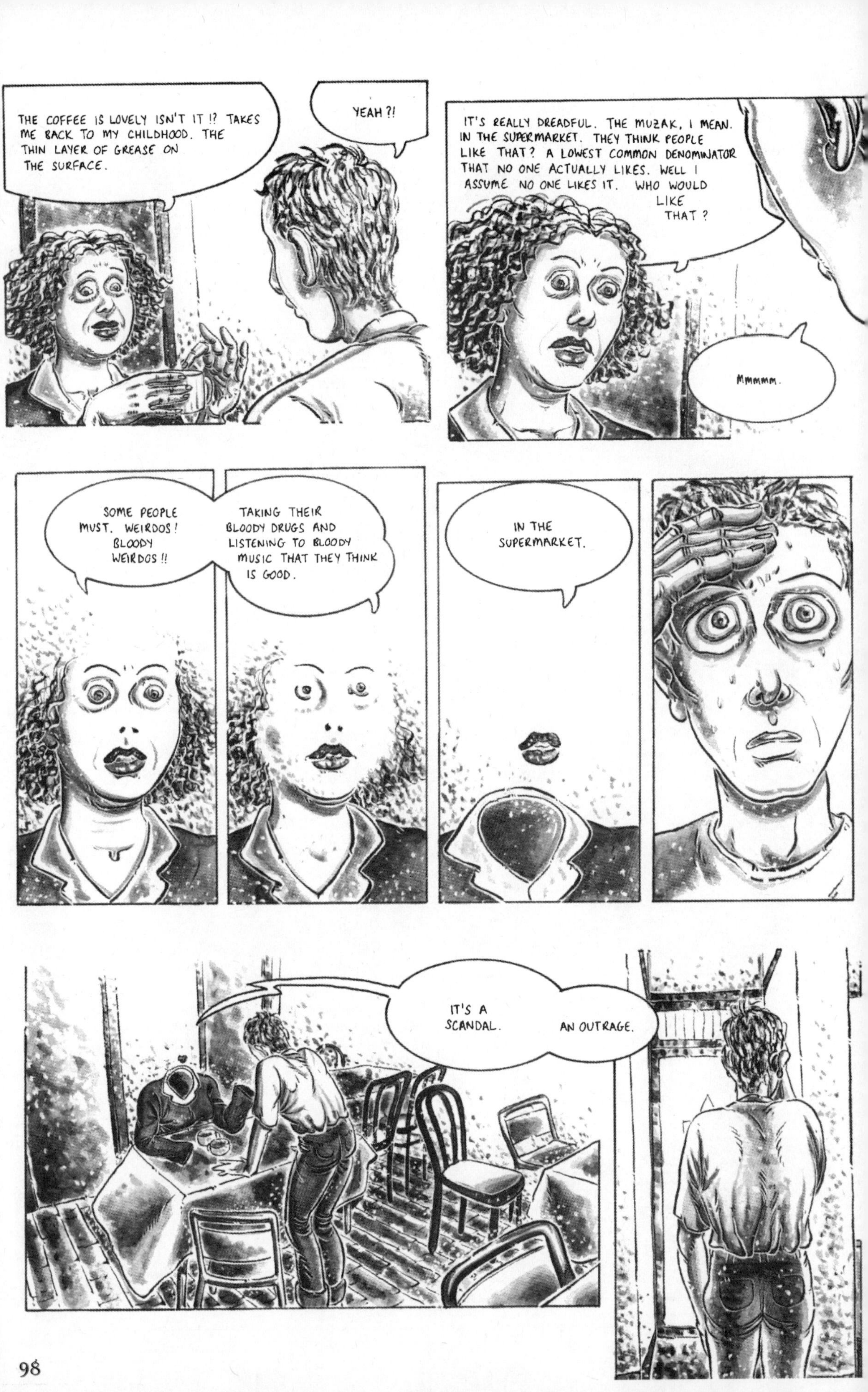
THE COFFEE IS LOVELY ISN'T IT !? TAKES ME BACK TO MY CHILDHOOD. THE THIN LAYER OF GREASE ON THE SURFACE.
YEAH ?!
IT'S REALLY DREADFUL. THE MUZAK, I MEAN. IN THE SUPERMARKET. THEY THINK PEOPLE LIKE THAT? A LOWEST COMMON DENOMINATOR THAT NO ONE ACTUALLY LIKES. WELL I ASSUME NO ONE LIKES IT. WHO WOULD LIKE THAT?
MMMMM.
SOME PEOPLE MUST. WEIRDOS! BLOODY WEIRDOS !!
TAKING THEIR BLOODY DRUGS AND LISTENING TO BLOODY MUSIC THAT THEY THINK IS GOOD.
IN THE SUPERMARKET.
IT'S A SCANDAL.
AN OUTRAGE.

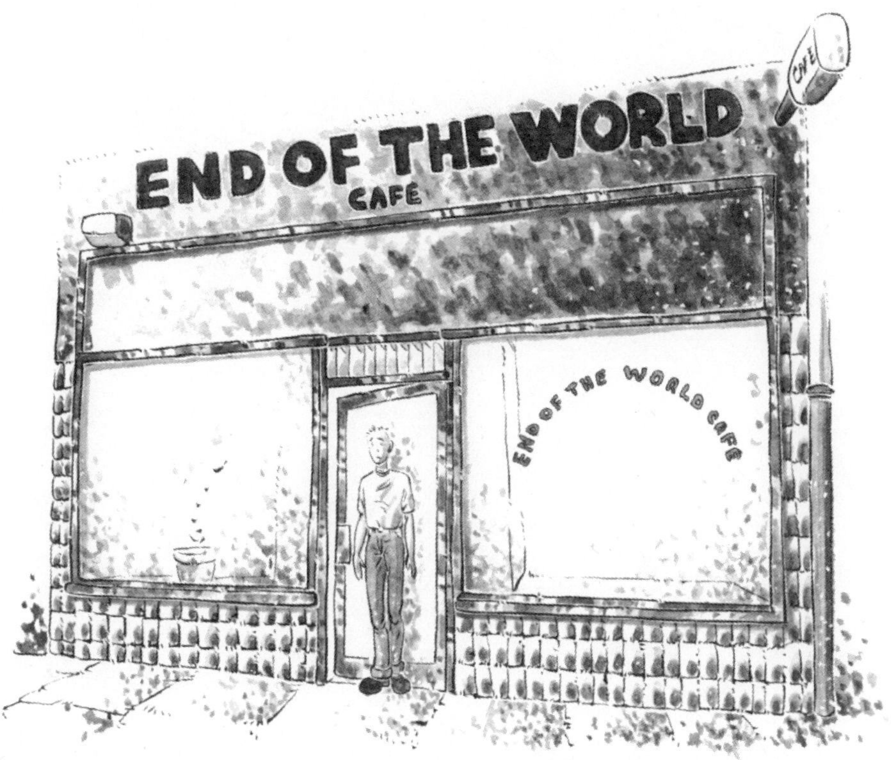
END OF THE WORLD
CAFÉ
CAFÉ
END OF THE WORLD CAFÉ

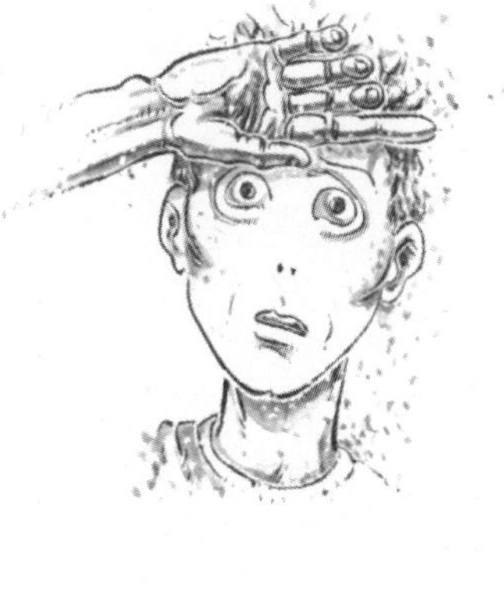

The End

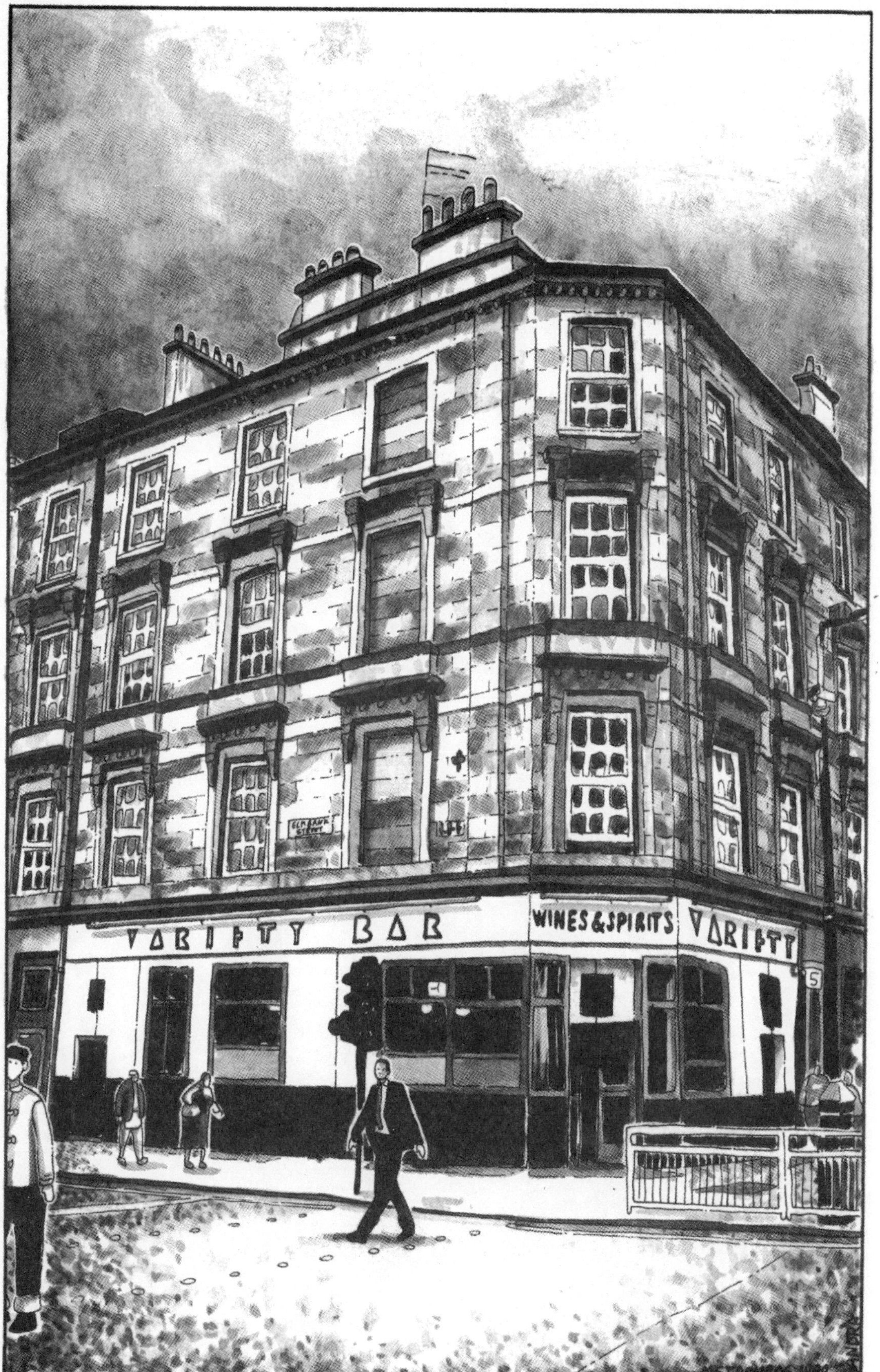
VARIETY BAR
WINES & SPIRITS
VARIETY

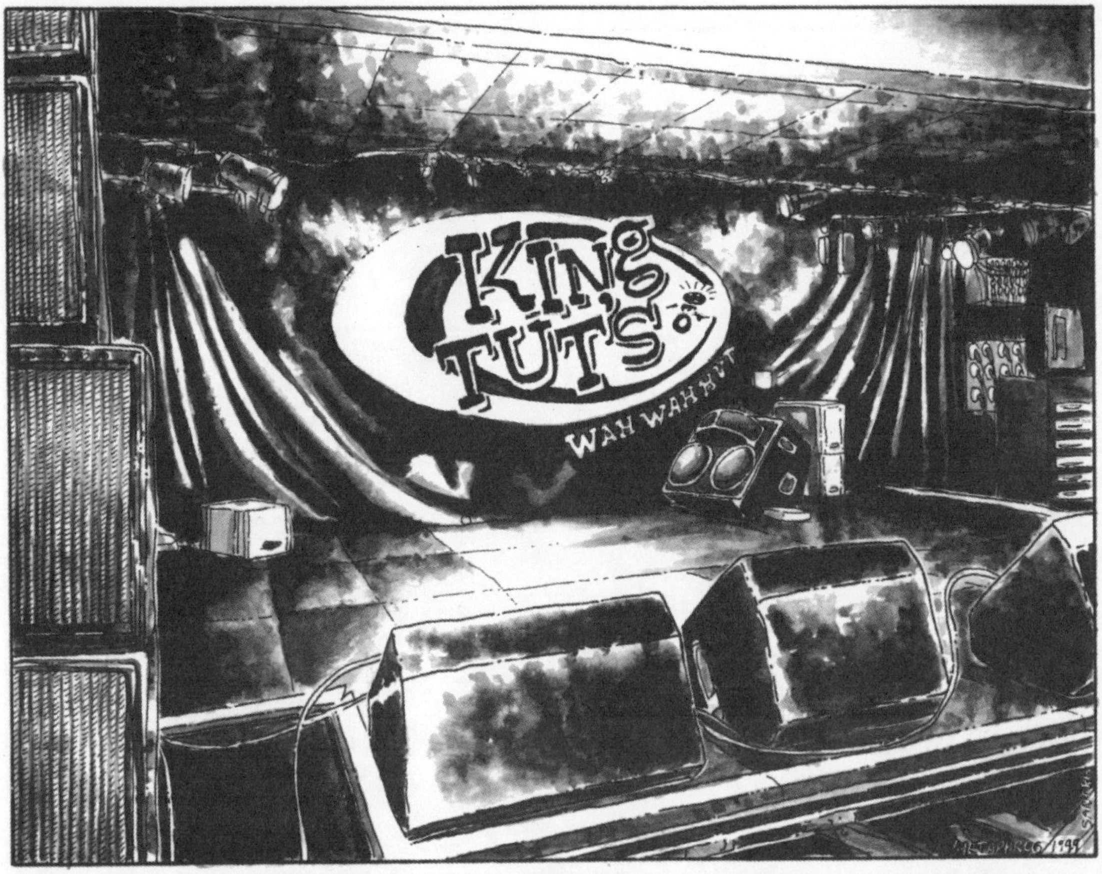
KING TUT'S
WAH WAH HUT
METAPHROG/1999

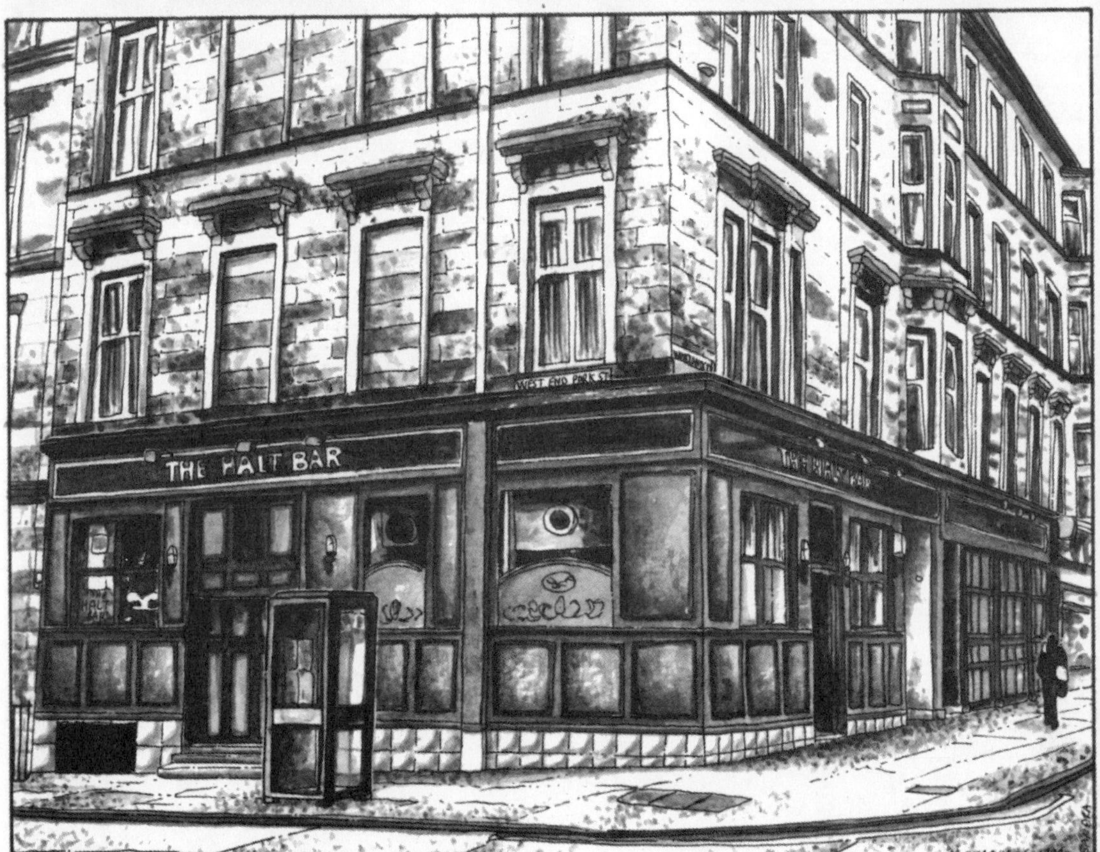
WEST END PARK ST
THE HALT BAR
THE HALT BAR
METAPHROG 1999

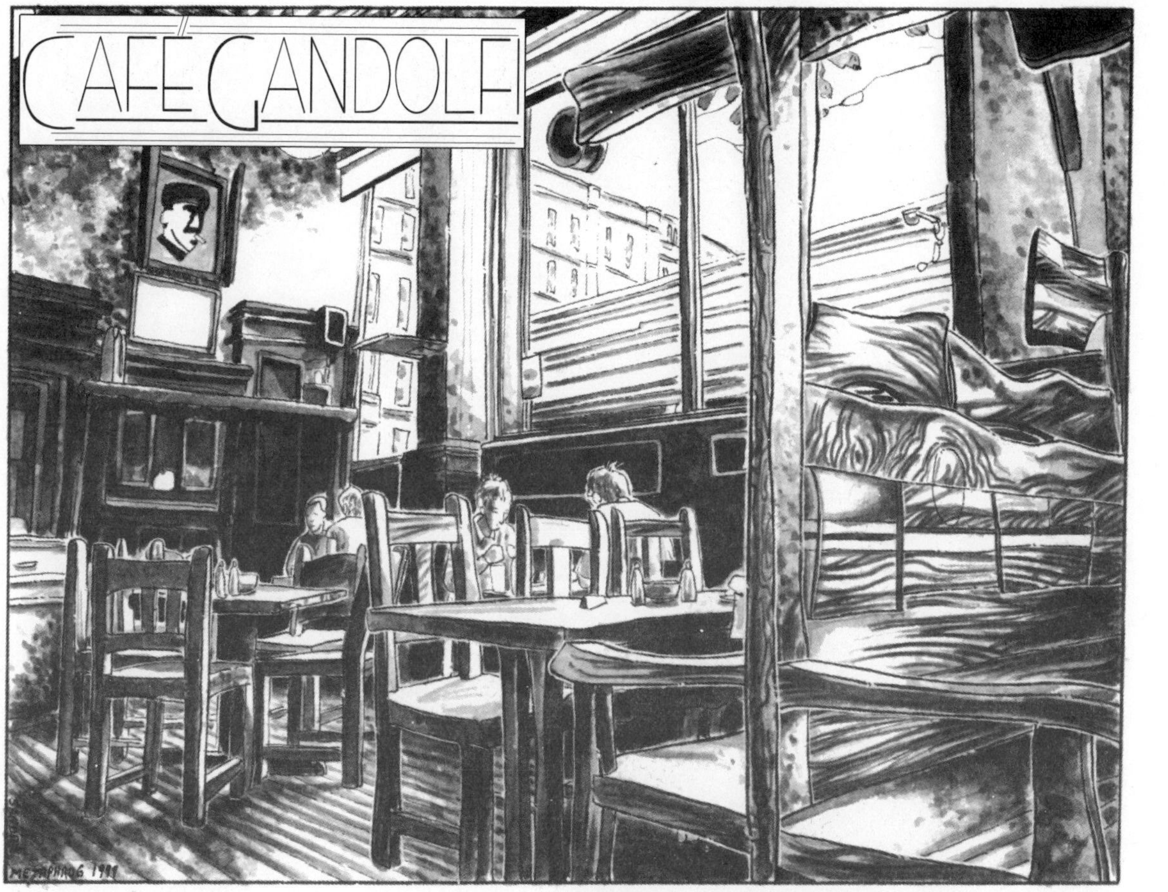
CAFÉ GANDOLFI
METAPHROG 1999

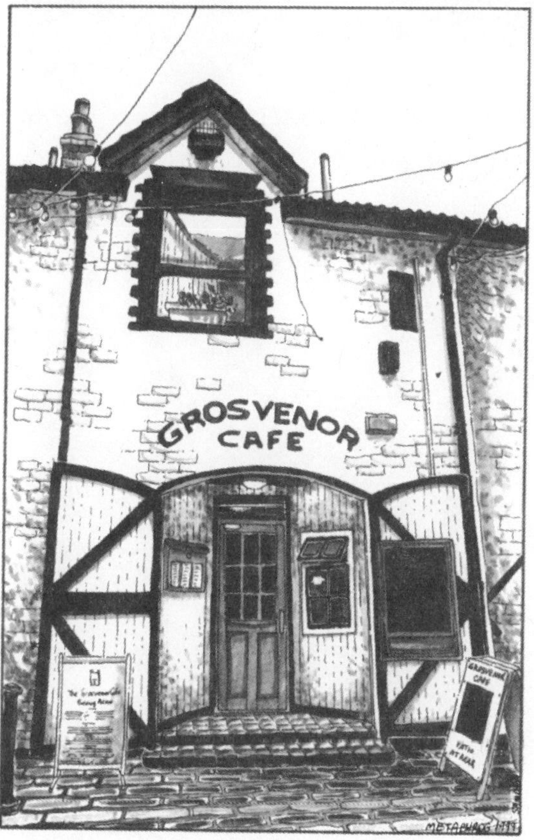
GROSVENOR CAFE
METAPHROG 1999

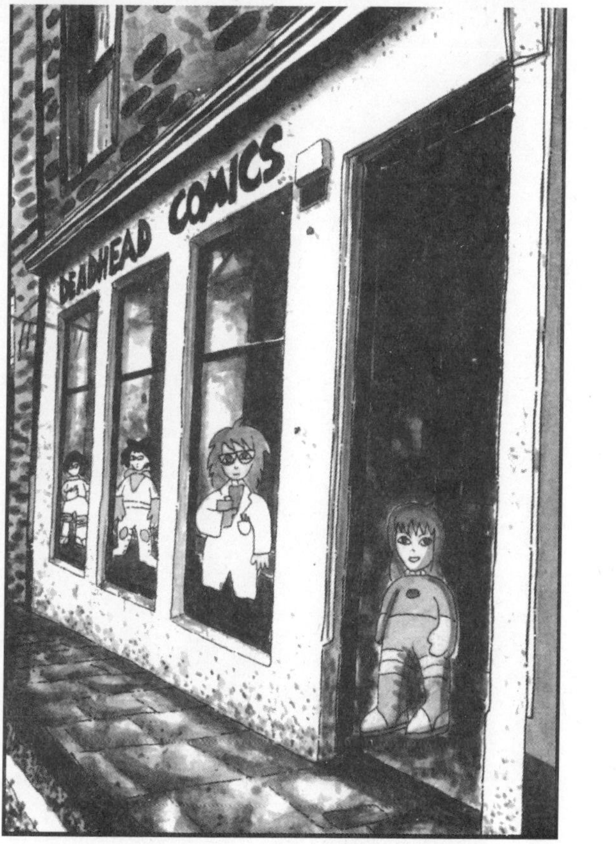
DEADHEAD COMICS

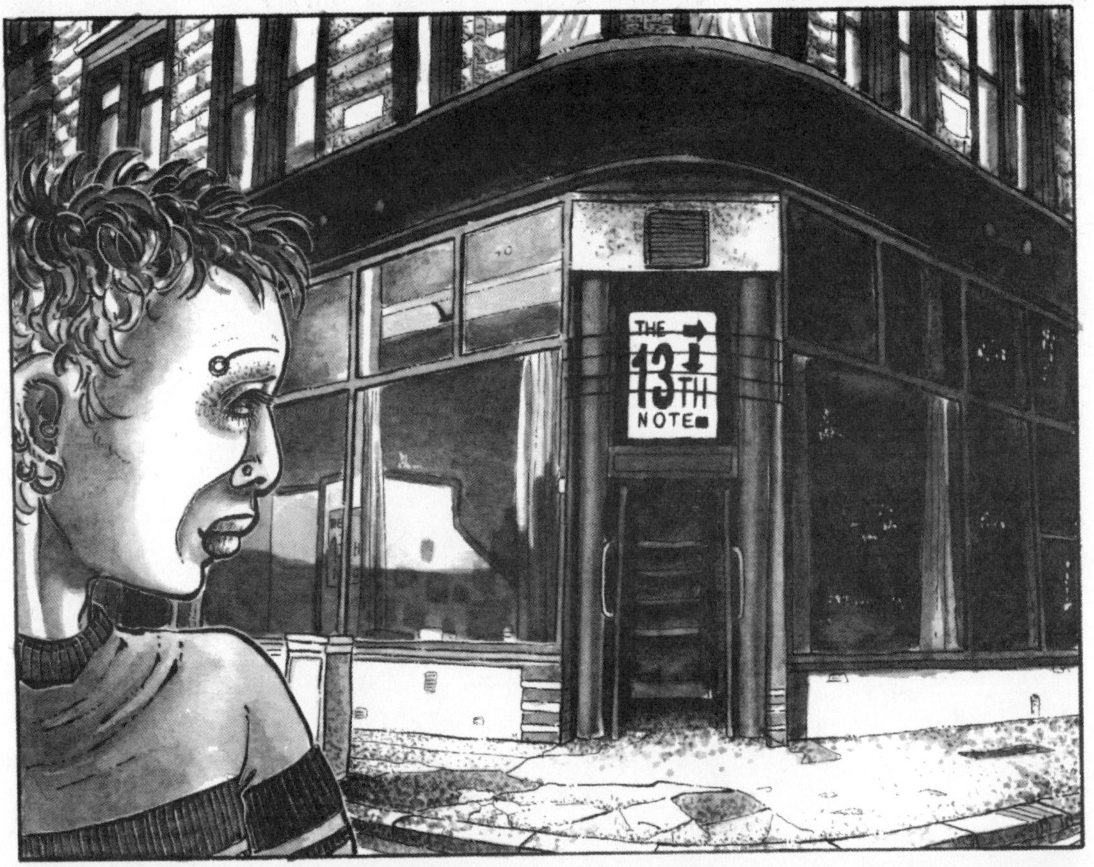
THE 13TH NOTE

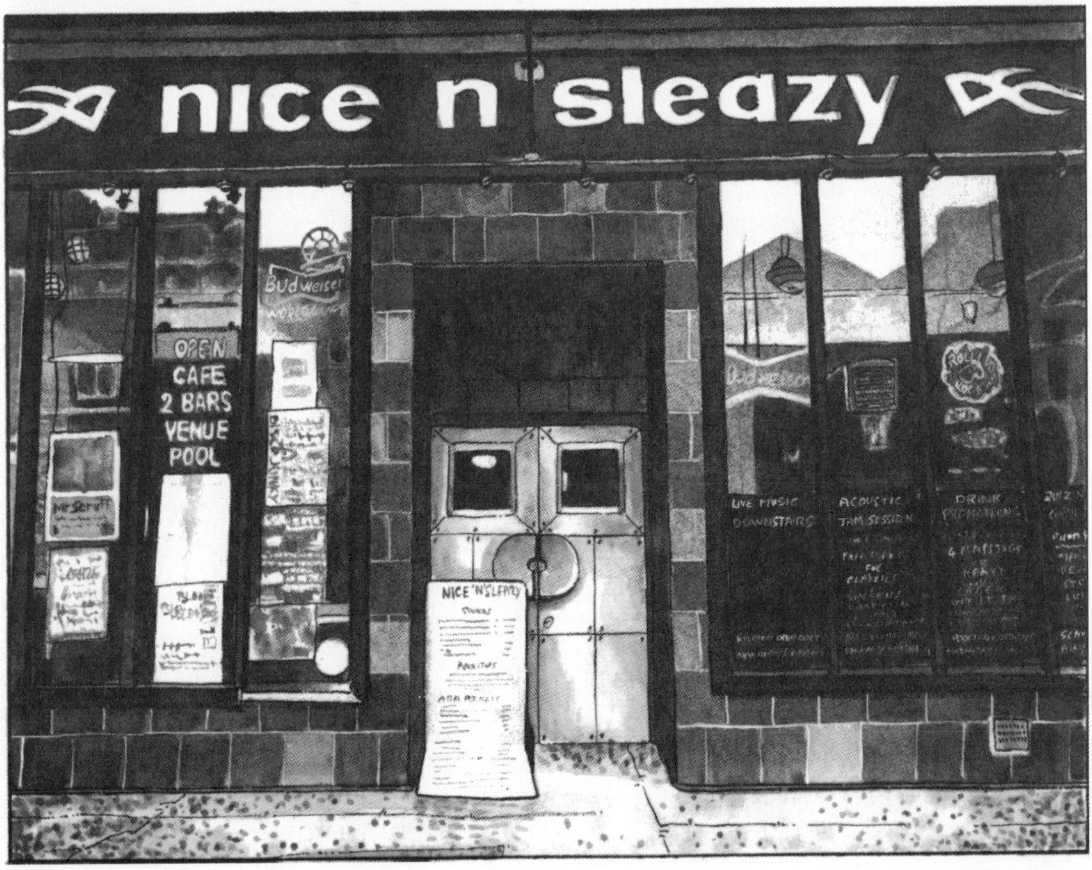
nice n'sleazy
Budweiser
OPEN
CAFE
2 BARS
VENUE
POOL
LIVE MUSIC DOWNSTAIRS
ACOUSTIC JAM SESSION
DRINK PROMOTIONS

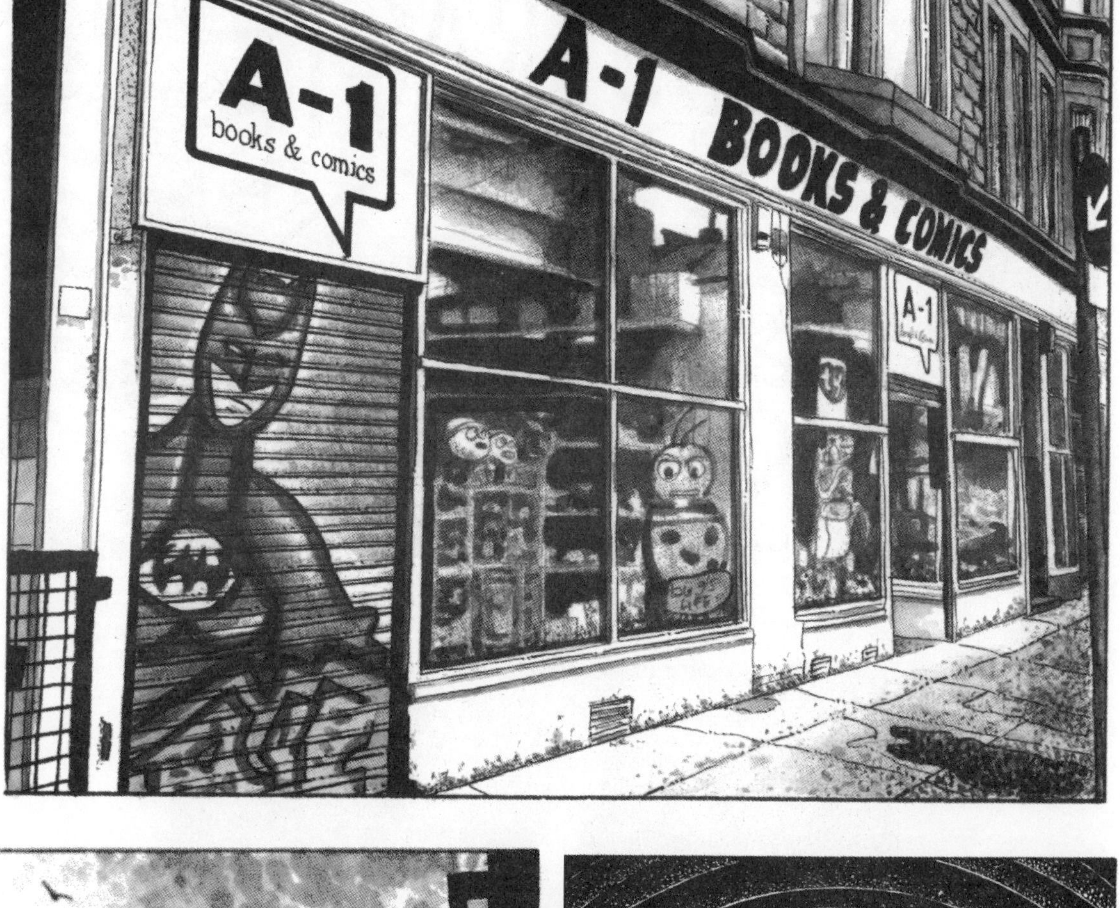
A-1
books & comics
A-1 BOOKS & COMICS
A-1

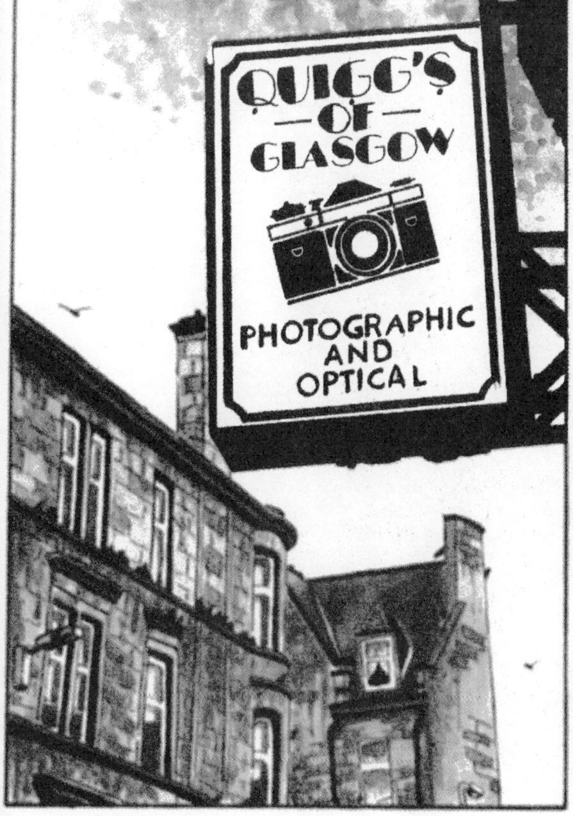
QUIGG'S
—OF—
GLASGOW
PHOTOGRAPHIC
AND
OPTICAL

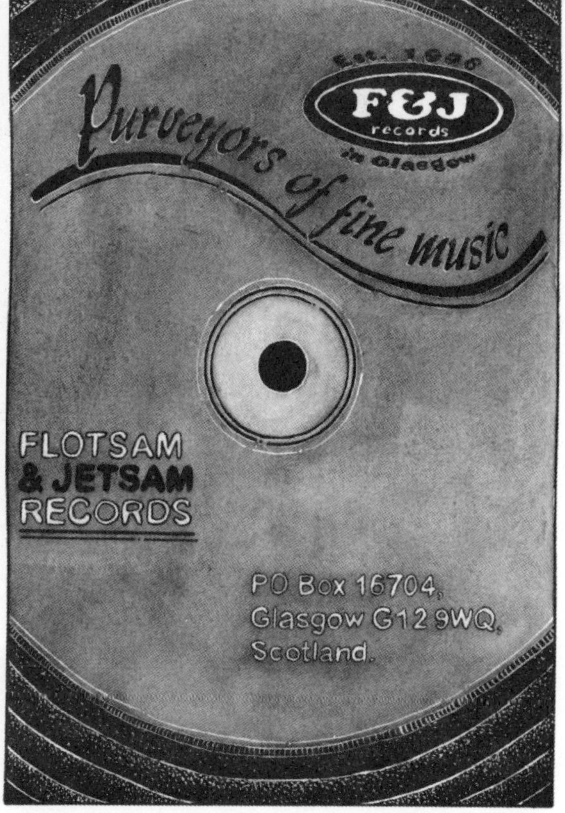
F&J
records
in Glasgow
Purveyors of fine music
FLOTSAM
& JETSAM
RECORDS
PO Box 16704,
Glasgow G12 9WQ,
Scotland.

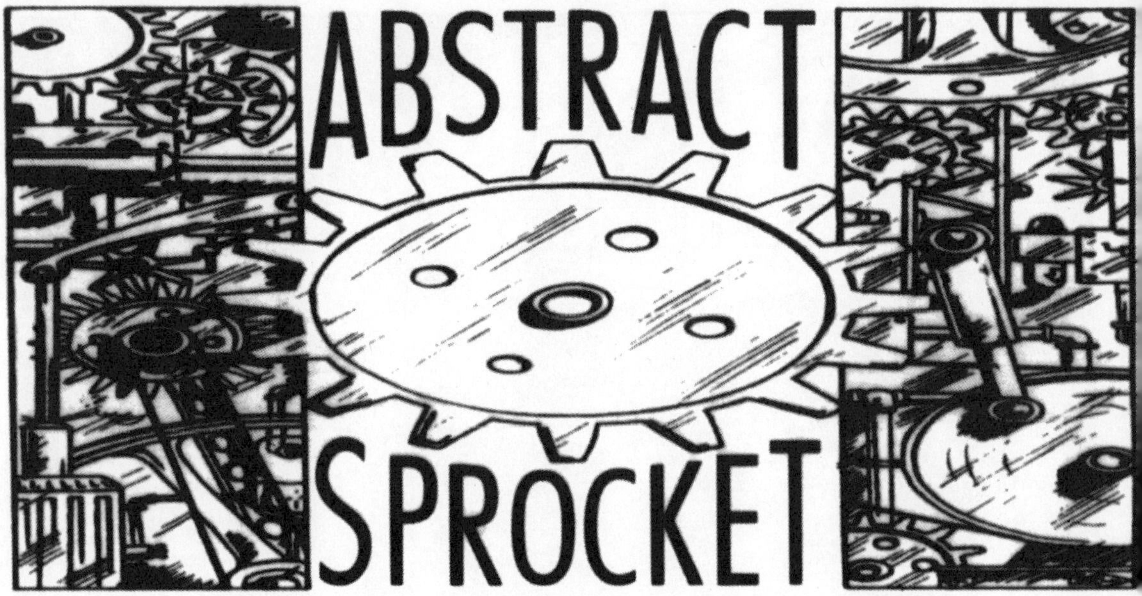
ABSTRACT
SPROCKET

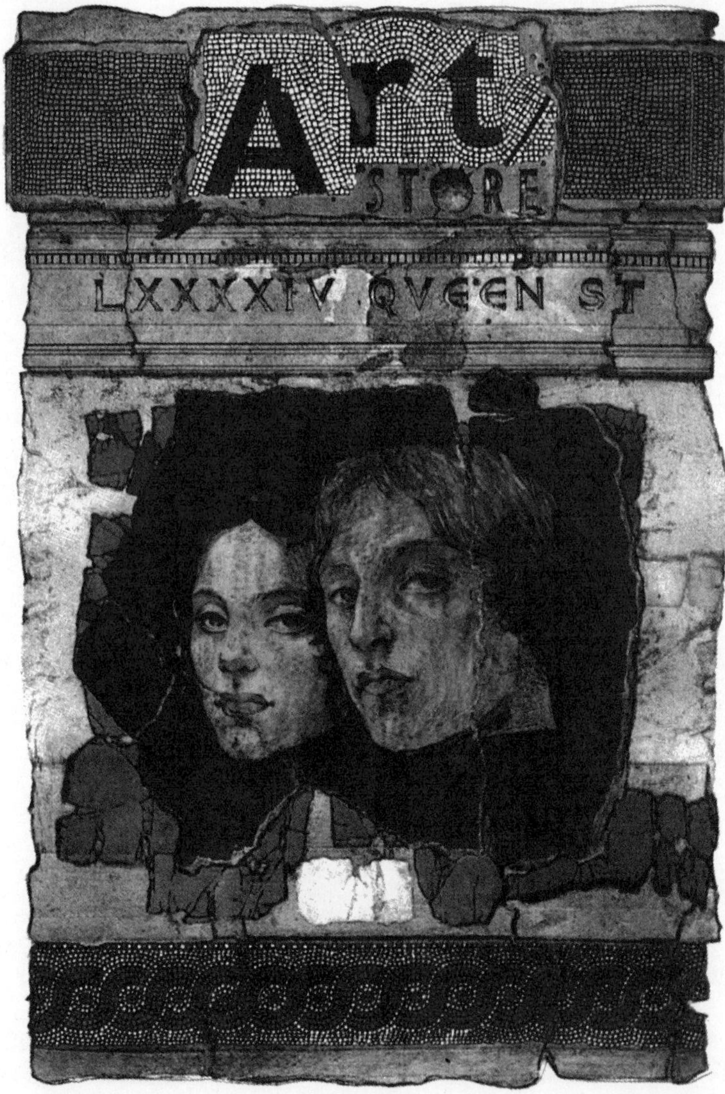
Art
STORE
LXXXXIV QVEEN ST

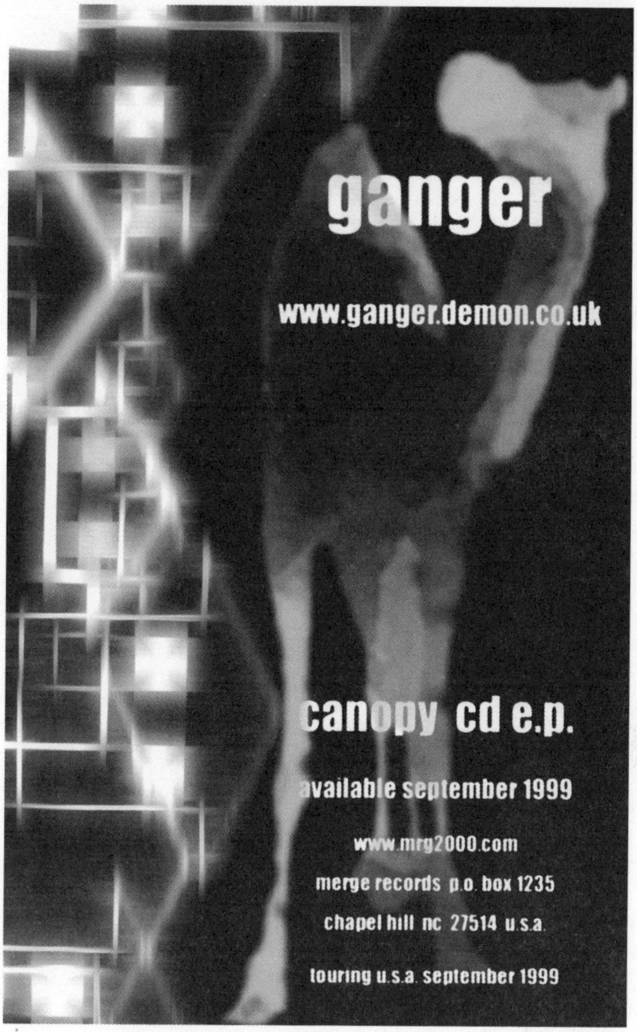
ganger
www.ganger.demon.co.uk
canopy cd e.p.
available september 1999
www.mrg2000.com
merge records p.o. box 1235
chapel hill nc 27514 u.s.a.
touring u.s.a. september 1999

The Variety Bar, 401 Sauchiehall Street, Glasgow G2. Tel: 0141 332 4449.
King Tuts Wahwah Hut, 272 St Vincent Street, Glasgow G2 5RL. Tel: 0141 221 5279.
The Halt Bar, 160 Woodlands Road, Glasgow G3. Tel: 0141 332 1210.
Café Gandolfi, 64 Albion Street, Glasgow G1. Tel: 0141 552 6813.
at Habitat, in Buchanan Galleries, Glasgow
The Grosvenor Café, 31-35 Ashton Lane, Glasgow G12. Tel: 0141 339 1848.
Deadhead, 27 Candlemaker Row, Edinburgh EH1 2QG. Tel: 0131 226 2774.
e-mail: gafin@ministryofsound.co.uk
The 13th Note Café, 50/60 King Street, Glasgow G1 5QT. Tel: 0141 553 1638.
The 13th Note Club, 260 Clyde Street, Glasgow G1 4JH. Tel: 0141 221 0414.
Nice 'n' Sleazy, 421 Sauchiehall Street, Glasgow. Tel: 0141 333 0900.
A1 Comics Glasgow, 31-35 Parnie Street, Glasgow G1 5RJ. Tel: 0141 552 6692.
635 Great Western Road, Glasgow G12 8RE. Tel: 0141 357 6944.
Glasgow's Collectable Card Game & Role Playing Centre, Argyle Market,
28 Argyle Street, Glasgow. Tel: 0141 226 5414.
Quiggs of Glasgow, 7-11 Parnie Street, Glasgow G1 5RJ. Tel: 0141 552 6823.
Flotsam + Jetsam Records, PO Box 16704, Glasgow G12 9WQ.
Abstract Sprocket, 29 St. Benedict's Street, Norwich NR2 4PF. Tel: 01603 624410.
The Artstore, 94 Queen Street, Glasgow G1 3AQ. Tel: 0141 221 1101.
Ganger, Merge Records, PO Box 1235, Chapell Hill nc 27514, USA. www.ganger.demon.co.uk

Special thanks to:

David and Kenneth at A1,
Dean and Lisa at Abstract Sprocket,
Michael at The Artstore,
Gordon, Hubby and Sandy
at Flotsam and Jetsam Records
(look out for Amphetameanics/
Newtown Grunts split),
Gafin and Emma at Deadhead,
John at The Halt Bar,
Seumas at The Café Gandolfi,
James and Stuart and all at Ganger,
Mrs Winning at The Grosvenor Café,
Dave, Dave and Fiona at King Tuts,
Ariki and Mig at Nice 'n' Sleazy,
Jim, Lee and Les at Quiggs,
Craig at The 13th Note,
Gerry at The Variety Bar,
Findlay, Harry, Joe, Ross, Martin, Pat
and Tommy at Clydeside Press.

Matt, Graeme and all at Borders,
Simon and Murphy at Eight-O-Three Records,
John, Brian, Simon, Stephen, Jackie, Joan and
John at John Smith and Son, Michael Zarlenga,
Sylvie and Christelle at Blackwells,
Elizabeth at the fruitmarket gallery, Lucy and
Mark at Waterstones, Neil Johnstone at
Edinburgh International Book Festival,
Nick Younger, Stewart May and Scot Cahill
at Tower, Mike Hart and all at
Compendium, Joe Walls and all at Rough Trade,
all at The Café Gandolfi.

**Thanks to our families and friends
and all the people who have helped,
encouraged and supported us:**

David and Rhoda Chalmers,
Jane and Fraser, Andi and Nic,
Jean-Pierre et Claudine Milice, Sébastien
Milice, Caroline Milice et Pierre,
Dave and Debs, Erik and Mr and
Mrs Nienhuis, Jim Mackie, Bob, Helen,
Lachlan and Machar, Adrian Hunter,
Jason, Ian and Diane, Maura McCallion
and John Larkin, Graeme and all at
Chemikal Underground, Alex, Dave
and all at Fat Cat Records, Alan, Martin
and Barrie at Rub-a-Dub, Philippe Ouvrard,
Hansje and all at Het Raadsel, Kees,
Klaas and Toon at Lambiek, Melle and
all at Vandal Com-X, all at Gojoker,
Noël at Un Regard Moderne,
Valéry et Nathaly at La Comète de
Carthage, Fabien at Album, Corinne
et Eric at l'ABD, Dominic Black,
Lucinda, Brian Morton, Craig Pilling
and Emily D. at SBN,
Brian Donaldson and Rob Fraser
at The List, Brian Beadie, Barry McDonald
and Keren McKean at Go!,
Brian McIver, Andrew Crumey,
Liam McDougall, Xavier Gros, Win!,
Gio Spinella, Ferg Handley and all
at the CCG, Simon, Gillian, James,